PERGAMON INTERNATIONAL LIBRARY
of Science, Technology, Engineering and Social Studies

*The 1000-volume original paperback library in aid of education,
industrial training and the enjoyment of leisure*

Publisher: Robert Maxwell, M.C.

CORPORATE PLANNING:
THE HUMAN FACTOR

THE PERGAMON TEXTBOOK
INSPECTION COPY SERVICE

An inspection copy of any book published in the Pergamon International Library
will gladly be sent to academic staff without obligation for their consideration for
course adoption or recommendation. Copies may be retained for a period of 60
days from receipt and returned if not suitable. When a particular title is adopted
or recommended for adoption for class use and the recommendation results in a
sale of 12 or more copies, the inspection copy may be retained with our compli-
ments. If after examination the lecturer decides that the book is not suitable for
adoption but would like to retain it for his personal library, then a discount of
10% is allowed on the invoiced price. The Publishers will be pleased to receive
suggestions for revised editions and new titles to be published in this important
international Library.

Other Titles of Interest

DUBRIN, A. J.,   *Casebook of Organizational Behaviour*

DUNCAN, J. W.,   *Statistical Services in 10 Years' Time*

HUSSEY, D. E.,   *The Corporate Planners' Yearbook 1978–79*

HUSSEY, D. E.,   *Corporate Planning: Theory and Practice*

HUSSEY, D. E.,   *Introducing Corporate Planning*

KERR, A. L. C.,   *The Common Market and how it Works*

LANGE, O.,   *Introduction to Econometrics*

MAROIS, A.,   *Towards a Plan of Action for Mankind*

SZALAI   *Cross-national Comparative Survey Research:*
AND PETRELLA,   *Theory and Practice*

CORPORATE PLANNING: THE HUMAN FACTOR

by

D. E. HUSSEY

Harbridge House Europe

and

M. J. LANGHAM

Hay Management Consultants

PERGAMON PRESS

OXFORD · NEW YORK · TORONTO · SYDNEY · PARIS · FRANKFURT

U.K.	Pergamon Press Ltd., Headington Hill Hall, Oxford OX3 0BW, England
U.S.A.	Pergamon Press Inc., Maxwell House, Fairview Park, Elmsford, New York 10523, U.S.A.
CANADA	Pergamon of Canada, Suite 104, 150 Consumers Road, Willowdale, Ontario, M2J 1P9, Canada
AUSTRALIA	Pergamon Press (Aust.) Pty. Ltd., P.O. Box 544, Potts Point, N.S.W. 2011, Australia
FRANCE	Pergamon Press SARL, 24 rue des Ecoles, 75240 Paris, Cedex 05, France
FEDERAL REPUBLIC OF GERMANY	Pergamon Press GmBH, 6252 Kronberg-Taunus, Pferdstrasse 1, Federal Republic of Germany

First edition 1979

British Library Cataloguing in Publication Data

Hussey, David Edward
Corporate planning, the human factor.–(Pergamon international library).
1. Corporate planning
I. Title   II. Langham, M J
658.4'01   HD30.28   78-40532

ISBN 0-08-022464-4 (Hardcover)
ISBN 0-08-022475-X (Flexicover)

For Bibliographic purposes this volume should be cited as:
Hussey D E and Langham M J *Corporate Planning: The Human Factor* Pergamon Press Limited

Printed and bound at William Clowes & Sons Limited Beccles and London

Contents

46450

The Authors

MIKE LANGHAM has varied practical experience in management development and organisational behaviour. His early career experience was in line management production and administrative functions in companies with interests in engineering, building products, and pharmaceuticals.

For the past ten years he has held senior appointments in management development and training initially in a large building products company and, latterly, for four years as Assistant Director Management Studies, with the Roffey Park Management College.

He qualified for his BA degree over four years with the Open University, reading psychology, sociology, and related subjects. He is also qualified as a member of the Institute of Personnel Management (MIPM).

Since 1976 he has been a consultant with HAY-MSL Ltd., based in Manchester, and specialising in organisation design and development and management development.

He is a behavioural scientist with essentially an applied and pragmatic approach to his work with business organisations.

DAVID HUSSEY is a leading international authority on corporate planning, and is one of the few writers with extensive practical experience as a corporate planner in industry. For twelve years he held senior appointments in companies with interests in mechanical engineering, food, pharmaceuticals, chemicals, horticulture, shipping, and road transportation. Since 1976 he has been a consultant with Harbridge House Inc., where he is a partner in the London office.

His books are *Introducing Corporate Planning* (1971), *Corporate Planning: Theory and Practice* (1974) (joint winner of the John Player Management Author of the Year Award), and *Inflation and Business Policy* (1976). He is the originator and editor of and the major contributor to *The Corporate Planner's Yearbook* (1974) and (1978), published by Pergamon Press for the Society for Long Range Planning.

He was a founder member of the Society for Long Range Planning, and a former vice-chairman.

He was educated in Rhodesia, attained his BCom with distinction in business economics from the University of South Africa and also qualified as a Chartered Secretary (ACIS). Before his return to the United Kingdom he was employed in the field of economic planning and research, working for the Federal (formerly Rhodesian) Government until the dissolution of the Federation in 1963.

Acknowledgements

All quotations are acknowledged in the text. We should like to thank the authors and publishers who have allowed us to quote from their works. A summary of permissions is given below.

The University of Chicago Press gave permission to reprint the tables from Gary A. Steiner, *The Creative Organisation*, 1965.

Quotations from Christopher Tugendhat, *The Multinationals*, appear with the permission of Eyre & Spottiswoode (Publishers) Ltd.

Pergamon Press Ltd. for quotations from the following publications: R. B. Higgins (1976), Re-unite management and planning, *Long Range Planning*, Vol. 9, No. 4; B. Taylor (1976), New Dimension in Corporate Planning, *Long Range Planning*, Vol. 9, No. 6; P. H. Grinyer and D. Norburn (1974), Strategic planning in 21 British companies, *Long Range Planning*, Vol. 7, No. 4; W. Solesbury (1974), *Policy in Urban Planning*.

The Industrial Society for permission to quote from D. Robertson and J. Henderson (1975), *A Guide to the Industry Act*.

H. Kirby Warren, *Long Range Planning: The Executive Viewpoint*, 1966, pp. 18, 29, 51, 54, 57, 59; reprinted by permission of Prentice-Hall Inc., Englewood Cliffs, New Jersey, U.S.A.

Professor George Steiner is thanked for allowing us to make extensive use of the findings of his research published in *Pitfalls in Comprehensive Long Range Planning* (1972), Planning Executives Institute.

Mr. G. Morris of European Manpower Advisory Services Ltd. for permission to quote from his paper 'Participative approaches in corporate planning'.

Jonathan Cape Ltd. for permission to quote from Edward de Bono (1971), *Practical Thinking*.

George Allen & Unwin gave permission to quote from J. R. R. Tolkien (1974), *Tree and Leaf*, and C. Levinson (1972), *International Trade Unionism*.

McGraw-Hill Book Co. (UK) Ltd., B. W. Denning (1971), *Corporate Planning: Selected Concepts*.

William Heinemann Ltd., Peter Drucker (1964), *Managing for Results*.

Henry Mintzberg, The manager's job: folklore and fact, *Harvard Business Review*, July-Aug. 1975, copyright 1975 by the President and Fellows of Harvard College; all rights reserved. Permission to quote given by *Harvard Business Review*.

Shell Chemicals UK Ltd. for permission to use and quote, without restriction, material on the Directional Policy Matrix.

Penguin Books Ltd. for permission to quote from the following: Definitions of *creative* and *learning* from James Drever, *A Dictionary of Psychology*, Penguin Reference Books, revised edition, 1964, copyright the estate of James Drever 1952; Robert Borger and A. E. M. Seaborne, *The Psychology of Learning*, Pelican Original, 1966, copyright Robert Borger and A. E. M. Seaborne, 1966; Quotations and a diagram from P. R. Whitfield, *Creativity in Industry*, Pelican Books, 1975, copyright P. R. Whitfield, 1975.

Hodder & Stoughton Educational, T. P. Jones. Creative Learning in Perspective (1972), Hodder & Stoughton Ltd.

The Editor, *The McKinsey Quarterly*, for permissions to quote from The meaning of strategic planning, by R. C. Ackoff, Vol. 11, No. 1, Summer 1966.

Macmillan Publishing Co. Inc., New York, George A Steiner (1969), *Top Management Planning*.

Methuen & Co. Ltd., E. Stone, *An Introduction to Educational Psychology*.

Quotations reprinted from C. S. Rogers, Towards a theory of creativity, *A Review of General Semantics*, Vol. 11, 1954, by permission of the International Society for General Semantics.

British Nationalisation 1945–73, R. Kelf-Cohen, Macmillan, 1973, by permission of Macmillan, London and Basingstoke.

Quotations from *Innovation in Marketing*, T. Levitt, copyright 1962, McGraw-Hill Inc.; used with permission of the McGraw-Hill Book Co.

S. J. Parnes, Education and creativity, *Teachers College Record*, Vol. 64, 1963; used with permission of *Teachers College Record*.

Pergamon Press Ltd. for a quotation from D. E. Hussey (1974), *Corporate Planning– Theory and Practice*.

The American Psychological Association gave permission for reproduction of the communication networks diagram in H. J. Leavitt (1951), Some effects of certain communication patterns on performance, *Journal of Abnormal and Social Psychology*, Vol. 46, pp. 38–50 (1951).

Prentice-Hall Inc., New Jersey, for permission to quote from: Amitai Etzioni (1964), *Modern Organisations*, and E. Schein (1965), *Organisation Psychology*.

Mayfield Publishing Co. (formerly National Press Books) for the use of the Johari Window concept in J. Luft (1963, 1970), *Group Processes: An Introduction to Group Dynamics*.

Pat Colville allowed us to quote from his MPhil research, 'A sociological study of the relationships between incumbents of managerial roles, the behaviour of managers and the structure of Organisations' University of Surrey, 1975.

Phaidon Press Ltd. gave permission for a quotation from M. Allbrow (1970), *Bureaucracy*, Pall Mall Press Ltd.

McGraw-Hill Book Co. gave permission to quote from R. Likert (1967), *The Human Organisation*, and F. Fiedler (1967), *A Theory of Leadership Effectiveness*.

Professor H. A. Turner is thanked for permission to summarise an extract from his paper 'The trend of strikes', Leeds University Press, 1963.

Addison-Wesley Publishing Co. gave permission to quote from Richard Beckhart (1969), *Organisation Development: Strategies and Models*.

The executive committee of HAY Management Consultants London are thanked for permission to use concepts and approaches to performance appraisal and organisational climate.

Professor C. Perrow kindly gave permission for us to quote from a paper presented to the British Sociological Association meeting of the Industrial Sociology group 1972, 'Technology organisations and environment: a cautionary note'.

W. John Giles and Robin Evenden of the Roffey Park Management College, Horsham, Sussex, gave permission for the use in standard and modified form of a number of management course notes and handouts.

Allan Little gave permission for us to quote from his article, When is a manager not a manager? (1977), *Journal of Chartered Institute of Secretaries.*

Longman Group Ltd. for a quotation from Raymond Vernon (1971), *Sovereignty at Bay.*

Tom Kilcourse gave permission for us to use a modification of a diagram from *Participation—an Analytical Approach* (1976), Industrial Training International.

John Wiley Ltd. gave permission to quote from J. G. March and H. A. Simon (1958), *Organisations*, and F. Herzberg (1959), *The Motivation to Work.*

Introduction

Perhaps the seeds of this book began to germinate when we came together in 1974, one of us a practitioner of corporate planning and an established author on the subject, the other an applied behavioural scientist. Our task at that time was to introduce a workable approach to performance management into a large engineering company as an integral part of its planning process. Our joint work on this assignment seemed to stress a requirement to interrelate the planning process with the actual behaviour of managers in an organisation. There was then, as there is now, a need to find the "middle-ground" between the objective, logical, analytical approach to planning, born out of rational thinking, and the subjective, social, emotional behaviour of organisational members.

We are not the first to notice this need, and a brief — usually very brief — mention of it occurs in many of the numerous and valuable books on corporate planning. Similarly, the equally valuable body of literature on organisational behaviour rarely trespasses on planning territory. For some reason the two streams of thought had not been brought together in a book born of both experience and conceptual knowledge.

For the organisational development man, many of the planning books (though not all) will seem very analytical and far removed from his job as he sees it. Similarly, the planner who explores the behavioural literature will find something of an information overload in the volume and variety of published work on the human aspects of business. Little has been done to mine this lode of literature so that it enriches thought on the corporate planning process.

Research into organisational behaviour is not an end in itself. The knowledge gained should be used to improve organisations and business operations. If, as Etzioni (1964)* suggests, "most of us are born in organisations, educated by organisations, work for organisations and spend much of our leisure time paying, playing and praying in organisations", it would seem to make sense to relate what we know about organisational behaviour to the corporate planning process. Planning, after all, sets out to change or influence the present and future of organisations.

In practice the planner has to cope with problems of motivation, conflicts of management style, the reconciliation of widely differing individual aims, variations in the quality of managers, the difficulty of encouraging creativity and problems of internal power politics. In addition, increasing social change is affecting the business organisation, not only internally, but also in its relationships with the environment in the form of government and trade union intervention and in the call for greater participation in planning and decision making by those with an "investment" (whether of money, labour, or however defined) in the future of the business.

Thus in the early chapters of the book we look at people, management, and planning in terms of the individual and groups in the firm, creativity, motivation, organisation and management style, and organisational development from the particular viewpoint of planning, leading to a consideration of the role of the planner in change processes. Thus far the link is essentially between "people and planning" where we are considering what actually happens rather than perhaps what should happen in organisations. The role of the planner in change situations is seen as both proactive and reactive and provides the pivot for us to consider "planning through people" in later chapters. Thus from Chapter 9, Objectives, we are concerned with matching the requirements of the planning process in practice to the operation of the organisation using the lessons learned about human behaviour from earlier chapters.

In Chapters 15–18 we focus on significant developments affecting the planning process both within and external to the organisation and in considering The Multi-national Enterprise, Manpower Planning, Participation: The Social Need, and Corporate Planning and Union Involvement: The New Dimension, we seek to find pragmatic approaches which will allow the ideals of logic and theory to work successfully in practice in the human organisation.

*A. Etzioni, *Modern Organisations*, Prentice-Hall, 1964.

We have drawn together the theory and concepts of planning with those of organisational behaviour and added to this our experience of relating the two areas in practice. In considering the extensive and valuable body of literature available we have attempted to select that which has proved valuable to us in practice and which has enabled us to find the "middle ground" referred to earlier. Above all we have sought to write a practical handbook, a volume which will be not only read in the conventional sense but referred to, thumbed through, and used as a practical management tool.

The aim of the book is to provide a text which, while drawing its basic strength from its practical bias and application for practising managers, including practitioners of planning and organisational development, will also have considerable relevance for academics and students.

This book is not solely the product of our unaided efforts. We owe a debt of gratitude to many colleagues and friends who have provided encouragement and constructive help during the writing. In particular Ben Bennett, Robin Evenden, and John Giles of the Roffey Park Management College have provided of intellectual stimulation and debate; John Murray of HAY-MSL has given professional support.

The environmental model in Chapter 1 owes much to ideas developed with Roger Smalley of Harbridge House: the strategic review concept was the brain-child of Basil Denning of Harbridge House, and has influenced our thinking beyond the few pages in which it is mentioned. Mary Dargue has found time and energy, in the middle of her own studies, to type some of the manuscripts. Thanks are also due to Mrs. Sheila Webb who typed the other half of the manuscript.

Many others knowingly and unknowingly have contributed to our thinking — to them all we offer our thanks.

D. E. H.
M. J. L.

December 1977

CHAPTER 1

The Human Factor in Management

Management is one of those strange activities which many people practise but which few can define. Ask any manager if he knows what management is and he will say that of course he knows as he does it every day. Press him hard and the chances are that his definition will be woefully inadequate and differ from that of his colleagues in many significant ways.

This is not really surprising, as management has many facets, and those who stand too close will not always see them all.

We shall return to the definition of management later in this chapter. Before doing this, we should like to use the diagram in Figure 1.1a to explore the complexities and interrelationships of the organisation and its environment in so far as these affect the objectives of the organisation and the means (strategy) chosen to achieve them. In other words we are examining some of the things that particularly affect the planning elements in the management role. What is especially important, and the theme of this book, is the implications of the human factor on all aspects of our model. Although our diagram looks complicated, it is perhaps needless for us to stress that it represents a gross oversimplification of the real world.

In Fig. 1.1a the environment in which the organisation operates — the external world of business — is represented by a hexagon. This shows a number of factors which influence the business under broad headings such as "economic" and "legal" and showing lines of force which connect each factor to each other. The full meaning of this part of the diagram, including ways in which the company can consider it in its corporate planning, is the subject matter of a later chapter. For our purpose now we wish to stress only the multi-dimensional, multi-facet, complex world in which every organisation operates. To see all this in our diagram requires some exercise of the imagination.

Within this integrated world, contributing to it, and drawing its opportunities and limitations from it, there is the organisation. For our example we have taken the business firm, but the concept applies to all human organisations. Most times, the impact of the world on the firm may seem greater than the impact of the firm on the world.

The firm exists because it has markets, and the markets themselves are also in a dynamic relationship with the environment. It is not hard to see how social trends, inflation, or the law can affect the size and structure of a market; nor how growth of a market such as motor-cars influences the environment itself. A market is a compound of buyers and sellers, which in turn is born out of the external environment and modified by the actions of the firm.

But the firm, although it cannot exist without a market, does not exist solely to serve that market. There are other groups of people who are concerned with the activities and aims of the company, and some of these are powerful enough to alter the way in which it responds to the market.

We have used the "stakeholder" concept to identify these groups and include those with a "stake" or interest in the company in one of the

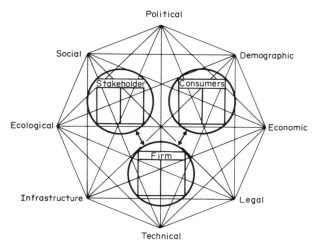

Fig. 1.1. The organisation and its environment.

(a) The full model.

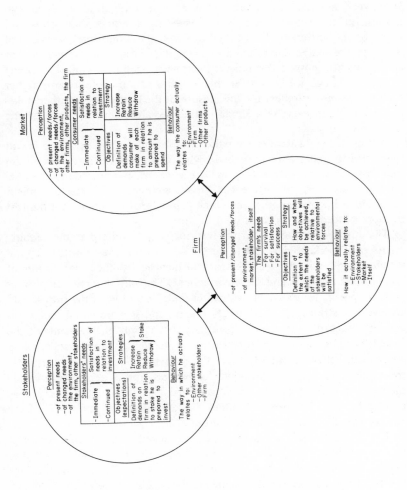

Fig. 1.1. The organisation and its environment.

(b) Expansion of the centre of the model.

boxes inside the hexagon. The stakeholders listed are shareholders, employees, suppliers, customers, and the community, all of which have an interest in the continuation of the business, although their objectives might be very different. We are used to thinking of companies being closed down by the shareholders, and are becoming accustomed to the idea that employees also possess this power. Customers can do the same, by ceasing to buy, although we would see this in terms of a market collapse rather than a vote by customers for the closure of the business. The other stakeholders also can exercise a similar influence, although they take drastic steps only rarely.

Not all the stakeholders want the same thing from the firm, and few of them clearly understand themselves what they do want or communicate that understanding to the firm in precise terms. Within groups of stakeholders there may be differences. One shareholder, for example, might be dividend hungry, another may seek capital growth, while a third might be more concerned with control.

The management of the firm has not only to interpret the requirements of its stakeholders but to decide which objectives it will meet and which it will not. Stakeholders are influenced by their perception of the firm, its markets, and the environment. The way in which employees perceive profit, for example, will affect their view of what the firm should achieve, its strategy, and its wages policy, and is a potential recipe for conflict. According to their perceptions of not only the elements of the model, but also their own requirements as individuals, so the stakeholder groups will behave: it is partly from the behaviour of the stakeholders that the management of the firm draws its own perception and in turn causes the organisation to behave in a particular way. Again, the interpretive process includes the personal values, biases, ambitions, and needs of the key individuals in the management group.

The firm's market (or markets) are also hedged around with the perception and behaviour of the individuals who make up the market, whether they are individual consumers or those responsible for buying for industrial markets, or the middlemen (e.g. retailers) between the manufacturer and consumers.

Similar behavioural implications could be shown around each of the facets of the business environment hexagon, except that to do so would make Fig. 1.1a unintelligible.

A partial answer to the question What is management? is that it is the task of interpreting stakeholders' needs and influences to define corporate objectives, and planning and implementing strategies which achieve these objectives and exploit the market opportunities; all within the context of the business environment. But just as each of the elements of our model is affected by human behaviour, so, too, is the task of management very much a "people" matter. Objectives are attained through the use of people who have to be motivated, organised, and are certainly the single most significant element in the entire management process.

There are three keys to successful management in the circumstances described in Fig. 1.1. First is an understanding not only of the dynamic relationships of the model but a realisation that it is continually changing and that today's solutions will not necessarily be right in the future. Next is an acceptance of the importance of the human factor. Thirdly should be the realisation that the only effective way of bringing the first two keys together is through a process of corporate planning.

To take the discussion further we present alternative views of the way in which managers think and act. These are deliberately written to polarise the views into two extremes of argument, but most readers will be able to identify some at least of the people they know in these descriptions.

View 1

Managers are rational people, dedicated to objective decision making, who will always make a careful study of the available facts before reaching a conclusion. They believe management to be a science capable of yielding precise answers, and consider that the correctness of a conclusion provides sufficient motivation for those who have to implement it. They believe there is one achievable optimum solution to every problem, and that all rational men, given the same facts, would make the same decisions.

View 2

Managers are as likely to act from emotion or "feel" as from rationality. They are given to making decisions without necessarily establishing a full basis of hard fact. They believe management to be an art, with many possible conclusions which can be drawn from one set of circumstances. Consequently rational men may not all choose the same solution and will not necessarily agree with the decision reached. Motivation of people becomes a critical task of management, since people have to be persuaded to implement decisions which are different from those which they may have reached themselves.

View 1 embraces much of the "scientific" view of management, and comes across very strongly in many books on corporate planning, operational research, finance, and management techniques. It appeals to logic but underplays the importance of people.

View 2, on the other hand, reflects much of the writing of the behavioural thinkers, and stresses the numerous human aspects of management, the political nature of management, and the significance of the human factor. It tends to underplay much of the economic rationale of management and to undervalue the degree to which rational analysis can lead to better decisions.

The aim of this book is to combine the two views and to present an approach to planning which balances both and which uses this balanced view to provide a solution of how to survive and prosper in the environment and situation postulated in Fig. 1.1.

Let us return to the problem of defining "management", which is where this chapter started. Sears (1965),[1] in an excellent survey of the terminology of management, states in a résumé of progress since the term "scientific management" was first coined:

"Fifty years of progress in the arts of management, of theorising, of communication, and of coinage of discipline-oriented buzz words have followed. Yet in 1962 another meeting of individuals, acknowledging a sense of urgency but under no specific pressure, met for this stated purpose.

". . . The more specific long-range goal was to make beginnings in clarifying some of the language of management, and its underlying disciplines, and in carving out a general theory of management — a conceptual scheme of ideas or statements — that explains or accounts for phenomena of management. . . ."

These goals were not achieved. Professor Koonz made these summary comments on the two days of presentations of papers and discussion.

"Semantic confusion was evident throughout the discussions . . . differences in using the word manager itself. . . . In fact, one head of a major company who had done and supervised meaningful research in management in his company for a number of years made the strong statement that much of what had been said by many members present was almost incomprehensible to him because he did not know how they were defining their terms. . . .

". . . Management theory is somewhat a jungle of confusing semantics, varying concepts in the field of management, unwillingness, and inability to understand, and failure to appreciate the usefulness and nature of a working conceptual scheme theory."

This division of opinion on definitions is reflected in the work of a study group set up by the Society for Long Range Planning in its first weeks of existence. The study group deliberated for some months and at the end of that time produced a series of definitions of keywords, such as "objectives". Unfortunately no one who was not a part of the work group would agree with any of the definitions, and the attempt came to nothing.

For us, much of the meaning of the term "management" comes across in this definition by Koonz (1962):[2]

"Managing is the art of getting things done through and with people in formally organised groups. It is the art of creating an environment in which people can perform as individuals and yet co-operate towards the attainment of group goals. It is the art of removing blocks to such performance, a way of optimising efficiency in reaching goals."

It is interesting to contrast this view with that of Drucker (1955):[3]

"Indeed, we can only answer our question: What is management and what does it do? by saying that it is a multi-purpose organ that manages a business, and manages managers *and* manages workers and work. If one of these were omitted, we would not have management any more — and we also would not have a business enterprise or an industrial society."

Drucker sees the fundamental function as being economic: "The first definition of management is therefore that it is an economic organ, indeed the specifically economic organ, of an industrial society, every act, every decision, every deliberation of management has as its first dimension an economic dimension."[4] In managing a business, management exercises an active role to make what is desirable an actuality. "Management is not just a creature of the economy, it is a creator as well. And only to the extent which it masters the economic circumstances, and alters them by conscious, directed action does it really manage."[5]

Managing managers is the process of creating an enterprise from financial, physical, and human resources. Motivation, organisation, leadership, and performance standards are among the elements which managers provide, which change a collection of individual resources into a functioning enterprise.

"The final function of management is to manage workers and work. Work has to be performed; and the resource to perform it with is workers — ranging from totally unskilled to artists, from wheelbarrow pushers to executive vice-presidents . . . and it is management, and management alone, that can satisfy these requirements. For this must be satisfied through work and job and within the enterprise; and management is the activating organ of the enterprise."[6]

The views of Koonz and Drucker have certain common elements, although they are by no means identical. Both stress management's role in making things happen, the significance of organisation, and the importance of people. However, the Koonz definition does not stress the role of management in establishing group goals, whereas Drucker stresses this very clearly as part of management. It is significant that Drucker's concept restricts "management" to business, which immediately raises the question of whether non-profit making, non-commercial activities require management.

Our belief is that they do, and a short exploration of management in the context of local government may serve as an example of all similar "non-business" activities.

Knowles (1971)[7] observes:

"It is not easy to see just where management resides in local government. Is it with the council members? Or with the principal officers? Or shared between both? It must reside somewhere, of course, but the fact that this is not immediately apparent is significant and accounts for the absence of unity and sense of direction characteristic of an unfortunately large number of authorities."

This confusion is not the intention of central government,[8] which emphasises "it is of first importance that the internal organisation of the new authorities should be based on sound management principles and structures".

However, according to Knowles (1971),[9] ". . . most council members do not think of themselves as managers, nor do they relish the idea of management. Few see themselves as policy makers." He also doubts that most members fulfil any task of management at all. He[10] also suggests that many town clerks think of management as being synonymous with co-ordination.

It was once fashionable to regard officials in local government as administrators rather than managers, under the belief that elected members defined policy and officials merely executed it. Two official reports shatter this illusion. The report of the Maude Committee on Management in Local Government (1967),[11] more familiarly referred to as the Maude Report, states:

"It is the members who should take and be responsible for the key decisions on objectives, and on the means and plans to attain them. It is they who must periodically review the position as part of the function of directing and controlling. It is the officers who should direct and co-ordinate the necessary action, and see that material is presented to enable members to review progress and check performance."

The report of the Study Group on Local Authority Management and Structures (1972),[12] note the title, expresses similar views.

All this sounds very much like a description of management, and would fit the Koonz definition if not that of Drucker. The fact that some authorities claim that there is confusion in the practice of management does not diminish the argument that local authorities have to be managed.

The view of Stewart (1971),[13] suggests a model of a planned process of management which should be practised by every local authority:

"(a) The organisation identifies certain needs, present and foreseen, in its environment.

(b) It sets objectives in relation to those needs, i.e. the extent to which it will plan to meet those needs.

(c)   It considers alternative ways of achieving those objectives.

(d)   It evaluates those alternatives in terms of their use of resources and their effects.

(e)   Decisions are made in the light of that evaluation.

(f)   Those decisions are translated into managerial action.

(g)   The result of the action taken is monitored and fed back to modify the continuing process, by altering the perception of needs, the objectives set, the alternatives considered, the evaluation, the decision made or the action taken."

In Table 1.1 we provide a brief comparison of management in local government and in business. The differences are immense, and the difficulties of practising good management principles in local government are enormous. But the task of managing is very much there despite the absence of profit as the economic *raison d'être*.

Sears (1965)[14] refers to the three pages of definitions and explanations

TABLE 1.1
Differences between management – local government and business

Local government	Business
1. Officers work under direction of elected politicians	1. Managers work under the direction of a board of directors
2. Objective is service to the public	2. Objective is to produce a profit for shareholders
3. Law specifically limits scope of activities (*ultra vires*)	3. Few specific legal limits other than the general law of the land
4. Subject to public criticism and investigation	4. Responsible to owner of the business
5. Dual nature of management (elected members and paid officers)	5. Single line of management responsibility
6. Frequent lack of a chief executive with overall authority	6. Normal to have a chief executive
7. Fragmentation of interests, not all of which appear related (e.g. weights and measures, and housing)	7. Greater unity of interests. Normal organisation on profit centre basis rather than as a variety of activities all competing for one source of cash

Table 1.1 (*cont.*)

Local government	Business
8. Fundamental importance of the committee system in the management process	8. Committees where used are generally an aid to management rather than the method of management
9. Council members unpaid, drawn from those available, not always high calibre people and elected for a defined period of time. Variety of motives for service	9. Managers and directors normally paid, may be removed if of low calibre and usually motivated by desire for personal gain
10. Although autonomous, subject to controls of and interference from central government. Plans may be upset on instructions from Central Government for national economic reasons, which have no direct relationships with local government objectives	10. More freedom to act and implement plans once made
11. Overriding strength and influence of professionalism, often acting as a force against unity	11. Professional influences much less marked, and rarely become more important than the company
12. Difficulty of measuring the result (that is output) of much of local government activity in meaningful terms	12. The difficulty sometimes exists in certain areas (e.g. public relations), but many measurement techniques have been devised, and profit criteria are frequently suitable
13. Activities, once started, tend to be carried on because they have been started and not necessarily because they are needed	13. Also happens in companies, but challenge more likely, particularly if financial performance slips
14. The outlook of many officers (conditioned by frequent mistrust of members, professionalism, the *ultra vires* rule, and lack of interest in corporate view) tends to conservatism and lack of innovation	14. Some companies also breed conservative managers, but many provide a climate which encourages creativity, innovation, and forward thinking
15. Expense without direct and obvious benefit to ratepayers may be difficult to justify – e.g. the setting up of an information system	15. Company management is judged by results. Where these are adequate, management authority to do what it believes necessary is unlikely to be challenged
16. Geographical unity in sphere of operations	16. No limit to possible variations of geographical operations

of management which appear in the *Encyclopaedia of the Social Sciences.*
One definition indicates part of the range of usage:

".. . the process by which the execution of a given purpose is put
into operation and supervised. The combined output of various types
and grades of human effort by which the process is effected is again
known as management, the human sense. Again, the combination of
those persons who together put forth this effort in any given enterprise is known as the management of the enterprise. The term therefore covers the process of managing, the combined human ability involved in managing and the personnel required to manage."

We could continue quoting, for there are numerous authorities to refer
to. But perhaps the time has come for us to summarise how we see
management. Figure 1.1 shows what management is about. We feel easy
with the Koonz definition, subject only to the qualification that management has an active role to play in the identification of group goals, and is
sometimes the only arbiter of conflict over what those goals should be.
We agree with Drucker that management is a creating task, and that it is
not just a creature of its environment. But we believe that management is
required in. virtually all human activities which bring together a group of
people to achieve a common goal (or goals). As a concept it is as valid in
government or the running of a charity as it is in business. Above all, it
has to do with people.

Using this assumption we are bound to consider the concept of group
goals more closely. It is one thing to suggest that management is required
to bring together groups of people to achieve a common goal or goals,
quite another for the manager to do this effectively. In a society which is
increasingly pluralistic in thought and need, attempts to focus a work
group on unitary goals becomes an increasingly difficult task. Indeed, we
may ask who decides which goals the organisation will pursue, a particularly difficult question to answer especially where we recognise that the
term "stakeholder" covers a range of different represented interests from
worker right through to shareholder or owner.

An organisation may expect the manager to manage or unify the goals
of work groups without (a) recognising the considerable constraints
inherent in individual and group behaviour, and (b) giving the manager
enough information, participation, and freedom to operate within the

company in a manner most likely to produce effective results. Little (1977)[15] has pointed out that the position of the manager, particularly at middle levels, is becoming increasingly isolated due to the decline in the material position of most managers by the erosion of differential structures (through the joint effects of trade union pressure and government pay restraint) and the lack of meaningful involvement in key company decisions at this management level. In later chapters we look more closely at both the behavioural constraints in managing groups and in the need and means to promote greater participation by managers in planning decisions.

Although we may, for the purpose of analysis, separate the quasi-scientific or systematic approaches to the management of a business from the dynamics of human behaviour in the firm, of necessity we expect the manager to integrate and combine both aspects in order to reach acceptable compromise. While we may discuss the concept of unitary versus pluralistic goals, the organisation expects management to successfully achieve organisational goals in highly pluralistic group situations. But perhaps, in the complex interaction of human behaviour and organisation goals, a more effective compromise may be found by looking at the manner in which organisational members, as stakeholders, seek to *satisfy* rather than *optimise* or *maximise* their returns from the company. March and Simon (1958)[16] have promoted a theory of organisational equilibrium which suggests as a basic postulate that "an organisation is a system of interrelated social behaviours of a number of persons who may be called participants in the organisation. Behaviour in an organisation is related to the manner in which the individual balances the inducements offered against the contributions expected." The decision to participate in an organisation is dependent upon inducement-contribution equilibrium, and such a state, it is argued, "implies an underlying structure within the organisation which exhibits both a high degree of interrelationships and substantial differentiation from other systems within the total social setting". In this way we may see how the work organisation differs from other organisations, e.g. social groups, and we may see how the "satisficer" effect applied at all levels in the company can provide for a compromise of both personal and organisational aims.

The idea of inducement-contribution balance, however, calls for a pragmatic analysis of individual and group perceptions about the operation and future development of the business (Fig. 1.1).

The human factor in management has received extensive analysis by behavioural scientists using a wide range of approaches and theoretical bases. We have sought to select that research, theory, and practice which most closely matches the management of people in organisations to the planning process. Thus we look in detail at the individual and the firm in terms of both formal and informal behaviour of both an individual and group nature. We discuss the requirement for and value of creativity within the firm. We also look both theoretically and practically at motivation, organisational style, organisational development, and change in relation to the planning process. In so doing we are implicitly relating these areas to the management of the human resource and this management function to the planning process. This provides a platform from which further areas in the planning process can be outlined always with the major focus being on human behaviour.

There is therefore throughout this book a linking of organisational behaviour with management and of these two phenomena with the planning process.

We suggest that a major function of the chief executive and his immediate colleagues involves planning since the role of chief executive will usually include accountabilities such as: "formulate and gain acceptance for strategies and policies which support the company's performance objectives" or "ensure the profitable development of the company by providing effective long term corporate plans".

Clearly, the management role involves planning and the planning process must operate effectively within, and for the benefit of, the human organisation. Within the boundaries of this book, therefore, the need for an academic definition of "management" becomes unnecessary since we are looking pragmatically at people and planning aspects of the management process.

We begin our study in the next chapter with an exploration of corporate planning and its place in the management process.

References Chapter 1

1. M. V. Sears (1965) Management, in *Planning and Control Systems: A Framework for Analysis*, R. Anthony, Harvard, p. 117.

2. H. Koonz (1962) Making sense of management theory, *Harvard Business Review*, July–August.
3. P. Drucker (1955) *The Practice of Management*, Pan, 1968 edition, p. 29.
4. P. Drucker (1955) op. cit., p. 19.
5. P. Drucker (1955) op. cit., page 23.
6. P. Drucker (1955) op. cit., p. 26.
7. R. S. B. Knowles (1971) *Modern Management in Local Government*, Butterworths, p. 10.
8. HMSO (1966–9) *Royal Commission on Local Government in England*, Cmnd 4584, para. 45.
9. R. S. B. Knowles (1971) op. cit., p. 62.
10. R. S. B. Knowles (1971) op. cit., p. 83.
11. HMSO (1967) *Maude Committee on Management in Local Government*, vol. 1, para. 145.
12. HMSO (1972) *The New Local Authorities: Management and Structure Report of Study Group* (Bain's Report).
13. J. D. Stewart (1971) *Management in Local Government: a viewpoint*, Charles Knight, p. 30.
14. M. V. Sears (1965) op. cit., p. 126.
15. A. Little (1977) When is a manager not a manager? *Journal of Chartered Institute of Secretaries*, September 1977, pp. 17–19.
16. J. G. March and H. A. Simon (1958) *Organisations*, Wiley, New York.

CHAPTER 2

Corporate Planning

Corporate planning has been established as a management process for over a decade. The need for organisations to plan their future has never been in dispute, although some may doubt their ability to do this, while others have been disappointed with results because they held the wrong expectations of corporate planning. Early attempts at planning frequently underestimated the importance of the human factor, and tended to see planning through systems eyes or as a mathematically based science, rather than as a management process.

Organisations need to plan for many reasons. We live in a world of change, and planning provides an attempt to adapt the organisation so that it can gain an earlier warning of major changes and take the appropriate action. In the 1960s most of the writings on planning drew attention to both the extent and rapidity of technological developments which tend to have been accelerating throughout the century and particularly since the post-war years. During this time the life-cycle of many old products has declined, and an ever-increasing range of new products and new industries have come into being. Technological complexity has increased, bringing major problems in research and development lead times, cost, capital requirements, higher risks, and potential obsolescence. Whole industries can become outdated (e.g. the British textile industry), and products can be overtaken by substitutes before they have had a chance to move into the maturity phase of their life-cycle.

One has only to compare the jumbo jet with the Tiger Moth, the Tiger Moth with the hot-air balloon, and the hot-air balloon with centuries when man's dream of flight was unfulfilled, to demonstrate how the pace and complexity of technology has increased in more recent years. The bow and arrow was a simple weapon to invent, and lasted centuries: many modern, complex weapons may be outdated before the first production prototype has been built.

The lesson of the 1970s is that although technology is important, it is not the only significant environmental change factor which organisations face. The pace and severity of economic, social, political, and related legal changes has reached a point when they may be potentially more damaging to the unprepared company than technological change. The reason for this is that there is always a reasonable lead time (for those who seek it) with technological change. There may be very little warning with the other change areas. The oil crisis of 1972–3, which sparked off a massive round of inflation, came as a surprise to almost all organisations. Some socio-political changes are more predictable than economic crises, but only for those organisations which develop an awareness of change, and understand the impact of the environment on their activities.

Where an environmental factor can be predicted within limits of reasonable probability this should be done and corporate strategy modified so that opportunities are seized and threats avoided. Where the unforeseeable happens the organisation must react speedily. Both the ability to integrate environmental factors with strategy and the ability to see sudden threats and take appropriate action require a well-developed approach to corporate planning.

The need for planning also arises from certain other factors in modern organisations. At the structural level there is the problem of complexity. The size of organisations has tended to increase, resulting in giant businesses such as General Motors or major undertakings such as the Greater London Council. In the United Kingdom nationalisation has com-bined businesses into vast organisations which rank with the largest created by private enterprise. The *Times Top 1000* (1975)[1] lists include six nationalised undertakings among the ten largest employers in the United Kingdom including all the first five places. Even traditionally small-type businesses, such as road transport, have been combined into major concerns, e.g. the National Freight Corporation.

Size is a problem even when the products are homogeneous. A further dimension of complexity is added when the organisation possesses a diver-sity of products which are not related to each other in either marketing or manufacturing terms. Add the dimension of multi-country operation, and the need for planning as a co-ordinating function becomes readily apparent. To get the different components of the organisation moving in the same direction (and the right direction) calls for planning of a higher order. Problems of size and of the multi-national will be returned to in later chapters.

The risks of modern business may be only slightly higher than in the past, but the size factor means that the results of failure can be more far reaching, bringing down not only the organisation itself but having wide-spread implications on society and the economy. A small business may collapse with damage to very few people other than the owners. Failure of a large business must have major effects on employment. A mammoth business may also impact seriously on exports or gross national product if it goes to the wall. Planning is therefore needed to reduce the risks associated with modern economic activity. Better planning would almost certainly have saved Rolls-Royce from the collapse caused by too heavy an involvement in the one project which had the power to crush the company.

These needs are real and important. Modern conditions require the addition of two more, which are of such recent origin that they have so far appeared in few of the books about corporate planning, and have manifested themselves with very different intensity in different countries, although one may be justified in predicting that the long-term trend for all countries will be very similar.

The first of these needs is the social requirement for greater involvement in planning and decision making by all employees of the company. Early works on corporate planning stressed the need to design an approach that had wide management participation. Now the arena is widening and the requirement is for a wider and more open approach to management which gives greater effect to industrial democracy. The methods by which this may be achieved are still open in many countries, including the United Kingdom. Whether they result in worker representations on the board, or a corporate plan negotiated with the workforce through the planning agreements procedure is, at this moment, undetermined. What is apparent is that if managers still wish to lead, rather than be driven, they have an even greater need to improve their planning abilities and those of the organisation which employs them.

Closely related to this need is another: the results of the second modern conditions. This is a closer association of business and government in planning the future of the country. In France this approach is already well developed through the National Plan. In the United Kingdom there is the much looser planning agreements concept and the National Economic Development Council. Even in the United States forces are arguing for a greater measure of centralised planning. To respond to this trend, which is undoubtedly here to stay, organisations need to plan.

Corporate planning as a concept requires some attempt at definition. It is a comprehensive future-oriented, continuous process of management, which is implemented within a formal framework and which is responsive to relevant change in the external environment. It is concerned with both strategic and operational plans, and through participation develops plans at the appropriate levels within the organisation. It includes methods of monitoring and control, and is concerned with both the short and the long term.

This definition links a number of elements which are critical to the success of corporate planning.

Comprehensiveness. Planning is comprehensive in scope. It attempts to integrate the entire organisation in terms of the relationship of activities and units, the functions within each unit, the short-term and long-term implications, and strategic and operational decisions. The aim should be for the entire organisation to strive to achieve a common, overall objective, so that each component of the organisation has a particular part to play which should be covered by the planning process.

Future-oriented. By its very nature planning is a future-oriented activity. Corporate planning makes a deliberate attempt to extend planning beyond the time-horizon of the annual budget. The exact period chosen should fit the specific requirements of the business and should take into account factors such as the lead time of decisions, the normal business cycles of the organisation, or the length of time it takes to develop a new product. Most British industrial companies have at least one in-built four-year cycle which should be considered in the manpower element of their plans: the apprenticeship period.

Five years has tended to become the most popular planning horizon, partly because it embraces the lead times of most organisations, but mainly, we suspect, because it is a period which can be conceived by the human mind. Beyond five years, unless tied to something very specific in the progress of the company, the period tends to become very unreal.

However, there is nothing magical about five years. Nor is there any reason why a diversified organisation should impose the same planning horizon on every subsidiary and every function. A common core period may be required for consolidation, but apart from this there is no reason why the planning time-horizon should not be tailored to fit the need of the individual business units.

Even a company that practises five-year planning may use forecasts of considerably longer periods.

Continuous process of management. Corporate planning is not a management technique. It is a complete way of running a business, and has a requirement for certain forms of management style (see Chapter 6). The corollary of this is that some management styles are not compatible with corporate planning. The word "planning" in this context is slightly misleading and means more than the dictionary definition would suggest. Many writers have attempted to break the management task into elements: some examples are summarised in Table 2.1. The significant point is that corporate planning embraces most of the elements listed. In addition to planning, it involves organising, motivating, communicating, co-ordinating, and controlling. The task of making plans is closely related to the task of implementing them: corporate planning covers both.

The process is continuous and ongoing. The idea of organisations sitting down occasionally to produce a five- or ten-year plan is very far from what is needed and is not what happens in most organisations. The reality is that organisations require considerable flexibility in their approach, that the corporate plan tends to be a rolling plan reviewed at least once per year when the first year is dropped and another added at the end, and that there should be a very close link between planning and other management tasks. It is in this last area that many companies fail. A plan that is strongly linked to the budgetary processes, personal performance standards, or management appraisal systems is more likely to be

TABLE 2.1
Elements of management task functions or process distinguished by certain writers

Name	Reference	Elements identified
P. Drucker	*Practice of Management*, Pan, 1969, pp. 409–12	Set objectives, organise, motivate and communicate, measure, develop people
H. Fayol	*General and Industrial Management*, trans. C. Storrs, Pitman, 1969, pp. 3, 5–6	Planning, organisation, command, co-ordination, control
E. L. F. Brech	*Organisation*, Longmans, 1966, p. 14	Plan, motivate and co-ordinate, control
W. H. Newman	*Administrative Action: The Techniques of Organisation and Management*, Prentice-Hall, 1963	Planning, organising, assembling resources, supervising, controlling
L. F. Urwick	*The Pattern of Management*, University of Minneapolis Press, 1956, p. 52	Forecast, plan, organise, direct, co-ordinate, control, communicate
G. F. Milward	*An Approach to Management*, Macdonald and Evans, 1946, pp. 35–6	Forecasting, planning and programming, organisation, command, co-ordinate, control
H. Koonz	*Towards a Unified Theory of Management*, McGraw-Hill, 1964, pp. 248–9	Planning, organising, staffing, direction, control

Note: The reader is referred to R. N. Antony, *Planning and Control Systems: A framework for analysis*, Harvard University Press, 1965, for a more detailed treatment of this subject.
Source: D. E. Hussey (1976), *Inflation and business policy*, Longmans.

part of a total management process than one which is treated as an annual *ad hoc* exercise.

Formal framework. Another keystone in the corporate planning process is a measure of formality. This is necessary to ensure that plans are made on time and in a sensible way; the right factors are considered so that plans are both meaningful and capable of interpretation by others in the organisation besides the authors; plans can be co-ordinated and consolidated because there is a common basis; documents can be produced which set targets and performance standards and can be used subsequently for monitoring and control purposes.

The problem with formality is that it can, if it becomes too rigid, destroy creativity. The challenge is to devise an approach to planning which has the best of both worlds, and this what much of this book is really about.

Necessary formality means that the corporate planning processes can be conceived as a system. An example of this approach will be given later in this chapter. Whether the system becomes a rigid paper exercise or something that has meaning depends very much on the attention given to the all-important human factor in management.

Relevant external change. Some attention has already been directed to this aspect at the beginning of this chapter. What is important is that corporate planning is a process which helps the organisation look outwards as well as inwards. It is this concentration on the relationship of the company with its environment that is one of the features which distinguishes corporate planning from other management processes.

Participation. It is possible for an autocratic chief executive to make plans for his organisation in an autocratic way, and this often happens. Such plans may benefit by attention to the disciplines and systems elements of the planning process. By corporate planning we mean something considerably deeper: a process which allows widespread involvement in planning of people from throughout the organisation, which at the very least means that all managers play some part in planning the operations for which they are responsible, and have some chance to contribute to wider strategic thinking. The nature of this involvement, and the time-horizon on plans may vary with the level in the organisation. At the other extreme participation may include a measure of industrial democracy.

Participation does not remove from senior management either the right or the duty to make decisions (although it may be associated with delegation which allows decisions to be made at the appropriate level in the organisation). The chief executive still has the obligation to lead his organisation along what he considers the most appropriate strategic path. Participatory corporate planning ensures that there is a consensus viewpoint about what is the most appropriate strategy, and that there is a common basis of understanding about what the organisation is trying to achieve.

Strategic and operational plans. There are at least two levels of planning which are different, but closely related, and which should be integrated in the corporate planning process. Ansoff (1966)[2] demonstrates the difference between the two levels with his famous cow analogy. He sees the operating problem as concerned with maximising performance in the organisation's current market activity areas, which he likens to "seeking the best way to milk a cow". Strategy is on a different plane and is concerned with allocating the firm's resources to the activities it considers to be in its best interests, but which are not necessarily the same as its current activities, "... but if our basic interest is not the cow but the most milk we can get for our investment, we must also make sure that we have the best cow money can buy". Strategic planning may include changing the cow. Operating planning can only be concerned with being a more effective milker.

Hussey (1974)[3] states:

"This does not mean that strategy does not take account of current operations. Indeed it must, for the decision to remain in them is in itself a matter of strategy. Where strategic decisions encompass all the possible paths that the company might take to reach its objectives, and where the definition of what those objectives should be, is of itself a matter of strategy: operating planning is concerned only with getting the most out of what is currently being done."

More precise definitions are provided by Denning (1971)[4] who sees strategy as "... the determination of the future posture of the business with special reference to its product–market posture, its profitability, its size, its rate of innovation, its relationships with executives, its employees and certain external undertakings". He sees operating plans to be "... the forward planning of existing operations in existing markets with existing customers and facilities".

The distinction is important because the type of information considered and the types of decisions reached are different. It is easier to obtain widespread and deep participation in operating planning than in strategic planning, although strategic participation is no less important.

Corporate planning is probably one of the most confused areas of management, and therefore is one of the most misunderstood concepts. Warren (1966)[5] stated that: "It is not, however, a process of making tomorrow's decisions today, but rather a process directed toward making today's decisions with tomorrow in mind and a means of preparing for future decisions so that they may be made rapidly, economically and with as little disruption to the business as possible." He also pointed out the common confusion of planning with one of its major parts (e.g. forecasting or budgeting) with one of the key areas in which it is required (diversification, acquisition), or with one of its common characteristics (e.g. believing long-range planning to be separate and different from other types of planning).

As mentioned earlier, planning is also perceived in a different light depending on the mental set of the individual. It has been seen as extended budgeting: a systems approach; part of a quantification approach, heavily dependent on computer models and optimising techniques; a socioeconomic activity; and a human behavioural activity. It has been postured as part of a management information system, and even described as an exercise in management development. The problem is that there is something of value in each of these approaches. The answer is to use them all, and to develop an integrated approach which draws from each.

With this intention in mind it is of value to examine corporate planning as a system, for whatever else it might be it certainly can be defined from a systems viewpoint. The system can be looked at in two ways: the hierarchy of plans which constitute the total corporate plan and the flow of information between them, and the flow of work through the year which contributes to the development of the plan. As each view adds perspective, both will be used.

There is a caution. What is presented here has to be a generalised approach. It embraces the broad principles but requires adaptation to fit individual organisations. What is important is to ensure that the final approach fits the requirements of the business.

Figure 2.1 gives a view of the hierarchy of plans and is based on a

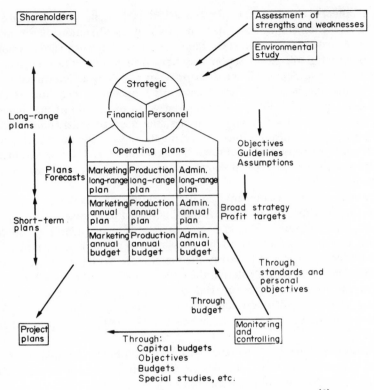

Fig. 2.1. Generalised planning system. (From Hussey, 1974[3].)

relatively simple company organised on functional lines. It is not difficult to extrapolate this to take account of the complexities of multi-division, multi-location, and multi-country companies.

The diagram relates strategic and operational plans, short-term and long-term plans, project plans, and methods of monitoring and controlling. The three boxes at the top of the diagram represent factors which must be taken into account in strategic planning, and through this in operational planning.

At the top left-hand side there are the stakeholders in the business. Traditionally we think of the strongest influence being exercised by the shareholders, although the previous chapter showed the importance of other stakeholders, not so much in choosing the direction of the enterprise or making management decisions, but by action when earnings slump or prospects look grim. Action may vary from voting with their feet by selling out and depressing the share price, or by taking action (much rarer) to change the board. Whatever the direct influence of shareholders on a business, and this is likely to be greatest when ownership of the shares is concentrated into a few large holdings, the need to satisfy shareholders will have a significant effect on corporate objectives and the resultant strategies. Organisations without shareholders (e.g. local government) will have a different type of stakeholder whose influence may take a very different course.

Employees of the company can also be defined as stakeholders, and will have certain expectations which increasingly need to be taken into account in strategic planning. The high growth rate of one dynamic group was fixed as much for the need to offer managers an exciting career with good promotion prospects as to satisfy the shareholder. With current trends and developing patterns of legislation the organisation's employees will become more and more significant in strategic planning, although the extent to which this is regarded as a constraint on freedom of action rather than a positive social benefit depends on the personal outlook of top management.

Customers, suppliers, and society are sometimes also defined as significant stakeholders. Again the degree to which their stake is recognised depends on the views of individual top managers.

The values of the stakeholders are felt positively as an influence on objectives, and negatively in constraints on strategic freedom.

On the top right-hand side of the diagram are two boxes dealing with what is sometimes called the internal and external appraisal. The first represents those factors about itself which the company should define by self-appraisal: its strengths and weaknesses. The second is a continuing study of relevant trends in the external environment, and consists of forecasts of these trends and assessments of their impact on the organisation. Together the two parts of the appraisal reveal a pattern of possibilities: opportunities, threats, profit improvement through the correction of weaknesses, and the strengths on which the organisation can build.

The strategic planning process is illustrated by the circle. It has three related elements which are mutually interdependent: strategy, finance, and people. It is also part of an iterative process which shows elements of strategic decisions being passed to operating units in the form of assumptions, objectives, and guidelines, and a corresponding modification of strategic thinking as a result of plans and forecasts flowing up from operational levels. How these elements are formulated is, of course, very important: objectives can be simple edicts from the top or they can be arrived at after much internal discussion and widespread participation.

The diagram moves from the agreement of the longer-term plans to the annual planning process. The long-term plans provide broad statements of strategy and specific targets which are translated into detailed action plans and budgets. It is this process which begins to relate corporate and departmental objectives with meaningful personal objectives and standards of performance and forms a potential link with management appraisal systems, training needs assessments, and management development.

At the bottom left-hand corner there is a box labelled project plans. These may result at any of the levels of planning and may vary in complexity from a scheme to build a new factory in Siberia to a way of improving profits by replacing some existing machine tools. Sometimes they may require heavy capital investment. Sometimes the expenditure may be mainly revenue, as in the launch of a new product that can be made on existing plant. The importance of project plans is that they provide for a formal evaluation of all significant projects before the company embarks on a particular course of action. This is one place where the bias of the planning system should lean heavily towards analytical and mathematical techniques. Project plans should also take a forward looking view, and the evaluation may cover a time-span which can be longer than the normal corporate planning period.

The last box, at the bottom right-hand corner, is an activity — monitoring and controlling. This impinges on all the various types of plans shown, using various approaches so that progress can be observed and measured and appropriate action taken. The control mechanism is a very significant part of any planning process. In analytical terms feedback allows for a judgement to be made on the validity of planned actions, and enables early corrective action to be taken. In human terms, the monitoring process is an essential factor to aid self-motivation and motivation through the organisation's reward structure.

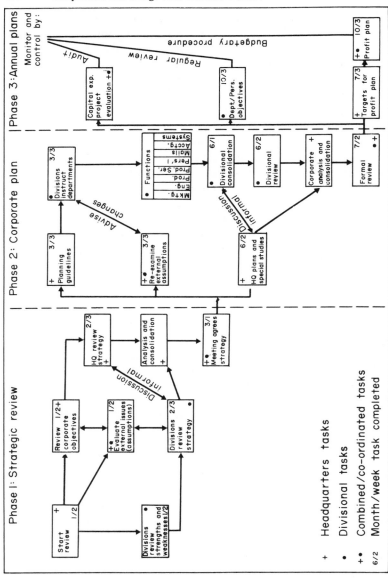

Fig. 2.2. Outline planning process. (From Hussey and Young, 1977[22].)

Figure 2.2 examines the planning process as an integrated system leading to the preparation of the various plans discussed above. The system can be divided into three main phases: the review of strategy, plan preparation, and action plans.

The purpose of the review of strategy is to enable an organisation to clarify its aims and intentions and set planning guidelines before committing the entire organisation to the time-consuming task of working out detailed plans. This step is more important in a complex multi-division company than in the simple type of organisation chosen to illustrate Fig. 2.1, and can avoid the frustrating task of having to re-write the detailed plans at subsidiary level after they have been rejected by headquarters. The first phase, therefore, incorporates a participative review of strategies against the changing pattern of opportunities, external change, and shifts in the organisation's own strengths and weaknesses. In many years the review will be a relatively simple study of changes from the previous plans, although periodically, perhaps every three years, a determined effort should be made to carry out a deeper and more fundamental examination to ensure that strategies are still appropriate. The review always gives the opportunity to question strategic thinking, and the periodic deeper examination ensures that issues are not being overlooked and that the organisation is avoiding the comforting trap of complacency.

This phase includes an evaluation of external issues relevant to the company, and the setting of planning assumptions. How this task can be approached is the subject of Chapter 10.

The review culminates in a series of meetings between different organisational units, and ultimately in a meeting between headquarters and divisions, where issues are debated and agreement reached on the path each division or business unit should take.

This joint approach leads directly into phase 2, through the publication by headquarters of planning guidelines for each of its units. These should contain no surprises as they are derived from the review meetings, and give guidance on planning assumptions, objectives, strategies, and capital availability.

Phase 2 also incorporates a new review of the external factors (in case they have changed) and progress with any special studies which might need to be carried out at headquarter level.

Within the framework of the guidelines the divisions prepare detailed plans for their area of responsibility. These will show what is to be achieved (objectives) and how it is to be achieved (strategies). Each divisional plan is broken down into sub-plans on a function basis. (There may, of course, be a greater network of divisions, subsidiaries, and subdivisions than the figure suggests.) Plans are consolidated at divisional level and reviewed by the appropriate management committee or board. After acceptance they pass to headquarters for corporate analysis and study, and consolidation into a corporate plan.

A second formal review follows, which allows corporate and divisional managements to explore deviations from the previously agreed strategies, the impact of any changes in internal or external circumstances on the agreed path, and the final shape of the plans in figures, particularly the expected profits, cash flows, and manpower. At this point some formal analysis should also be made of the risks and the sensitivity of the results to changes in key factors.

The completion of phase 2 leads naturally to the final stages of the cycle (shown only in summary form in Fig. 2.2) which embrace three groups of tasks. One is the annual budget, the targets for which derive from the plans. This ensures that the budget is firmly linked to the overall planning process but not so rigidly that there is no flexibility to modify the actions and figures if circumstances change.

A budget once agreed should be regarded as a form of "contract" between different levels of managers, and should be drawn up on a participative basis. Closely allied to the budget are the departmental and personal objectives (which relate to the action plans of Fig. 2.1).

The third group of tasks is the same as the project appraisal box in Figure 2.1.

The monitoring and controlling process goes on continuously.

Any system is only as good or bad as the people who operate it. In our opinion real success with the corporate planning process demands a management which is able to blend the formality of the system with the human problems of motivation and add to this a reasoned mix of analysis and rational decision making.

There is little doubt that the complexities of the modern world demand an approach to decision making which is logical, analytical, and which takes due note of facts. This may not always automatically lead to the right decision, but should go a long way to avoiding the sort of horror story reported by Kelf-Cohen (1973):[6]

"In the history of the nationalised industries, there are many instances where Government backs the industries in their plans of capital development, only to find that there was inadequate justification for the plans and that much of the money advanced was lost. But the relations of Government and Transport Commission from 1956 to 1960 are the classic case of a Government utterly misled – time and time again. The central feature of the reorganisation was the electrification of the London Midland main line; yet in 1960 it was revealed that the project had never been properly costed and that the Commission had no idea whether it would ever be profitable."

This nightmare-type of decision process is by no means restricted to government and the nationalised industries, and major and far-reaching decisions are still made in many businesses on the flimsiest of data after the most rudimentary study and with next to no thought. The world calls this entrepreneurial flair and sometimes it works. Often it results in something decidedly less than optimum.

There are numerous reasons why few organisations get the best out of analysis. Not least among these is the fact that decision making in organisations has political and emotional facets. Organisations do not function on pure logic. They are run by people, not computers, and any attempt to make decisions more analytical must take cognisance of the human factor in decision making. Analytical approaches must be integrated with the behavioural aspects of decision making.

Mintzburg (1975)[7] draws together a number of researches into how managers spend their time:

"If you ask a manager what he does, he will most likely tell you that he plans, organises, co-ordinates and controls. Then watch what he does. Don't be surprised if you can't relate what you see to those four words. . . . The fact is that these four words which have dominated management vocabulary since the French industrialist Henri Fayol first introduced them in 1916, tell us little about what managers actually do. At best they indicate some vague objectives managers work to."

He maintains that the evidence does not fit the classical view (see Table 2.1) of what management is about.

He maintains that there are four myths about managers which are disproved by the evidence:

(1) "The manager is a reflective, systematic planner."[8]
(2) "The effective manager has no regular duties to perform."[9]
(3) "The senior manager needs aggregated information, which a formal management information system best provides."[9]
(4) "Management is, or at least is quickly becoming, a science and a profession."[10]

The gaps between what managers do, what we popularly believe they do, and what they ought to do give us a good clue to why corporate planning is more difficult to implement successfully in practice than the logic of the theories would suggest. Some of these problems are discussed at some length in Chapter 13. Most are in some way connected with behavioural problems of one type or another — not least being the difficulty of enforcing a formal and structural approach to issues which historically have been handled by informal and unstructured responses. Human attitudes and behaviour are rarely changed solely by an exhortation from the chief executive to do corporate planning. These issues will be returned to later in the book.

Corporate planning has now reached a stage when many of the opinions and acts of faith which used to dub for "proof" of what was good or bad, are now being replaced by research-based evidence. Despite the results of the Mintzburg analysis of studies of management behaviour referred to above, there is proof that a significant number of companies attempt some form of corporate planning, and that despite the disappointment and disillusions found by some investigators (see Chapter 13), the number of "planning" companies has shown a healthy increase over time.

Brown, Sands, and Thompson (1969)[11] found that 90% of US manufacturing companies were practising some form of formal corporate planning. As is so often the case, the United Kingdom was at this time lagging behind. Denning and Lehr (1971-2)[12] demonstrated that 25% of companies from *The Times* top 300 (financial companies and nationalised industries were excluded) were undertaking corporate planning in 1967, but that the distribution of planning companies was restricted to seven industry groups, and was much more likely in subsidiaries of overseas companies than in British based companies.

The general nature of the Denning and Lehr findings is in part supported by a survey which Knowlson (1974)[13] conducted for the Society for Long Range Planning among its members in 1974. This asked when corporate planning was first introduced into the organisation and showed that:

> Only 15% of the sample of 385 organisations were undertaking corporate planning in 1967.
>
> The Median year for all organisations for the introduction of planning was 1970.
>
> Introduction occurred earlier in some industries than in others.

Some results of this survey are shown in Table 2.2. Although the general indications support the pattern observed by Denning and Lehr, the significant differences in sample, universe, and timing should not be forgotten. Some of the activity groupings are based on very small samples.

The rather surprising industry distribution of early planning companies may possibly go some way to explaining the results of the survey by Kempner and Hewkins (1968),[14] which maintained that few British companies had implemented corporate planning. The size of sample and method of sampling of the survey could have easily led to this erroneous conclusion.

Grinyer and Norburn (1974)[15] state that their work "suggested very wide adoption of corporate planning". Grinyer and Norburn (1974)[16] also obtained findings which lend some weight to the Mintzburg analysis referred to earlier.

> "Although our findings suggest that the real decision making system is informal and often ill defined, they also highlight the need for top managers to be well informed and to use more information. Financial performance, as has already been suggested, tends to be associated with the use of more items of relevant information to indicate the need for a review of strategy and in the review itself.
>
> "If this interpretation of the significance of our findings is correct a number of warning notes should be sounded to those concerned with strategic planning and decision making:
>
> "(1) The important decision making process is informal and political. Performance is more likely to be improved by fostering

TABLE 2.2

Survey of corporate planning: activity of organisation and when corporate planning was introduced

Main activity of organisation	Replies in group	Number with corporate planning %	Year of Introduction									
			Before 1963	1963/4	1965/6	1967	1968	1969	1970	1971	1972	1973
Mining or quarrying (not coal)	5	80			1				|2|	1		
Food, drink or tobacco	30	97	2		2	1	3	6	|4|	3	2	7
Chemicals or pharmaceuticals	35	89		3	3	3	5	|2|	2	6	7	2
Oil, coal, gas or electricity	10	100			2	1	1	|2|	1		3	
Metals and metal manufacture	17	88	1		3	1	|5|	1	1	5		3
Mechanical engineering	22	91	1	1	1	1	4	|3|	3	2	2	1
Electrical eng. and electronics	17	88	5	1		1	|2|	2	2	1		1
Motor vehicles, aircraft, ships	13	77	2		1		1	|3|	3			
Textiles, fibres or footwear	8	87		1	1		1		1	|2|		
Other manufacturing industry	51	90	2	2	5	2	7	|5|	10	6	4	2
Construction	20	80	1	2		3		|2|		7	1	3

	Total	No.	%										
Transport (inc. post office)	16	16	100				2	2	|5|	1	3	1	2
Retailing and Distributive trades	13	8	62	1						|1|	1	1	4
Banking, insurance, finance	39	35	90	1			1	4	4	5	|4|	8	8
Consultancy	36	26	72	1	1	1	3	6	|1|	4	4	1	3
Research	6	2	33							1	1		
Education and training	12	11	92	1	1	1		1	1	|3|	2		1
Central govt. administration	3	1	33								|1|		
Representative org. govt. agency	9	8	89			2			2		|4|		
Other non-manufacture industry	23	19	83	1	1		2		1	2	|2|	4	5
Grand total	385	330	86	21	12	25	19	43	40	|46|	55	34	43

Source: Knowlson, 1974 (13)

Note: | | = Median year of introduction.

more informal communication and a better use of information than by expending a lot of effort on designing and operating formal procedures enshrined in planning manuals.

"(2) Formal planning systems can do no more than provide a framework for the real, political, decision-making system. If they define responsibilities, or objectives, too rigidly they may be made obsolete by the changing political process. They will then be ignored.

"(3) Strategic planners will influence decisions only by becoming embedded in the political process. Since they carry no line decision making authority, they cannot make decisions, they can only influence them. This influence is likely to depend on the planner's understanding of the company and its informal channel of danger signals to key decisions taken, and his ability to collect, analyse, and present data on specific strategic alternatives in a way that decision takers can easily understand and use.

"(4) Too much information is wasted because it is thought inappropriate and over-elaborate by decision takers. Yet financial performance is related to use of more relevant information. Clearly the relevance of information received by decision-takers in many companies should be reviewed and presentation of relevant items improved.

"(5) Thus, in general, there should be a greater emphasis on facilitating operation of the real, political decision taking process, and provision of appropriate information to participants within it, and less on formal procedures and beautifully documented plans. The latter may have a useful co-ordinating function but are too often either overtaken by unforeseen events or just ignored by those with real decision making power."

We would not agree with these conclusions in their entirety, and will be exploring some of the issues related to them in Chapters 6 and 7. The behavioural problems which are observed in this study perhaps begin to explain the disappointment some organisations have felt over their planning activities. Ringbakk (1969)[17] made a survey of forty planning companies in the United States. This established that most companies were dissatisfied by what they had achieved from their planning efforts. Not all the managements concerned practised planning as vigorously, or accepted it as firmly, as might have been assumed. A further general conclusion was that planning in many companies was still in an evolutionary stage. Considerable evidence has been produced from this and other studies (e.g. Warren, 1966[5]) on the reasons for planning failure. These will provide much of the material for later chapters.

There is some evidence to suggest that crisis was the cause that set many of the earliest companies on the planning route. Irving (1970)[18] found in a survey of twenty-seven "planning" companies carried out in 1969 that more than a third had begun planning as a direct result of major changes at board level, and in practically all cases planning was initiated as the result of the perception of a need to meet a factor of change which the company faced or anticipated. Denning and Lehr (1971/2)[12] found technological change to be a major factor in early planning companies. The wider spread of planning activity suggests that crisis-response is no longer the most significant trigger. This is all to the good, since corporate planning is a complex process of management that thrives best in a healthy company. It is not an alternative to facing up to the real problems that beset the company.

Many individuals have made personal statements about the value and benefit of corporate planning. More specific evidence is provided by two major surveys, which provide statistical proof.

Thune and House (1970)[19] analysed the results of matched pairs of "formal planning" and "informal planning" companies in six industry groups (drugs, chemicals, machinery, oil, food, and steel) over periods varying from seven to fifteen years – depending on the date of introduction of planning – up to 1965. Planning companies were found to out-perform informal planning companies on three of the five economic measures chosen for the study: earnings per share, earnings on common equity, and earnings on total capital employed. Results for the other two measures, average sales, and stock price appreciation were also better for planners, but the results lacked statistical significance.

Planners were also found to out-perform themselves when pre-planning results were compared to those of post-planning. Data was only available for three of the economic measures: sales, earnings per share, and stock price appreciation, but on each of these formal planning showed better results.

Validation of the findings came from a comparison of the performance of planning and non-planning companies for a period before the introduction of planning. There was no significant difference in results.

The second study, Ansoff *et al.* (1970)[20] examined the effects of planning on the success of acquisitions, and was based on a sample of companies with a four-year period free of acquisitions, followed by an acquisition period during which no more than one year elapsed between any successive acquisitions, and followed by a post-acquisition period of two years.

The study examined acquisition behaviour at the strategic (defining corporate objectives and acquisition strategies) and the operational (identifying the means of acquisition, establishing search criteria, allocation of supporting budgets, and similar activities) levels. Thirteen variables were used to measure performance, with up to three ways of measuring each.

A comparison of "extensive" and "non-planners" found that the former achieved better results on all variables except one (total asset), and that the performance of planners had a more consistent pattern.

Some individual "non-planners" did out-perform the best of the planners, but a much higher proportion of non-planners had poor performance.

Vancil (1970)[21] studied the accuracy of forecast results in plans, although accuracy does not necessarily demonstrate a planning benefit. He was able to show that accurate forecasts were found where there was top management involvement, association of subordinates in the setting of goals, a discipline which linked the plan to the annual budget, and a philosophy that an important purpose of the plan was to provide a frame of reference for the operational budget. This takes us right back to the behavioural aspects of planning: and even more so in the researcher's feeling at the end of the study that over-concentration on accuracy could be a bad thing in that it could result in self-fulfilling prophecies at sub-optimum performance. Many planners have claimed that the process is more important than the plan, which seems to be the tentative conclusions of Vancil's work.

This chapter has explored the nature of corporate planning, the shape of the process, and has shown that, although a widely practised and often successful approach, it is not universally practised, nor does it always lead to the satisfaction of those using it. Partly an analytical process, it also relies very heavily on the behavioural aspects of management. Good planning is a blend of both.

Later we shall return to the various components of a planning process. But first it is necessary to consider some of the behavioural issues: this we do in the next few chapters.

References Chapter 2

1. *The Times* (1975) *Times Top 1000 1975/6*, Times Books.
2. H. I. Ansoff (1966) Planning as a practical management tool, paper presented at a Corporate Planning Seminar, Bradford University.
3. D. E. Hussey (1974) *Corporate Planning: Theory and Practice*, Pergamon Press, Oxford, p. 116.
4. B. W. Denning (1971) *Corporate Planning: Selected Concepts*, McGraw-Hill, pp. 2 and 4.
5. E. K. Warren (1966) *Long Range Planning: The Executive Viewpoint*, Prentice-Hall, p. 18.
6. R. Kelf-Cohen (1973) *British Nationalisation 1945-73*, Macmillan, p. 79.
7. H. Mintzburg (1975) The manager's job: folklore and fact, *Harvard Business Review*, July–Aug. 1975, p. 49.
8. H. Mintzburg (1975) op. cit., p. 50.
9. H. Mintzburg (1975) op. cit., p. 51.
10. H. Mintzburg (1973) op. cit., p. 53.
11. J. K. Brown, S. S. Sands, and G. C. Thompson (1969) Long range planning in the USA – NICB survey, *Long Range Planning*, March, Vol. 1, No. 3.
12. B. W. Denning and M. E. Lehr (1971/2) The extent and nature of long range planning in the United Kingdom, Parts 1 and 2, *Journal of Management Studies*, Vol. 8, May 1971; Vol. 9, Feb. 1972.
13. P. Knowlson (1974) *Organisation and Membership Survey, March 1974*, Society for Long Range Planning, p. 27.
14. T. Kempner and J. W. M. Hewkins (1968) *Is Corporate Planning Necessary?*, British Institute of Management.
15. P. H. Grinyer and D. Norburn (1974) Strategic planning in 21 British companies, *Long Range Planning*, Vol. 7, No. 4, Aug. p. 8.
16. P. H. Grinyer and D. Norburn (1974) Op. cit., p. 87.
17. K. A. Ringbakk (1969) Organised planning in major U.S. companies, *Long Range Planning*, Vol. 2, No. 2, Dec.
18. P. Irving (1970) *Corporate Planning Practice: a study of the development of organised planning in major U.K. companies*, University of Bradford, MSc dissertation.
19. S. S. Thune and R. J. House (1970) Where long range planning pays off, *Business Horizons*, Aug.
20. H. I. Ansoff, J. Avner, R. G. Brandenburg, F. E. Portner, and R. Radosevitch (1970) Does planning pay: The effect of planning on success of acquisitions in American firms, *Long Range Planning*, Vol. 3, No. 2, Dec.

21. R. F. Vancil (1970) The accuracy of long range planning, *Harvard Business Review*, Sept–Oct.
22. D. E. Hussey and R. Young (1977) Corporate planning at Rolls–Royce Motors, *Long Range Planning*, Vol. 10, No. 2.

CHAPTER 3

The Individual and the Firm

Prior to the Industrial Revolution most people worked either as a member of a small group, e.g. in farming, or individually, e.g. wool spinners, cloth makers. The rapidly developing technology of the century from 1750, however, brought the introduction of mills and factories and the large-scale exploitation of minerals which led to the growth of manufacturing industries employing hundreds of people at single sites using highly mechanised production techniques. The phenomenal growth of the manufacturing industry and corresponding commercial services called inevitably for larger and larger organisations staffed by many thousands of employees. In an era where technological innovation could produce vast rewards there were major upheavals of the old social order of the landowner and his workers, giving rise to the new rich, the mill or factory owner employing the thousands who were leaving the land to seek work in growing towns and cities. Not surprisingly the major accent on technology produced research and treaties into more effective ways of managing the vast labour forces employed in different industries. The fourth quarter of the nineteenth century and the early years of the twentieth century were the setting for such notable theorists as Fayol (1949)[1] on organisation and management and Taylor (1947),[2] the father of scientific management. At this time also the noted sociologist Max Weber (1925)[3] was advancing his theory of bureaucracy in an attempt to explain the manner in which large organisations sought to control and effectively harness the partial degree of commitment or allegiance given by its members. Weber suggested that the old order of master–servant authority based on traditional grounds, or the established belief in the sanctity of

41

immemorial traditions and the legitimacy of the status of those exercising authority under them, had given way to a different kind of authority, that based on rational grounds — the belief in the "legality" of necessary rules and regulations and the right of those elevated to authority under such rules to issue commands. Weber further expanded on the use of rational authority in organisations through his description of the features of a bureaucracy. In brief outline these are as follows:

"(1) The staff members are personally free, observing only the impersonal duties of their offices.

(2) There is a clear hierarchy of offices.

(3) The functions of these offices are clearly specified.

(4) Officials are appointed on the basis of a contract.

(5) They are selected on the basis of a professional qualification, ideally supported by a diploma gained through examination.

(6) They have a monetary salary, and usually pension rights. The salary is graded according to position in the hierarchy. The Official can always leave the post and, under certain circumstances, it can be terminated.

(7) The Official's post is his sole or major occupation.

(8) There is a career structure, and promotion is possible either by seniority or merit and according to the judgment of superiors.

(9) The Official may appropriate neither the post nor the resources which go with it.

(10) The Official is subject to a unified control and disciplinary system." [Allbrow (1970)[4] from Weber (1964).]

These features of a bureaucratic organisation are intended to illustrate the nature of the control exerted by the organisation on individual members. One should bear in mind that, in this sense, the term "bureaucracy" is used in a descriptive sense rather than in the evaluative sense of an overstaffed, ponderous, slow administrative machine for which the term is sometimes used today. Weber was, then, intent upon describing the manner in which large organisations function and control their members, and creating an understanding of the unique manner in which the organisation can continue to function despite the fact that over a period of years its membership changes with people joining and leaving to suit their own purposes in life. A number of writers have used Weber as the basis for the further analysis of the organisation as an entity which can be examined in its own right and, further, be said to exist *despite* people. Such an entity may be looked upon as a machine or self-sustaining system which, by its relentless operation and developing efficiencies, will affect all those working within it whilst being unaffected by the actions of any individual member. Of course, this view is challenged by other writers who subscribe to the view that an organisational functioning is best understood by analysing the behaviour of the individuals and groups who make up that enterprise and that an organisation cannot and does not exist without people. The former viewpoint is often referred to as "structuralist" since it seeks to explain an organisation in terms of the formal structure, roles, and rules supporting the operation. The latter viewpoint may be referred to as "interactionist" because it seeks to understand organisational functioning in terms of the behaviour, action, and interaction of organisational members. In considering the individual and the firm, we need to look more closely at both viewpoints in order to examine how the individual both affects and is affected by the organisation of which he is a member. A structuralist analysis of organisations may use Weber's ten bureaucratic features as a blue print for efficiency, or, in the terms of some management theorists, as a means of achieving the organisation's end goals. Such an analysis will focus on the normative actions — or "what should happen" — in the organisation, rather than "what actually happens", and show that it is possible to control the efforts of people through payment, but also more effectively, perhaps, by mobilising skills and professional commitment in a rational sense, to the achievement of organisational goals. Further than this, Perrow (1970)[5] suggests that an organisation may attempt to control external influences, which arise because of changes in the environment and personnel characteristics, by creating specialised (staff) positions and through devices such as regulations and categorisation. It could be argued that the immersion of successive generations into the rational requirements of organisations has resulted in a socialising effect such that individuals readily assimilate the rules and regulations and offer commitment in order to use their fund of knowledge and skills in the pursuance of quite acceptable and natural organisational goals. This argument may appear, at first sight, somewhat tautological, or, at least, the proverbial chicken and egg — Which comes first? Does the organisation control the individual so totally? How can the individual influence not only what happens inside the organisation but also his own career and life space? The structuralist viewpoint of the organisation taken further suggests that the effects of bureaucratic socialisation may be seen most clearly in the employment of professionals – those who are professionally qualified and have membership of a professional body or reference group. Consider this comment by Perrow (1972)[6]

"The less the expertise, the more direct the surveillance and the more obtrusive the controls. The more the expertise, the more unobtrusive the controls. The best situation of all, though they do not come cheap, is to hire professionals, for someone else has socialised them and even unobtrusive controls are hardly needed. The professional, the prima donna of organisation theory is really the ultimate eunuch – capable of doing everything well in that harem except that which he should not do, and in this case that is to mess around with the goals of the organisation, or the assumptions that determine to what ends he will use his professional skills."

It is a nice point – the organisation overcomes the partial allegiance which individuals have either by overt control and direction or, more subtly, by hiring those who have already been socialised into organisation norms and standards through professional education and training and will not, therefore, question the basic tenets and goals for which the bureaucracy exists. This line of reasoning can be taken further to suggest that an organisation, existing as an entity in itself, can control individual behaviour by satisfying economic needs (wage payment) and by providing intrinsic rules and procedures, the breaking of which is labelled as incompetent behaviour. The structuralist mode of analysis may lead ultimately to the view that most action in a bureaucracy is instrumental and that although employees, particularly managers, feel they have control over their work and their destiny, this is not, in fact, the case. The major problem facing an organisation in relation to the individuals it employs is really one of sheer size necessitating the use of formal roles and rules within an extended hierarchy and chains of command. Often it is difficult to know where the real power lies since, although it may be perceived that it lies ultimately with the chief executive or board of directors, as we have seen, changes at this level as at any other level will not usually affect the continuing operation of the business in the broad bureaucratic sense. Furthermore, individuals lower down in the organisation may feel a real sense of alienation, removed completely from the power source and having little control over their work and working life. Many studies of workers engaged in routine, instrumental jobs have highlighted the basis of such alienation and its effects in terms of motivation and commitment to the organisation (see Blauner, 1964,[7] Gouldner, 1954[8]). It could be argued that the underlying or latent reasons for frequent industrial disputes in certain types of industry lies in the desire for greater control and participation in organisational decision making by employees regardless of what the manifest reasons for a dispute might be.

The analysis of organisational behaviour from a formal, structuralist point of view (for all its inherent assumptions and difficulties) is the approach quite often adopted by management consultants and planners because it allows for rational decisions to be made about rational needs and behaviour (since behaviour not conforming to organisational goals is seen as deviant or incompetent) and the construction of an organisation structure and reporting system against the responsibilities of functional management. This approach has distinct advantages in that it is neat and uncluttered with considerations of the vagaries of human behaviour; it also allows decisions and suggestions to be made on how the organisation should operate and, in certain respects, how the analytical process can be quantified. The major drawback in such analyses is that they fail to take account of what actually happens in organisations in terms of the effects of individual and group behaviour on the functioning of the firm. Such considerations are necessary for a proper understanding of the conditions under which planning or change processes are likely to succeed.

The view of an organisation as a system of overlapping groups of individuals and in terms of inter-individual behaviour has been referred to earlier as the interactionist perspective. It differs from the structural viewpoint in the level of analysis, and researchers are usually seeking to show how the interaction of individuals and groups either provides the structure of the organisation or at least interprets and modifies what we have called the "formal" structure. Thus the organisation, as depicted by organisation charts and reporting diagrams, is not what it seems to be.

Research into the behaviour of small groups, and the effects of this behaviour on organisational functioning, has been carried out since the end of the First World War. The use of the concept of formal and informal groups has been used to draw distinctions between planned and actual behaviour. Many studies have been concerned with comparisons of systems of rewards and punishments affecting the individual as a member of a work group and as a member of the organisation. It is important to realise that managers, staff, and workers belong to a number of different groups, some of which exist in a formal sense (e.g. management teams, committees, sections, shifts) and others which can be said to be informal (e.g. friendship or common interest groups). Some of these groups operate to further organisational goals, whilst others are in conflict with or at the least indifferent towards such goals. An individual both affects and is affected by the standards (or "norms") and behaviour of groups to which he belongs. Most of us can recall times when decisions we have made have been based less on expediency or the need to meet company objectives and more on the needs or requirements of our colleague group. It has been suggested that, in fact, individuals have to cope with a system of "dual control" based on two kinds of rewards and punishments. The model in Fig. 3.1 suggests that management offers a set of rewards for conforming to organisational requirements while at the same time the individual receives a further set of rewards for conforming to the informal group norms. Where the two control systems are in conflict, the individual finds himself pushed and pulled by management and his work group. There is

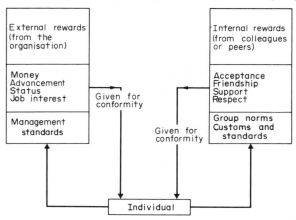

Fig. 3.1 Individual and group behaviour — the dual control system. (From Zaleznick and Moment, 1964[9].)

much research available, which suggests that, when faced with such a situation, the individual will usually conform with group requirements since pressure from the group is closer, more pervasive, and can have a more powerful immediate effect. Thus in planning, as in managing, it is important to recognise and find ways of coping with group pressures and harnessing group effort to planning activities. It will be recognised that whilst pressure from a formal group, e.g. a representative committee, may be obvious and clearly presented, this will often not be the case with informal groups where it may be difficult to ascertain either the leadership or the full extent of the membership and the degree of commitment to the group itself. Nevertheless, failure to recognise informal group pressure can lead to the best of plans or decisions being thwarted. We have undoubtedly all heard of cases of new management systems or techniques being installed with great ceremony and at great cost which, after a short time, have failed or become debased and virtually worthless. Examples exist in companies of the installation of elaborate systems of management by objectives promoted at chief executive level and implemented right down the management hierarchy, which have not worked successfully because the commitment of middle and junior management has not been obtained. When such cases are analysed it is apparent that middle or junior management "groups" have provided support for individuals to either ignore or so modify company policy that the system is rendered ineffective. Oddly enough, most managers are in favour of some form of objective performance measurement system of the MBO type, and cases of failure to implement such a system are often rooted in the suspicion by management groups of the ulterior motives of senior executives or the feeling that the "organisation" is somehow curtailing or withdrawing the manager's authority to make his own assessment of his staff. But whatever the reasons for failure, this example is used to illustrate the real pressure which middle management, as a group, can exert on company policy and operation.

So far we have suggested that the planner will find it useful to consider the effects of the organisation as an "entity" on the individual and the effects of his or her membership of both formal and informal groups. If the individual both affects and is affected by these situations we might usefully examine some of the theories and research which offer suggestions on how the individual copes with and adjusts to pressures of membership of the organisation. The studies outlined form part of the extensive range of research into organisation behaviour but have been selected because they offer practical thinking "models" for the planner to take account of in his work.

The importance of informal behaviour in organisation functioning is well demonstrated by the research of Strauss *et al.* (1963)[10] and his concept of "the negotiated order". In an empirical study of doctor-nurse-ancillary worker and patient relationships in a psychiatric hospital situation, Strauss points to the manner which individuals break, stretch, modify or re-define organisational rules by striking bargains with other members of the organisation. In this way informal rules governing behaviour in a particular ward would be agreed between parties involved, e.g. doctor and ward sister, and remain in force for a relatively short period of time then be discarded until some particular issue arose which called for the negotiation and agreement of a further rule to cope with that contingency.

Thus the need to "get things done" in an organisation may be facilitated by a process of negotiation between people resulting in relatively short-term understandings or agreements establishing rules or norms about the way in which specific things will be ordered. Readers will undoubtedly be familiar with such arrangements: a recent example from the research of Langham (1976)[11] concerned the bypassing of a formal communication link between a regional office manager and staff management at head office where the office manager had made an "arrangement" with a relatively junior clerk in head office to deal with certain issues affecting the region rather than use the formal laid-down channel between himself and the deputy staff manager. When questioned about this his response was that, since it took weeks to get information through the formal channel, he preferred to contact the junior clerk, who was three or four grades junior to the deputy staff manager, but who nevertheless could provide information to enable the office manager to "get things done". The negotiation process may be affected by such factors as the differences in professional training and qualification of the individuals concerned, their respective position in the hierarchy, individual beliefs and standards, but particularly also in the degree of trust developed and maintained between the interacting parties.

It goes without saying that trust is a major feature of all negotiating situations and is illustrated best by reference to the formal negotiating stances adopted by unions and managements which feature in reports in the national press. Looking at the negotiated order as a means of analysing ongoing organisational behaviour, however, should provoke thought and questions on the extent to which the specialist role in the planner has to build and work within a climate of trust in order to negotiate and successfully obtain the scarce resource of time and commitment from operating management. It is generally accepted that trust is very much a reciprocated factor in that one party to a negotiation will invest the degree of trust in the other party which he feels is commensurate with the degree of trust being invested in himself. In other words there is a balance of trust between the two parties which can easily be strained, hence we often hear the comment that trust takes years to build but can be broken or lost within minutes.

It will be seen that the concept of a "negotiated order" at once raises issues for those working in and attempting to influence organisations. Although the work of Strauss arises out of studies of hospitals, clear parallels can be drawn with other types of organisations. The work particularly draws attention to the interplay of professionals and non-professionals not just in terms of hierarchical position where behaviour should follow the formal organisation structure but in terms of the informal behaviour required where a crude "pulling of rank" approach would not gain sufficient agreement and commitment to necessary working arrangements. The idea of a balance or reciprocation in the behaviour of organisational members can be further extended by looking at the theory of "social exchange" advanced by Homans (1958).[12] He has suggested that the nature and extent of interaction in organisations can be analysed on the basis of the stimulus–response model in psychology, where two people can provide rewards and punishments to each other in working together. If we add to this exchange of rewards and punishments the concept of opportunity cost culled from economics, then it can be suggested that one individual will relate to and work with another to the extent that the rewards associated with that relationship (normally in social/behavioural terms) are balanced against the cost in terms of the time and effort required by the relationship. Thus, in the example of the office manager and junior clerk mentioned earlier it could be suggested that the pay-off for the junior clerk is her perception of importance and enhanced status in working directly for a fairly senior manager coupled with the recognition and expressions of gratitude received from that manager. For the office manager, what he gives in recognition is balanced against what he receives in terms of rapid information and answers to queries. This kind of arrangement would break down if either party felt that they were having to give, in a relative sense, much more than they were receiving. In this particular example we can see that if the junior clerk felt or perceived that she was just "being used" it is likely she would break off the arrangement by referring the office manager to the formal channels to be used. The reverse would, of course, also apply. The approach of Homans has been extended by Blau (1963)[13] in an extensive study of a Federal Law Enforcement Agency. The purpose of Blau's study was to investigate the social cohesion and the exercise of authority within departments by looking at the relationship between formal rules and the actual behaviour of departmental members. In the Federal Law Enforcement Agency each agent investigated particular firms against a range of complex business legislation and was measured on his performance in reaching decisions in respect of particular aspects of law enforcement on the basis of evidence uncovered. There arose situations where the agent found himself in difficulties concerning a particular case, and the procedure laid down was that, in such circumstances, he should seek advice and help from his immediate supervisor. However, within the agency appraisal system the immediate supervisor was responsible for carrying out appraisal and performance rating of his agent subordinates. Consequently agents were reluctant to go to their supervisor for help with a problem case since they felt that such action would reveal their inadequacies in handling cases and reflect adversely on their competence. The agents overcame this conflict of needs and desires by establishing an "unofficial" network of contacts amongst agents in which advice was sought and offered in informal consultations. Such consultations represent an exchange of values, in Blau's terms, where both participants gain something and both pay a price. The agent seeking the advice of a colleague on a problem gains information to enable him to perform better without having to expose his difficulty to the supervisor. In return this agent implicitly pays respect to the greater proficiency of his colleague and, as the cost of receiving assistance, acknowledges his inferiority in comparison with the more proficient agent. The agent being consulted gives up time and allows his own work to be temporarily disrupted in return for prestige and the implicit acknowledgement of his greater expertise. In this analysis the concept of rewards and costs can be seen as central to the interaction; indeed, it is suggested that the continuation of such an arrangement between two people may be dependent upon the perception of each one as to what is a reasonable balance between costs incurred and rewards received. Homans has called this "the rule of distributive justice".

The concept of exchange theory has been criticised on the grounds that it does not adequately cater for the intra-personal aspects of social behaviour and therefore it is difficult to assess, in economic terms, what the pay-off for each party may consist of. We can accept this criticism, however, and yet still use the social exchange concept to throw light on organisational behaviour, particularly the effects of intervention in a firm by specialists such as corporate planners. The use of the concept will channel the planner's thinking into such questions as How am I perceived by others? What am I asking for? What am I giving in return? and, most importantly, How can I, through my own behaviour as well as the techniques I am applying, create conditions which will support a balance of costs and rewards? Chapter 13 illustrates the dangers to specialist groups of ignoring this concept and isolating themselves from the organisation.

The theories and research we have outlined so far have illustrated the manner in which groups of individuals operate informally in order to cope with the formal rules and regulations of large organisations. It is appropriate to review also the manner in which individuals themselves cope with organisational demands which are in conflict with their own needs and demands. The work of Erving Goffman (1968)[14] is apposite since he has focused on "total institutions", i.e. organisations in which all aspects of an individual's life are governed by a single authority, where the individual is a member of a large group of others all treated alike, and where each day's events are tightly scheduled with clear expectations and requirements. Goffman's best-known studies were of hospitals for the mentally ill, and the fact that his findings arise out of such situations means that translation of such findings into other organisations which are less total, e.g. business organisations, must be tempered with the knowledge that the business organisation obtains only partial commitment from individuals who are members for only part of each day. Nevertheless, much of Goffman's work, particularly the influence of organisational forces on self-identity, can be usefully applied to business organisations.

When an individual enters an organisation he is likely to undergo

changes of identity in terms of how both he and others define his behaviour. Goffman suggests that the individual is concerned to "manage"
the impression he creates in the presence of other people, but that such
"impression management" is subject to the constraints of institutionalised
standards, incentives, joint values, and promptings which exist within the
organisation. Thus there is a requirement for the individual to become a
co-operator or conforming member. In conforming to institutionalised
standards, promptings, and so on, the individual makes what may be
referred to as a "primary adjustment" to the organisation. Such "primary
adjustment", however, merely describes the overt and superficial
behavioural contract between the individual and organisation. It does not
account for the manner in which the individual copes with the dissonance
created by organisational demands and requirements which conflict with
his own needs, aspirations, or values. The individual must, therefore,
reduce such dissonance by employing informal means of satisfying his
personal needs and values. This process is described by Goffman as
"secondary adjustment" and takes the form of rule bending or stretching
and the gathering together of material objects which will support the ego
identity and provide for some personal comforts within an austere institu-
tional setting.

The process of secondary adjustment is common in organisations; examples range from the alteration and personalisation of standard uniforms,
e.g. by nurses or security guards, to the bartering for and collection of
office equipment by clerical and administrative employees particularly in
status-conscious organisations where size and type of desk, carpet and
other trappings is an indicator of rank. In this way the clerk officially on
the same level as other clerks, who sees himself as "senior" by virtue of
length of service, age, job knowledge, and so on may reinforce that perception by careful acquisition of supporting status symbols. It is small wonder
that specialists such as O&M or job evaluators meet with resistance in their
attempts to assess and standardise procedures and jobs.

It is important to bear in mind that individuals may "perceive" the
same situations differently, one from another, since each individual's
beliefs, values, experiences, and needs, i.e. the "frame of reference", on
which an assessment or "perception" of a situation is based, are also different one from another. This is but a simple explanation of the complex
phenomena of intra-individual behaviour against which we must relate the

requirements and rules of the organisation. Colville (1975)[15] has studied the effects of organisation structure on managerial behaviour in the airline industry with particular reference to the newly appointed or promoted manager. This study is particularly illuminating in that it has approached the study of managerial behaviour within both the formal *and* informal framework whilst focusing on the meaning and perceptions which individual managers attach to requirements arising out of both formal and informal practices. The term "incumbency development process" is used to describe the activity which an individual experiences from the moment he assumes a role title in an organisation. The research outlines the diverse nature of role learning and the establishment of relationships and understandings. Such processes are unique in the sense that every individual has personal experience and subjective perceptions and expectations. Other members within the organisation serve vital roles, however, in exerting restraints, controls, and boundary limitations upon the behaviour the individual is able to exhibit or even use furtively.

Colville goes on to explain that the incumbency development process is:

"A development in the sense that it is a learning activity combining what experience and knowledge an individual brings to a situation and its actors and the interaction which then goes on between the individual and that situation. The individual will learn how to adapt his experience, knowledge and methods of interaction to suit and accommodate objectives which he either defines or has defined for him by others. This process is therefore one of perceiving, interpreting and applying meaning. . . . Each individual undergoes a process which will include for example the appreciation and interpretation of expectations. These expectations of behaviour are often unclear and may only be discovered by the individual through 'experimenting' with behaviour. Illustrations provided in the current research saw individuals using very subjective assessments to determine whether or not they could make decisions. The expectations in such situations had not been clarified and the individuals undertook their own means of clarification by acting in ways they felt to be appropriate. . . ." [Colville, 1975,[15] pp. 156-7.)

So we can conjecture from this that managers will push out, maintain, or reduce the boundaries of their authority — depending upon their own frame of reference — in order to establish for themselves a job size and level of authority within which they feel comfortable. In this way the manager can cope with the organisational constraints and incentives as he sees them, using behaviour which has previously been defined in "negotiated order", "social exchange", or "secondary adjustment" terms.

It is apparent that any process which attempts to formalise organisational goals and, more particularly, to plan and formalise long-term business strategy, must take into account the extent to which the actual operation of the firm is a combination of both formal and informal behaviour. The behaviour of the individual is not simply that which is indicated in a job or position description, nor is it simply behaviour which conforms to the organisation's rules and procedures. Other forces, arising from the membership of different groups, the relationship of such groups to organisational goals, and the need for the individual to rationalise his self-image, needs, and aspirations against the constraints and incentives provided by the firm must be considered. For the planner, attempting to influence the direction of organisational growth, there are no easy answers but there are some useful questions, indeed crucial questions, which he must ask in relation to the individual and the firm. This chapter should serve to raise some of those questions, and in later chapters we examine in more detail some of the issues pertinent to the planner as an influencer, and yet also member, of a complex organisation.

References Chapter 3

1. H. Fayol (1949) *General and Industrial Administration*, Pitman, London.
2. F. W. Taylor (1947) *Scientific Management*, Harper, New York.
3. M. Weber (1964) *The Theory of Social and Economic Organisation*, Free Press, New York (first published 1925).
4. M. Allbrow (1970) *Bureaucracy*, Pall Mall Press, London, pp. 43-45.
5. C. Perrow (1970) *Organisational Analysis*, Tavistock, London.
6. C. Perrow (1972) Technology organisations and environment: a cautionary note, paper presented at the British Sociological Association meeting of the Industrial Sociology group: in K. Thompson People and Organisations, Unit 1, *The Problem of Organisation*, Open University Press, 1974.
7. R. Blauner (1964) *Alienation and Freedom*, Chicago University Press.
8. A. Gouldner (1954) *Patterns of Industrial Bureaucracy*, New York Free Press of Glencoe.
9. A. Zaleznick and D. Moment (1964) *Casebook on Interpersonal Behaviour in Organisations*, Wiley, London.

10. A. Strauss *et al.* (1963) *The hospital and its negotiated order*, in G. Salaman and K. Thompson, *People and Organisations* (1973), Longmans, pp. 303–20.
11. M. J. Langham (1976) Unpublished research.
12. G. Homans (1958) Social behaviour as exchange, *American Journal of Sociology*, Vol. 63, pp. 597–606.
13. P. M. Blau (1963) *The Dynamics of Bureaucracy*, Chicago University Press, Vol. 63, pp. 597–606.
14. E. Goffman (1968) *Asylums*, Penguin, Harmondsworth.
15. P. Colville (1975) A sociological study of the relationship between incumbants of managerial roles, the behaviour of managers and the structure of organisations. MPhil thesis, University of Surrey.

CHAPTER 4

Creativity

"Creativity, because of its great value in planning, should receive more than passing notice in any discussion of major techniques for better planning" (Steiner, 1969[1]). Without an element of creativity, that most individual of human attributes, planning will almost certainly become an empty, repetitive chore. Few would argue over the need to harness individual creativity for the good of the organisation as a whole, yet in many enterprises creative inputs occur only outside the planning process. Indeed, it is possible to argue that the desire for more formal and rational approaches to management, and the stressing of the control function of a planning process, all act against normal creative instincts. We have already seen the necessity for a more systematic approach to managing for the future (including an examination of some of the philosophies which prevent the whole process from becoming an empty charade). It is now appropriate to take Steiner's advice and concentrate on creativity and ways of building it into the organisation.

Creativity is a word which is difficult to define, one reason being the many meanings which it has in normal usage. We are not discussing only the creative genius of a Leonardo da Vinci, or an Einstein, but refer to that quality of imaginative thought possessed to a greater or lesser extent by all human beings.

Drever (1954)[2] defines *creative* as: "Producing an essentially new product, constructive (somewhat wider); used of *imagination*, where a new combination of ideas or images is constructed (strictly when it is self-initiated rather than initiated); also of thought synthesis, where the mental product is not a mere summation."

Jones (1972)[3] believes: "Creativity is a combination of flexibility, originality and sensitivity to ideas which enable the thinker to break away from the usual sequences of thought into different and productive sequences, the result of which gives satisfaction to himself and possibly to others."

Whitfield (1975)[4] distinguishes between creativity and innovation:

"We have just used the word 'creative' to describe the idea that is to to be developed into an innovation, and in doing so have indicated something special, a quality which is also implied in words like novelty, inspiration, ingenuity, originality, invention, genius and imagination. All these words seem to have the idea of creativity in common, although separately describing an idea, the mental activity which forms it or the ability of the person to carry out this activity."

He sees innovation as ". . . the development of a creative idea into a finished article (or process or system since, from the start, we are concerned with more than just 'things' as innovations)".

The organisation is interested not in creativity for its own sake, but because the creative process leads to innovation, and innovation is the foundation of entrepreneurial activity. Creativity is not only the seed of innovation, but is needed at all stages in the successful development and marketing of the idea. "The road from a valuable idea to final commercialisation and profit is long and hazardous and creativity can and must flourish throughout the entire journey" (Steiner, 1969[1]).

Not all creativity operates for the benefit of the business. The creative process is present in all humans but in many cases does not result in an output that is of value to the company. The tea lady may have a creative outlet in embroidery, although this may have no relevance to her employer. Some creative effort may be devoted against the interests of the organisation. The shopsteward who devises a new method of industrial action may be applying both creativity and innovation, but hardly for the benefit of the company. The degree of creative ability varies considerably from person to person, and the highly creative individual is in a minority. While those endowed with a high level of creativity may come out with more and better ideas and concepts, we should not overlook the spark of creativity which lies in even the less-gifted members of the community.

The belief that creativity exists in every person is part of Maslow's (1943)[5] theory of human motivation. His concepts, including the self-actualisation drive, will be discussed in Chapter 5:

"The clear emergence of these needs rests upon prior satisfaction of the physiological, safety, love and esteem needs. We shall call people who are satisfied in these needs, basically satisfied people, and it is from these that we may expect the fullest (and healthiest) creativeness. Since, in our society, basically satisfied people are the exception . . ."

The message is clear, if we want to increase creativity.

Drucker (1965)[6] states: "There are more ideas in any organisation, including businesses, than can possibly be put to use. What is lacking as a rule is the willingness to look beyond products to ideas. Products and processes are only the vehicle through which an idea becomes effective." The entrepreneurial process means that an idea has to pass rigorous tests. Drucker emphasises that it has to have operational validity, economic validity, and must meet the test of personal commitment:

"The idea itself might aim at social reform. But unless a business can be built on it, it is not a valid entrepreneurial idea. The test of the idea is not the votes it gets or the acclaim of the philosophers. It is economic performance and economic results. Even if the rationale of the business is social reform rather than business success, the touchstone must be ability to perform and to survive as a business."

Drucker sees ideas as part of the process of making the future: "Tomorrow always arrives", and those companies which fail to innovate will suddenly find that they have lost their way. This is a rephrasing of the words of the sixteenth-century philosopher Sir Francis Bacon. "He that will not apply new remedies must expect new evils: for time is the greatest innovator." The creative process is an individual activity, although it can be fostered by group interaction when the various members of the group may act in a synergistic way towards each other. Rogers (1954)[7] identifies three "inner conditions of constructive creativity".

"A. Open-ness to experience: extensionality" This he sees as the dropping of pre-determined defensive categories of perception: "(trees are green; college education is good; modern art is silly) the individual is aware of this existential moment as it is, thus being alive to many experiences which fall outside the usual categories (*this* tree is lavender; *this* college

education is damaging; *this* modern sculpture has a powerful effect on me)."

"*B. An internal locus of evolution.*" Rogers sees this as the most fundamental condition. For the creative individual the value of his "product" is "established not by the praise or criticism of others, but by himself. Have I created something satisfying to me? Does it express a part of me — my feeling, or my thought, my pain or my ecstasy." This does not mean that he is oblivious to the opinions of others, but that outside views cannot take away the inner feeling of satisfaction.

"*C. The ability to toy with elements and concepts.*" "Associated with the openness and lack of rigidity of A is the ability to play spontaneously with ideas, colours, shapes, relationships — to juggle elements into impossible juxtapositions, to shape wild hypotheses, to make the given problematic, to express the ridiculous, to translate from one form to another, to transform into impossible equivalent. It is from this spontaneous toying and exploration that there arises the hunch, the creative seeing of life in a new and significant way. It is as though out of the wasteful spawning of thousands of possibilities there emerges one or two evolutionary forms with the qualities which give them a more permanent value."

Whitfield (1975)[8] observes:

"As a mental activity, the moment of creation appears to be largely outside our conscious control, although it is more likely to be stimulated when we have become immersed in a subject. A burning desire to find a solution, concentration, gathering and marshalling of facts, and striving for completion by reaching out for still vague ideas are all activities we can feel and largely control at a conscious level. They mobilise and direct energy to finding a solution, but they are really only precursors to the act of creation, which seems to have a quality of spontaneity making it difficult to track and explain."

Vernon (1970)[9] provides a number of readings on both introspective, personal views of creativity and its scientific evaluation. For us, part at least of the quality of creative thought is summed up in the allegorical story of the artist Niggle in *Leaf by Niggle*:

"There was one picture in particular which bothered him. It had begun with a leaf caught in the wind, and it became a tree; and the tree grew, sending out innumerable branches, and thrusting out the most fantastic roots. Strange birds came and settled on the twigs and had to be attended to. Then all around the tree, and behind it, through the gaps in the leaves and boughs, a country began to open out; and there were glimpses of a forest marching over the land, and of mountains tipped with snow." [Tolkien, 1947.[10]]

Whitfield (1975)[11] argues (following Kurt Lewin) that the degree of creativity possessed by an individual is the result of his "tension field". The strengths of the various vectors (which may change from time to time) pull the individual either to or away from a creative tendency. An imaginary tension field is shown in Fig. 4.1.

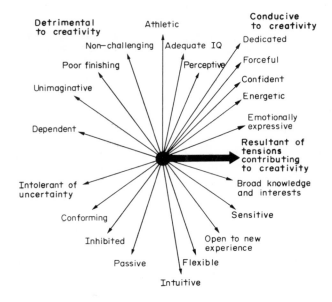

Fig. 4.1. Personality vectors. (From Whitfield, 1975[4].)

All the vectors fall into three broad classifications.

"1. Knowledge — specific and general information which acts as a store of building blocks for novel re-combinations.

2. Intellectual abilities — mental skills which enable knowledge to be used effectively, including its recombination into new forms.

3. Temperament — emotional aspects of personality pertaining to level of energy, mood and activity which make a person more likely to use his skills and knowledge and to take the risk of entertaining and developing the novel ideas which may arise from them."

Innovation is perceived by Whitfield (1975)[12] as a problem-solving process, the full cycle of which embraces seven steps. Creativity has a place in each step and is essential for at least step 4.

"1. Perceiving some need or problem.

2. Gathering relevant facts and classifying the true nature of the problem.

3. Seeking new information and analysing the whole picture.

4. Proposing alternative ideas for a solution.

5. Evaluating and selecting a final solution for implementation.

6. Implementing the solution.

7. Verifying that the solution is satisfactory."

Every organisation may at any one time have, as Drucker suggests, more ideas than it needs. At the same time it must stimulate creative thought for the process of time ensures that circumstances are continually changing and that the "bank" of ideas suitable for today's situation will become inadequate or inappropriate for the situation which will be faced in the future.

The organisation needs, therefore, to take special steps to ensure that it is creative, both in the generation of good entrepreneurial ideas and in the way these are translated into action.

Levitt (1962)[13] draws attention to size and innovation:

"One of the most important things to understand about marketing innovations is that the bigger and more novel they are, the greater is their capacity to change the ingrained consumer habits to which they address themselves. And the greater capacity, the greater is their chance of success.

"This also applies to the companies which do the innovating. The bigger the company, the better are its chances of making the innovation stick. But it has become a cliché among the top executives of some giant corporations to say that a large company cannot afford to introduce vastly new innovations because it has such an enormous dollar and consumer-franchise investment in the present. In short it has too much to lose. . . .

"The larger the company the more screening an idea gets. This almost invariably results in screening into extinction ideas which cannot easily be proved in advance with pencil and paper, that is, ideas which must, to a considerable extent, be accepted on faith and then tested out in actual operating situations. But the larger the company, the more it is likely to think in severely "professional management" terms. This means that radical new ideas have to be elaborately supported by feasibility studies, and then they must wend their laborious way tortuously upward through successive committee layers before coming up for final approval. This is almost invariably a strangling process, which kills off all but the most obvious and least risky propositions."

He goes on to contrast the less-formal management of small companies and their ability to bring in high-level executives at an early stage in new idea discussions, which in turn tends to lead to a greater corporate receptiveness to new ideas. The large company may have the capacity to innovate, but it is the smaller company that has the greatest propensity to actually do so.

The need for an organisational climate which fosters creativity is important, and there are differences between the creative organisation and others which are more stolid in their acceptance and application of the new. One of the reasons behind the need for a sympathetic climate is that the creative process is not completely logical. Although parts of the process can be directed so that the mind is focused on a specific problem area, the solution cannot be guaranteed. Indeed, it is uncertain whether an idea of value will emerge at all. Motivation, and the encouragement of creativity, is an important element in the process, and will not occur in a hostile environmental climate.

The fact that success is uncertain has considerable implications for the way in which the financial aspects of innovation are considered. Few successful companies can operate without financial control or without attempting to look at both costs and potential benefits. At the same time budget restrictions, over rigid capital evaluation criteria, short-term across-the-board expense reductions (10% off everything), and unimaginative approaches to setting research and development or marketing budgets (fixed percentage of turnover), are often enough to turn off the most creative of individuals. In some companies the rules are so rigid that innovation is next to impossible since they only allow backing for apparent certainties. If this is coupled with a "little boxes" approach to corporate planning ("list all the new products you intend to launch in the next five years with turnover and profits"), which sees the completion of a form as more important than the stimulations of men's minds, the possibility of innovation retreats even further. Add a rigid organisational framework, which acts against inter-departmental initiatives — and particularly a rigid structure subject to frequent reorganisation — and innovation has a lower probability of occurring than a snowstorm in Zaire.

There would seem to be a close link between the creative company and organisational style (see Chapter 6). At first sight it would appear a logical deduction that the less-directive styles of management would encourage a higher level of creativity than the authoritarian company. Yet companies run in a highly directive way do introduce new products, and indeed are often built around the creative genius of an autocrat. We would postulate that a directive style of management need not necessarily reduce creativity in a small company, and is not likely to do so when the men at the top are also the source of most new ideas. What we suspect is that in the larger companies creativity will have a greater tendency to be misdirected, and innovations produced which make technical sense, or satisfy an individual whim, but do not necessarily meet marketing needs or profit objectives. The engineering department, which continually innovates for technical excellence and without reference to the marketing department (and often without cross-departmental discussion of any kind), seems to us to offer a good example of the way in which the wrong organisational style can drive the company's creative talent in less-productive directions. In addition, authoritarian management can stifle creative ideas from those whose job is not specifically defined as innovation, and this type of organisation probably loses out on a lot of other aspects of innovations between development of the product and getting it to market.

TABLE 4.1

Comparison of creative individuals and creative organisations

The creative individual	The creative organisation

Conceptual fluency: able to produce a large number of ideas quickly	Has idea men
	Open channels of communication
	Ad hoc devices:
	  Suggestion systems
	  Brainstorming
	  Idea units free of other responsibilities

Originality: generates unusual ideas	Encourages contact with outside sources Heterogeneous personnel policy Includes marginal, unusual types Assigns non-specialists to problems Allows eccentricity

Separates source from content in evaluating information; motivated by interest in problem; follows wherever it leads	Has an objective, fact-founded approach
	Ideas evaluated on their merits, not status of originator
	Ad hoc approaches:
	  Anonymous communications
	  Blind votes
	Selects and promotes on merit only

Suspends judgement; avoids early commitment; spends more time in analysis and exploration	Lack of financial, material commitment to products, policies Invests in basic research; flexible, long-range planning Experiments with new ideas, rather than prejudging on "rational" grounds; everything gets a chance
Less authoritarian; relativistic view of life	More decentralised; diversified Administrative slack; time and resources to absorb errors Tolerates and expects risk-taking
Accepts own impulses; playful, undisciplined exploration	Not run as "tight ship" Allows freedom to choose and pursue problems Freedom to discuss ideas
Independence of judgement, less conformity Deviant, sees self as different	Organisationally autonomous Original and different objectives; not trying to be another "X"

The creative individual	The creative organisation
Rich, "bizarre" fantasy life and superior reality orientation; controls	Security of routine *allows* innovation; "philistines" provide stable, secure environment that allows "creators" to roam
	Has separate units or occasions for generating vs. evaluating ideas; separates creative from productive functions

Source: Steiner (1966)[14]. An earlier version appears in Gary A. Steiner, *The Creative Organization, Chicago, University of Chicago Press, 1965, pp. 16-18.*

Complete *laissez faire* may encourage creativity, but is unlikely to possess the drive and control needed to develop the ideas entrepreneurially. We advocate careful attention both to management style and the control methods and systems within the company. Control there must be, but it can be more imaginative and sympathetic than the methods practised by many organisations. Various solutions have been tried or postulated from time to time, and include: the hiving off of venture projects so that they are separate from the bureaucracy of big organisations, and have less stringent financial performance standards and controls; establishing risk funds which are available for use in developing "blue skies" innovations up to a certain ceiling figure, on a more easy evaluation scheme, where the company is willing to take risks although quantification is difficult; hiring sympathetic accountants. The last may be one of the cheapest and most effective methods of fostering innovation. The sympathetic accountant will give help and advice on evaluations supporting applications for funds, will make assessments within bands of probability when finite numbers are not available, and will generally try to help make things happen. This is in contrast to the hostile accountant who sees his role as preventing money from being spent, and regards anyone trying to obtain capital expenditure as an enemy to be put down.

Table 4.1 reproduces an analysis made by Gary Steiner (1966)[14] of the characteristics of the innovative person and the innovative organisation. It would be wrong to suggest that this analysis is complete, but it identifies many issues which are worthy of consideration.

One behavioural aspect of innovation should be stressed, for it explains why new things are sometimes slow to take off. Innovation suggests change, and change threatens many of us. What happens is that the comforting, known situation is challenged by the unknown. Depending on the nature of the change, the value of experience and present skills may be seen as at risk. Implied assumptions on which everyday actions are based may suddenly be removed, leaving a feeling of insecurity.

There is also risk in innovation because the new is unknown, and results may not work out as intended. Major changes may bring major risks: loss of prestige or authority, failure to achieve objectives, reduced chances of promotion, or even dismissal. Against these risks the known may appear positively attractive, and the innovator has to display a significant amount of courage.

Because people feel threatened they will often pour scorn on a new idea. They may oppose the innovation or try to frustrate it if it is imposed. This is not a new phenomenon. "New opinions are always suspected, and usually opposed without any other reason but because they are not already common." So wrote John Locke in 1890, and this remark still holds good. Aspects of implementing change will be discussed in greater detail in Chapter 8, when the problem of resistance to change will be re-examined.

Before we move into a discussion of the creative process and the ways in which an organisation can encourage or stimulate new ideas and innovation, it is worth stressing the importance of knowledge and skill in the development of creative ideas. De Bono (1971)[15] puts it succinctly: "knowledge is *not* creativity but within any particular field it is difficult to come up with new ideas unless you have some ideas to play around with in the first place".

Jones (1972)[16] observes: "The vast majority of innovators have been masters of the traditional method from which they departed. They have profited from what is already known because without it they could not tell what is new, or combine the older forms in a new pattern." These statements have two implications for organisations. The first, and obvious, implication is that the company which wishes to achieve anything other than mere haphazard and random innovations must employ people of the required skill. One can hardly expect a motor-vehicle manufacturer to innovate if he employs no skilled and specialist engineers.

The second implication goes back to the creative groups mentioned earlier. The range of skills which may be brought to bear on a problem may be numerous, and can rarely be possessed by one man. Often creativity can be increased by bringing together groups of people, with differing skills, who provide each other with flashes of insight, and by seeing the problem from differing angles, tend to stimulate creative ideas in the group as a whole.

Many have tried to analyse the creative process. We may distinguish the following stages.

(1) *Preparatory*: defining the problem, collecting basic information.

(2) *Incubation*: the results of the preparatory stage are digested, turned over in the mind, and conscious efforts are made to see a solution.

(3) *Illumination*: the solution suddenly appears. Jones (1972)[17] states: "At all levels of creativity, following a period of what can best be described as muddled suspense there will be sudden and unexpected flashes of insight. A solution or a novel idea appears out of nowhere and often in the midst of some other activity, as in the case of Archimedes in his bath. Poincaré insisted that a period of preliminary conscious work always preceded fruitful unconscious work, and Bertrand Russell describes the frustration of trying to force a mathematical hypothesis to completion by sheer concentration before he discovered the necessity of waiting for it to find its own subconscious development."

(4) *Reinforcement*: development of the idea, verification, testing out, and turning the flash of inspiration into something which makes sense and hangs together.

It is, of course, possible for the illumination or inspirational stage to occur even though the problem may not have been fully defined at the conscious level. It is also possible for a problem to be wrongly defined. In an organisation this suggests that careful attention should be given at this stage, as it is by no means atypical for a problem to be seen only in engineering or scientific terms and for the marketing aspects to be brought in too late. There may be a good engineering idea, but the "improvement" is not always wanted by the market.

The organisation which wishes to become more creative — and it can only do this through people — has three courses of action open to it. The first is to pay attention to the organisational issues discussed in this chapter, which can stimulate creativity, remembering that the removal of a negative influence may often do more to develop creativity than any action taken to try to stimulate it. Attention might also be given to the concept of creative groups, and the bringing together of the right kind of people in an environment conducive to their needs.

A second organisational aspect is to establish a formal and systematic approach to profit improvement, which gives every manager a role in finding ways to improve productivity and eliminate waste. Procter and Gamble have built in "method change" into the thinking of all managers over a number of years. Companies like Union Carbide have continuous profit improvement schemes which work to defined targets, stimulate ideas, and provide a mechanism for evaluating and implementing worthwhile concepts. This sort of approach is far more complex than a suggestion scheme and is much less haphazard. Fuller details of the operation of this type of initiative can be found in Hussey (1974)[18] and which is based on a study of the schemes of four companies.

The second course of action is to attempt to build up those elements of personality which contribute to creativity. This goes back to the numerous psychological studies of creative people, and is an attempt to sharpen elements of personality which those in question already possess. The better known of these include T groups and Coverdale training. Their use in this context is described in Whitfield (1975),[19] together with illustrations of related techniques. Both Coverdale Training and the T group are used to examine, understand, and overcome interpersonal blocks to organisational effectiveness. The nature of activities embodied in these approaches is outlined in Chapter 7.

A third possible course of action is to introduce and use techniques which stimulate mental activity and lead to the development of new ideas. Many of these techniques are for group application, where the contribution of each member fuels the further thoughts of the other members. Expressed at the simplest level, we are really discussing thinking. "You can probably remember things you were taught at school about geography (valleys, river deltas, rice-growing countries, etc.). But can you remember what you were taught about thinking?" (de Bono, 1971[20]).

de Bono's contribution to creativity is very much about thinking. He argues[21] that the process of thinking which causes creativity is lateral (that is sideways) thinking, which allows movement from one idea to another by a variety of ways, and cutting through the rigid sequences of logical thinking.

One of de Bono's methods for stimulating lateral thinking is to take a word at random from a dictionary and try to "connect it up" to whatever problem is being discussed. de Bono (1971)[22] states:

"At first sight it may seem unlikely that a random word will connect up with a specific problem. But in fact it often proves so very easy that when this is done at a lecture the audience believes the word and the problem have been deliberately selected beforehand.

"Problem: to solve traffic congestion in cities
   Random word: soap
   Connect up:

"1. Soap is slippery . . . lubricate traffic flow through street . . . remove street parking, bus stops, traffic lights . . . makes it possible to drive very easily in town but not to do much else . . . stopping of any sort only allowed in special stopping zones.

"2. Soap is used to remove dirt. . . . remove 'dirty' traffic areas (that is, traffic intensive areas) from residential and shopping areas.

"3. Soap is gradually worn away the more it is used . . . have a system whereby heavily used streets get worn away . . . and either get wider and easier to use . . . or more bumpy and more difficult to drive on . . . devise a self adjusting system whereby use increases use or slows downs use."

A second method is to use an "intermediate impossible", that is an idea which is known not to be true but which can become a bridge to an idea that is right. Thus the man seeking to cut down the time he spends maintaining his garden might postulate a lawn which he does not have to mow as the intermediate impossible. This could lead to ideas such as growing a short variety of grass, chemical control of grass height, replacing with an artificial lawn, or designing a garden with no lawn at all.

These two methods are part of a search for different ways of doing things. Part of de Bono's philosophy is concerned with liberation of thought from the idea that a particular concept or solution is absolutely right. This is a way of escaping from a particular point of view, with the opportunity this brings of studying new possibilities. Secondly, his philosophy includes an attempt to provoke new thoughts: ". . . Change may come about through escape from the old idea when this is no longer regarded as being absolutely right . . . through the generation of new ideas which provide alternatives to which one can move" (de Bono, 1971[23]).

One of the best-known techniques is one of the oldest and is reputed to have been devised by an advertising executive, Alec Osborn, in 1938. This is brainstorming, from the original concept of which a number of variants have emerged. The basic principles of brainstorming include the suspension of criticism and judgement during the ideas session; a deliberate attempt to let the imagination roam freely, including encouragement to suggest ideas which may appear silly or impossible on evaluation; the use of the group to stimulate ideas through personal reinforcement; and a deliberate attempt to generate as many ideas as possible in the belief that quality will emerge from the quantity.

Care has to be taken in organising a brainstorming session to ensure that those attending are not disappointed. Groups can become disillusioned with brainstorming if the problem is poorly defined, not worth solving, too large to be tackled in this way, or if the ideas generated are all mundane and already known, or if the group operates badly and stops brainstorming and starts criticising. Surroundings must be comfortable and undisturbed, those attending should be of mixed functions, departments, and personalities, and training should be given so that all present know how to operate the technique. In a company it is desirable not to have too wide a spread of organisational levels because of the difficulty individuals might have in shedding hierarchical relationships. Dominance of a session, either by personality or formal authority, by one or two people is to be avoided.

When a session is conducted it is a good idea to get the group to break the problem down into its lesser facets. The group must have a full understanding of the problem, and a measure of agreement and comfortableness over the way it and its facets are defined.

Ideas should be written up, ideally on large flip charts or blackboards so that all can see them as they are stated. Afterwards they should be typed out and sent to all those who attended the session.

Evaluation should be carried out afterwards, preferably by a team. It is good sense to ensure that the group is kept informed of what happens to their ideas and, if possible, for them to be given an opportunity to help implement the chosen ones. Apart from encouraging creativity and innovation, brainstorming can be a good method of developing group relationships and teamwork.

Some of the variants of brainstorming use similar ideas to those of de Bono. Random words can be used, through the association of ideas, to set the team on a new line of thinking. Alternatively a "wild idea" can be selected and used for the same purpose. Another approach is to turn the problem round to its opposite (e.g. instead of considering how to get to Paris, the opposite problem of how to leave Paris might be chosen): the aim of this is to help liberate thought.

Parnes (1963)[24] demonstrated that more good ideas are produced in the last half of a brainstorming session than in the first half, and that the production of good ideas increases as a subject's total quantity of ideas increases.

"The above findings support Osborn's theory that in idea production, quantity leads to quality. The results also seem to concur with William J. J. Gordon's (1961)[25] explanation of 'deferment' in the creative process. He describes deferment as 'the capacity to discard the glittering immediate in favour of a shadowy but possibly richer future'. The *non*-creative problem solver gets an idea, sees it as a possible solution to his problem, and settles for that without further ado. The *creative* problem solver is not satisfied with his first idea. Like the person who invests money to obtain greater rewards later, the creative person forgoes the immediate reward of applying his first idea in expectation of an ultimately better solution (greater reward). A further hypothesis suggested by Osborn's and Gordon's theories is that the *best* idea will come later in the production period."

Gordon (1961)[25] is the deviser of another technique, "synectics", one dimension of which has the team — it is essentially a team approach — imagining they themselves are part of the problem. They might, for example, be asked to imagine that they were part of the engine of a motor-car, and thus attempt to understand the problem from the inside.

All problem solving requires some attention to problem definition, and this step should never be neglected in favour of the more "glamorous" approaches to stimulate solutions. Once this has been done, there is much to be gained by seeking to improve the creative element in the company.

Like Parne's creative problem-solver, the company should not be prepared to run at the first strategic idea which comes to it to the exclusion of all other possibilities. "Consider all alternatives" (or more accurately, since alternative means literally one of two, "all options") is a well-known cry in planning.

To identify the options requires a creative contribution. And this can only come from people and the degree to which the organisation allows them to use their creative talents.

References Chapter 4

1. George A. Steiner (1969) *Top Management Planning*, Macmillan, p. 353.
2. J. Drever (1954) *A Dictionary of Psychology*, Penguin, p. 54.
3. T. P. Jones (1972) *Creative Learning in Perspective*, University of London Press, p. 7.
4. P. R. Whitfield (1975) *Creativity in Industry*, Pelican, p. 7.
5. A. H. Maslow (1943) A theory of human motivation, *Psychological Review* Vol. 50; reprinted in *Management and Motivation*. (V. Vroom and E. Deci, editors), Penguin, 1970, pp. 32–33.
6. P. F. Drucker (1965) *Managing for Results*, (Pan edition 1967), pp. 216–20.
7. C. R. Rogers (1954) *Towards a Theory of Creativity*; reproduced in *Creativity* (P. E. Vernon, editor), Penguin, 1970, pp. 143–4.
8. P. R. Whitfield (1975) op. cit., p. 9.
9. P. E. Vernon (editor) (1970) *Creativity*, Penguin.
10. J. R. Tolkien (1947) *Leaf by Niggle*, re-published in *Tree* and *Leaf* (1964), Allen & Unwin, p. 73.
11. P. R. Whitfield (1975) op. cit., pp. 32–3.
12. P. R. Whitfield (1975) op. cit., p. 21.
13. T. Levitt (1962) *Innovation in Marketing*, Pan (1968) edition, p. 137.
14. Gary Steiner (1966) The creative individual: his nurture and nature, *The McKinsey Quarterly*, Vol. 11, No. 2, p. 8.
15. E. de Bono (1971) *Practical Thinking*, Penguin 1976 edition, p. 162.
16. T. P. Jones (1972) *Creative Learning in Perspective*, University of London Press, p. 18.
17. T. P. Jones (1972) op. cit., p. 19.
18. D. E. Hussey (1974) *Corporate Planning: Theory and Practice*, Pergamon, Chapter 17, pp. 214–18.
19. P. R. Whitfield (1975) op. cit., pp. 73–83.
20. E. de Bono (1971) op. cit., p. 7.
21. E. de Bono (1971) op. cit., p. 160.
22. E. de Bono (1971) op. cit., p. 58.
23. E. de Bono (1971) op. cit., p. 147.
24. S. J. Parnes (1963) *Education and Creativity. Teachers College. Record*, Vol. 64, reprinted in P. E. Vernon (editor), *Creativity*, Penguin 1970, pp. 348–9.
25. W. J. J. Gordon (1961) *Synectics*, Harper & Row.

CHAPTER 5

Motivation: The Manager and Planning

One of the primary considerations facing the manager is that of motivation. The motivation of employees may both affect and be affected by the corporate plan. The corporate planner, being himself an employee, is motivated by a range of factors similar to those which affect other managers, but he also has a need to consider the motivation of both managers and subordinates in the context of an overall plan. The fact that any form of planning may affect the motivation and needs of individuals is in itself sufficient reason to consider some of the more important theories, research, and approaches to motivation, but there are a number of other reasons:

(1) Corporate planning as a formal systematic managerial process may tend to view man as a rational thinker and a reactive being. If this were the case then perhaps the job of the corporate planner would be a whole lot easier, but there would probably be no need for a book of this sort. The work of the behavioural scientists (or, more specifically, the motivation theorists) offers a many-faceted view of man and explanations of some of the reasons for success or failure in corporate planning.

(2) The process of planning may bring about changes in work structuring (e.g. job enrichment) or organisational design or management style, all of which may have an effect on the motivation of employees.

(3) One aim of corporate planning is improved business results, and much of the emphasis, by definition, is on the future. The design

and implementation of the corporate plan is in the present. For some managers, working within an overall plan may provide motivational stimulus. Indeed, an integral part of the planning process, as we shall see later, may involve agreeing objectives and monitoring performance towards those objectives. However, essentially the organisation is calling for high commitment from managers to achieving *future* results where most of their rewards are in the *present*. The potential rewards inherent in future plans may not be apparent in today's planning process, nor in today's results.

All of these reasons suggest that we take a closer look at the interaction between motivation and corporate planning and review some of the significant motivational research.

As a starting point we may define motivation in broad terms as "the will to work well". This definition is arrived at by considering the difference in performance between level of output in the perfect situation against the minimum level which management will tolerate (Behrend, 1961)[1]

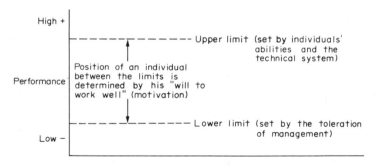

Fig. 5.1. Limits on performance and the role of motivation.
(From Evendon, 1970[21].)

Thus in Fig. 5.1 it is suggested that a performance gap exists between ideal performance and a level of performance below which management will not tolerate. The implications of this suggestion are that management may improve performance by:

(1) Improving the technical system (e.g. methods, procedure, controls,

planning, information system, equipment).
(2) Developing individual's skills and abilities (e.g. training).
(3) Possibly raising or lowering the level of toleration (although this may not be seen as a consideration).
(4) Positively influencing those factors which will affect the "will to work well", i.e. motivating employees.

When we begin to consider those factors which motivate (4) we shall inevitably take into account changes in the technical system (1) and people development (2) since the implications set out above are not discreet options but together make up the complex picture of man and organisation.

Historically, man and organisation has been viewed in a less complex manner, and there have been, since the turn of the century, a number of "schools of thought" or basic assumptions about the nature of man. We may briefly review the major schools.

Rational/Economic Man

The turn of the century saw the emergence of techniques of method study and work measurement (together referred to as work study). Prominent at this time were Gilbreth (1911)[2] the father of method study, and Taylor (1947),[3] noted for his "work measurement" techniques for assessing human effectiveness. Taylor based his methods on the assumption that man was rational thinking and motivated by economic considerations. It therefore made sense to apply scientific methods to work content in order to control the effort and decision making required by the worker so that jobs could be clearly defined and broken down into measurable elements. Thus as a measure of his success we could quote the experience of Mr. Schmidt at the Bethlehem Steel Company, who, under Taylor's guidance, managed to increase the amount of pig-iron he loaded from 12½ tons to 47½ tons per day and earn 70 cents more than he had done before (Munro Fraser, 1963).[4] Broadly speaking, the assumptions and strategies of the rational/economic movement were:

Assumptions	*Strategies*
"(a) Man is primarily motivated by economic incentives and will do that which gets him the greatest economic gain.	"Scientific Management" (1) Emphasis is on efficient task performance. Management's role is to plan, organise, direct, and control.
(b) Since economic incentives are under the control of the organisation, man is essentially a passive agent to be manipulated, motivated, and controlled by the organisation.	(2) *Incentives* — Individual bonus schemes which reward high producers. — Stimulate competition among workers and give special rewards to winners, e.g. bonus on promotion.
(c) Man's feelings are essentially irrational and must be prevented from interfering with his rational calculation of self-interest.	
(d) Organisations can and must be designed in such a way as to neutralise and control man's feelings and therefore his unpredictable traits."	(3) *Control exercised* — Close supervision with sanctions against poor performers. — Streamline information gathering mechanisms to enable management to identify and punish poor performing areas.
(Schein, 1965, p. 48.[11])	

The assumptions concerning rational economic man were taken as self-evident truths based upon the theories of classical economists and were largely untested by behavioural scientists. The "scientific management" movement was largely based upon these assumptions.

Social Man

The onset of the First World War brought a massive influx of both men and women into armament and other war-effort factories. Increasingly the welfare function became predominant, and concern for the conditions under which people were working became very real issues. During the

1920s a significant and lengthy motivation research programme was undertaken at the Hawthorne works of the Western Electric Company, Chicago. This research, carried out by a team under Elton Mayo and reported fully by Roethlisberger and Dickson (1939),[5] highlighted, amongst other things, the social needs of people at work. The study tested a range of factors influencing worker performance including payment systems (the rational economic motive) and working conditions. One of the most significant findings was with a group of girls in the Relay Assembly test room at Hawthorne where a range of changes in working conditions of both a positive and negative nature were tested (see Brown, 1954[6]), each change resulting in an increase in output. Additionally, a "control group" of girls formed for comparison purposes, and for whom no changes were made, also increased their output. This work, and other experiments at the Hawthorne works, were interpreted by the researchers as indicative of the social nature and therefore of the social needs of man at work. Much of the increases in output and work satisfaction could be put down to the feeling of recognition inculcated by the researchers and to the social relationships in the workplace. We therefore have a set of additional assumptions and strategies to add to those of the rational/economic.

Assumptions	*Strategies*
"(a) Man is basically motivated by social needs and obtains his basic sense of identity through relationships with others.	"Human relations" (1) A manager should not limit his attention to the task but should give more attention to *the needs of the people working for him.*
(b) As a result of the industrial revolution and the rationalisation of work the meaning has gone out of work itself and must therefore be sought in the social relationships on the job.	(2) Instead of controlling and motivating subordinates the manager should try to *understand their feelings*, especially those concerning acceptance and sense of belonging and identity.
(c) Man is more responsive to the social forces of the peer group than to the incentives and controls of management.	(3) Incentives should focus on *the group* rather than on the individual.

(d) Man is responsive to management to the extent that a supervisor can meet a subordinate's social needs and needs for acceptance."

(Schein, 1965, p. 51.[11])

(4) The role of the manager is to act as an intermediary between the men and higher management *trying to reconcile their needs.*

(5) The manager should try to encourage the *participation* of subordinates in order to encourage them to identify with the organisation.

Self-actualising Man

Since the work of Mayo and the Hawthorne experiments, a number of researchers have advanced the theories of social man (see Brown, 1954[6]; Zaleznick, 1958[7]) while others have advanced more complex theories of motivation. One of the most influential theorists has been Maslow (1954),[8] who has suggested a hierarchy of needs which includes higher level needs than social relationships. The hierarchy suggests at the lowest level physiological, e.g. food, drink, shelter, moving to safety and security needs, to social needs, e.g. those outlined in "social man" theories. Beyond this Maslow postulates two higher levels, viz. self-esteem/status and then self-fulfilment or self-actualisation, i.e. the realisation of an individual's own potential.

It is suggested that lower needs must be satisfied before higher needs become operative; thus a man who cannot earn enough to clothe himself is unlikely to be too concerned with a need such as status. The model is a useful heuristic device in that it poses a number of questions about employee motivation. Can we assume, for example, that when one level of needs is met man will strive for the next level up? What happens when one reaches self-actualisation — does motivation cease? Can man's needs be expressed in terms of a hierarchy at all? And can they be expressed in any real sense in this way? Perhaps these are questions best left to the motivation theorists (the interested reader who might like to pursue Maslow's philosophy in greater detail will find *The Further Reaches of Human Nature* published after his death in 1970 particularly illuminating).[9]

For the manager and planner looking at organisational operation, the idea of self-actualising man moves assumptions and strategies beyond those of rational economic and social man and leads us to take a much broader view of the inherent intellect and skills of individuals.

Assumptions	*Strategies*

"(a) Man's needs are arranged in a hierarchy from physiological and social to higher needs of esteem and self actualisation.
 	
(b) Man has an inherent need to use his capacities and skills in a mature and productive way, exercising autonomy and developing skills and flexibility in adapting to circumstances.
 	
(c) Man is primarily self-motivated and self-controlled — externally imposed incentives and control block mature adjustment.
 	
(d) Man's self-actualisation needs are not necessarily in conflict with effective organisational performance. Given opportunity man will voluntarily integrate his own goals with those of the organisation."
	"Self-actualisation"
	
	A manager should worry less about being considerate to employees and more about how to make their work intrinsically challenging and meaningful:
	  – Job enlargement.
	  – Sharing of influence.
	  – Greater decision-making involvement.

(Schein, 1965, pp. 57–58.[11])

The work of Maslow has been developed by other psychologists, notably McGregor, whose theory X and theory Y (McGregor, 1960)[10] offer two opposing views of human behaviour, theory X being akin to the assumptions of rational/economic man and theory Y supporting the assumptions of self-actualising man. The suggestion is that individuals have inherent needs which they will seek to satisfy and that management may best use forms of management-by-objectives rather than management-by-control to allow individual self-development. McGregor goes on to examine the idea of objective setting and agreeing targets, techniques which have become elements in the corporate planning process.

Each of the basic assumptions reviewed so far has been influential in shaping managerial behaviour and in suggesting management techniques, from work study through to management by objectives. The current work in motivation, in part, builds on the self-actualisation assumptions but offers a more flexible approach in keeping with the complex view of man (Schein, 1965, p. 60).[11]

Complex Man

"a. Man is not only complex, but also highly variable; he has many motives which are arranged in some sort of hierarchy of importance to him, but this hierarchy is subject to change from time to time and situation to situation; furthermore motives interact and combine into complex motive patterns (for example, since money can facilitate self-actualization, for some people economic strivings are equivalent to self-actualization).

"b. Man is capable of learning new motives through his organizational experiences, hence ultimately his pattern of motivation and the psychological contract which he establishes with the organization is the result of a complex interaction between initial needs and organizational experiences.

"c. Man's motives in different organizations or different subparts of the same organization may be different; the person who is alienated in the formal organization may find fulfilment of his social and self-actualization needs in the union or in the informal organization; if the job itself is complex, such as that of a manager, some parts of the job may engage some motives while other parts engage other motives.

"d. Man can become productively involved with organizations on the basis of many different kinds of motives; his ultimate satisfaction and the ultimate effectiveness of the organization depends only in part on the nature of his motivation. The nature of the task to be performed, the abilities and experience of the person on the job, and the nature of the other people in the organization all interact to produce a certain pattern of work and feelings. For example, a highly skilled but poorly motivated worker may be as effective *and satisfied* as a very unskilled but highly motivated worker.

"e. Man can respond to many different kinds of managerial strategies, depending on his own motives and abilities and the nature of the task; in other words, there is no one correct managerial strategy that will work for all men at all times."

The management strategies which accompany the "complex" view of men include: diagnosis of the motives and variable abilities of subordinates, recognition and use of valuable human differences and, thirdly, personal flexibility in employing whichever strategy is appropriate to subordinates' needs.

The strategies outlined for "complex man" relate us back to two points made at the beginning of this chapter. These were, firstly, a concern for the effects on motivation of changes in organisation or work method brought about within a corporate plan, and, secondly, a concern for the present motivation and commitment of employees to the payoff from future plans.

The first consideration leads us to look at the effect on motivation of job design and work structuring. The second consideration suggests that we look at the possible processual effects of incentives, or the effects of an individual's motives and needs at work, over time. Both of these areas are of considerable importance to the planner who may affect and be affected by the implied motivational factors.

The concept of complex man suggests a concern for the intrinsic qualities of the work itself. A number of research projects have investigated the job content as opposed to individual role content in an effort to distinguish those factors within the job which act as incentives. One of the most influential contributions in this area is the "dual factor" theory of Hertzberg (1959,[12] 1968[13]). This theory suggests that man has two sets of needs: his need as an animal to avoid pain and his needs as a human to grow psychologically. The research, which was initially conducted with

200 engineers and accountants, was based on a semi-structured interview during which the subjects were asked to recount times when they felt exceptionally good or bad about their jobs. The information so obtained suggested the kind of situations leading to positive and negative attitudes about the job and the effects of those attitudes. In this process a number of factors emerged, some of which are said to provide positive attitudes to the job and thus act as motivators, others of which merely "maintain" a level of performance. We can therefore modify the definition of motivation given earlier (see Figure 5.1) using the diagram shown in Fig. 5.2.

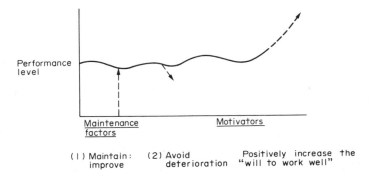

Fig. 5.2. Functions of maintenance and motivator factors.
(From Evendon, 1969[22].)

Motivation now means considering how far and under what conditions certain job factors will positively increase the "will to work well" rather than merely maintain a level of performance. The results of the early Hertzberg research are given in Fig. 5.3 and show that, in general, factors such as achievement, recognition, and responsibility can be classed as motivators whereas factors such as company policy and administration, working conditions and supervision are merely maintenance factors. In the diagram the length of the line indicates the frequency with which the factor was mentioned, whilst the depth of the line gives a comparison of the length of time the effects of each factor lasted. Since the original findings this work has been replicated over a number of job situations, both blue and white collar, with similar results to those shown in Fig. 5.3.

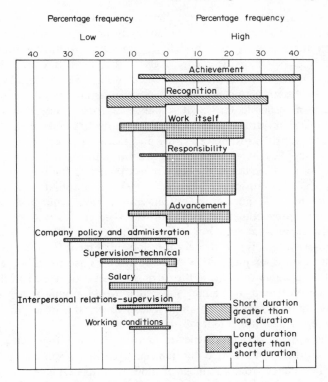

Fig. 5.3. Comparison of satisfiers and dissatisfiers.
(From Hertzberg *et al.*, 1959[12].)

The work has been influential in the growth of job-enrichment programmes in a variety of industries in the United States, the United
Kingdom, Europe, and elsewhere in the world. We shall expand on the
concept and application of job enrichment later in the chapter.

The dual-factor theory has been criticised on a number of grounds, and
not all replications have in fact supported the findings above. House and
Wigdor (1967)[14] offer a useful review of the evidence and some criticism
of the findings. In particular, as Vroom (1964)[15] has pointed out, individuals may be more likely to attribute good feelings to incidences over
which they have direct control, i.e. their own accomplishments and

achievements, and bad feelings to incidences over which they have no control, i.e. obstacles presented by company policy or supervision. Such rationalisations may stem from defensive processes within the individual. A further criticism of the theory suggests that there is a range of variables which may partially determine whether a given factor will be a satisfaction or dissatisfaction, some of these variables are job or occupational level; age of respondents; sex of respondents; formal education; culture; time dimension variable; and the respondent's standing in his group. Despite these criticisms, however, the dual-factor approach to motivation has been applied in a range of organisations to "enrich" the jobs of employees, i.e. to re-design the work so as to build back into the job those factors which are motivators, e.g. achievement, responsibility, and intrinsic work interest. A number of organisations have embarked on job-enrichment programmes, notably British Oxygen (clerical operation), ICI (sales representatives), Volvo (car assembly), and Richard Baxendale (electric fire assembly). The concept of job enrichment is one approach to the restructuring of jobs and is often referred to as vertical job enlargement. It is possible to increase the intrinsic interest of work and thus the motivation potential by training jobholders to do a number of jobs and allowing rotation between different jobs. This practice of job rotation is often referred to as horizontal job enlargement.

We have, then, two approaches to motivation which focus on job content — vertical and horizontal job enlargement. Examples of these approaches, culled from a number of industries, may be given as follows:

1. *HORIZONTAL JOB CHANGES – Job Enlargement*

Workers producing auto switches were operating on an assembly line where each worker performed a routine single operation in a short cycle time. The line was redesigned to allow each worker to produce an entire subunit and, therefore, to become engaged in a variety of tasks such as wiring, soldering, assembly, and testing. Further training was given to allow operations to rotate between different operations.

2. *VERTICAL JOB CHANGES* – *Job Enrichment*

2.1. Assemblers producing television sets on a routine short-cycle assembly line basis were regrouped into teams of between twelve and fifteen and became responsible for assembling complete television sets as a group. The group was responsible for its own parts stores and for deciding which group member should work in which tasks. In addition the group became responsible for the quality of output and for handling quality complaints.

2.2. Clerks in an order office processed incoming customer orders on a flow-line basis with each clerk carrying out a limited number of routines, e.g. vetting, pricing, credit control, typing checking, stock verification. The office procedure was redesigned to give each clerk the responsibility for dealing fully with a number of customers and for following the orders through all the administrative procedures. Clerks were encouraged to handle all queries and questions from customers and to provide a personal customer service routine for their particular customers.

2.3. Process operators in a 24-hour continuous operation plant worked as a team of eight where all were trained to rotate around the eight jobs on the plant and could do so by arrangement with the shift foreman. (This is an example of horizontal job enlargement.) The team of eight were asked to make their own decisions regarding job rotation and to assume responsibility for quality checks on the finished products taking "go"–"no go" decisions and reclaiming substandard materials to best effect. In addition the team put forward work improvement suggestions which were discussed with the foreman and implemented where possible, with reference to production management after rather than before the event. Wider improvement in planning and controlling the work and greater scope for taking decisions affecting the work methods were given to the group.

As we can see from the example quoted at 2.1 and 2.2, the process of job enrichment can involve changes in the make-up of the work group, section, or shift. This may mean changes in role content for individuals, where leaderless or autonomous groups are formed. The work of researchers at the Tavistock Institute, London (Trist *et al.*, 1963),[16] has been influential in suggesting the need to take into account the role of the individual as a member of a work group and the motives and needs of individuals at work in a psychological, social, and technical sense. One of the most important studies carried out by Trist and his colleagues was into the effects of technological change in coal-mining. Here, changes in methods of "winning" coal brought about the break-up of traditional semi-autonomous work groups (known as "marra" groups) which were also friendship groups. The new mining techniques called for continuous production on a flow-line type basis (i.e. the longwall and, later, continuous mining methods), which was obviously a more profitable and effective way of producing coal. However, the new techniques which followed the nationalisation of the British Coal Industry were associated with substandard results such as low productivity, low level of job satisfaction, inflated costs, and a high level of worker absenteeism. The benefits of increased automation were not manifest in actual production. The Tavistock study was long term and systematic, and served to highlight the importance of considering the social and psychological effects of technological change on worker motivation.

As a result of the study, mining techniques were redesigned to bring back into the jobs some of the elements of autonomy previously found in the traditional "marra" groups. This had the effect of increasing the intrinsic interest in the work itself and re-introducing elements of responsibility.

The concept of "complex man" has brought us a long way on from Taylorism and rational/economic man; indeed, many of the job-enlargement programmes can be seen as a move away from and in direct opposition to the structuring of work using work-study techniques.

The implication of motivation theories are of considerable significance to those who would establish a formal process of corporate planning. Firstly, the planners need to be aware of the negative effects of planning processes which are seen by individuals to threaten their status or self-actualisation needs. These may be seen at risk by, for example, a senior manager because he is forced to write down his plans for the first time (which may make him worried about giving commitment which he might prefer to avoid, or make him feel that his current approach to decision making is under attack), because he may be required to share his decision-making powers with managers under him or colleagues with other functional responsibilities, or because a new power figure, the corporate planner, may appear in the top management group. Issues arising from this type of threat are discussed in more depth in later chapters. It is sufficient to say here that any planning approach which promotes insecurity is to be avoided.

The planner, too, must design a planning process which assists motivation. It is very easy to produce a dreary form-filling exercise, with hundreds of little boxes which *must* be completed, which ensures that all creativity and initiative is stifled, and no opportunity is given for people to satisfy their higher needs. A positive approach to the design of the process, which deliberately takes note of motivational issues, is essential for success in planning. The opportunity that planning gives for a wider involvement in a more open style of management is, perhaps, a form of job-enrichment programme for managers.

Objectives can be used as a tool for motivating and, when linked to a process of monitoring and controlling which stresses the positive rather than the negative implications, can become a key part of a good planning system.

The planner should also consider the motivational aspects which will be affected by the plans themselves. Any significant change areas should be coupled with a plan which takes due notice of the motivational issues. An acquisition or merger situation may be seen as an issue of concern by both the employees of the buying and the selling companies. An awareness of what really motivates people throughout the organisation is essential if the best results are to be achieved.

It is important for the planner to be aware of the problems inherent in job design from the point of view of both job content and role content. Clearly, in situations where flow-line short-cycle work is performed, future plans will need to take into account the motivational problems which can ensue through boredom and alienation from the work itself. The use of work-measurement and method-study techniques may offer a neat and predictable set of practices for structuring output, and to that extent are appealing in the planning process, but they incorporate a number of foreseeable difficulties. On the other hand, if the plan involves work structuring to include job enlargement and the role changes embodied in autonomous groups, the planner will be well advised to consider the extent to which he should involve work groups in the planning process. There is a good deal of evidence to show that autonomous groups who participate in decision-making processes are more committed to the outcome and better motivated to achieve the ensuing joint targets or objectives. Such participation, however, is required on a continuing basis if the motivation and commitment of the group is to be maintained (Tannenbaum, 1966).[18] This will be true of all groups whether operatives, supervisors, or managers. The involvement of those affected by aspects of the corporate plan may be a way of overcoming the psychological defence mechanisms of individuals attributing good feelings to their own efforts (or involvement) and bad feelings to factors outside of their control. It is easy to see how likely it is that employees will attribute bad feelings to parts of a corporate plan which affect their working life but over which they have no control.

Perhaps one way of overcoming the problem of gaining the commitment of managers to planning in the present where the external rewards are in the future is through participation, involvement, and an enhancement of the intrinsic interest in the job. The planning process can indeed help this by providing personal learning and growth for the managers involved. We shall return to these issues in later chapters.

So far we have reviewed the effects on motivation of job design and work structuring, treating these factors from a management point of view as independent variables. In addition we have considered these factors in a static sense; in other words, suggesting that to enrich the job or recreate an autonomous work group should always result in increased motivation regardless of the timing of such changes. There is a further need, however, and that is to take into account the needs and the "orientation to work" of the worker. Goldthorpe and Lockwood (1968),[19] in their affluent worker studies, have pointed to the need to examine the wants and expectations of individuals relative to work and the meaning attributed to work by the worker. These studies showed that assembly-line workers doing what we might refer to as very de-enriched work (i.e. continuous-track short-cycle tasks) were prepared to accept these conditions in return for relatively high pay. A consideration of factors outside of the work environment, e.g. social class/life style, community membership, was seen to be necessary in order to understand more fully the motivation of the worker. The concept of "orientation to work" is seen to arise out of the social situation and as such suggests that the psycho/socio/technical system should take account of influences on the worker outside of the work setting. Ingham (1967)[20] has suggested that changes in the social situation of the individual and the context (e.g. work group/social group) within which decisions are made may effect changes in orientation. He postulates four alternatives (Fig. 5.4).

"Orientation"

	High economic/high non-economic	Low economic/high non-economic
"Orientation"	High economic/low non-economic	Low economic/low non-economic

Fig. 5.4. Motivation variables and orientation to work.
(From Ingham, 1967[20].)

Each of these alternatives may be operative at any point in time, hence the processual nature of motivation referred to earlier. The planner cannot assume that worker needs and orientation to work will be static. It is reasonable to suggest that factors external to the work such as market situation, government influence on income, etc., may also affect behaviour at any particular point in time. Thus it could be argued, for example, that propensity for industrial action will be higher in times of high demand and full order books than in slack periods when the chances of lay-offs are greater.

It is important, then, to consider the needs and orientation of the worker in the wider context of motivation, in addition to the intra-work consideration of job design, job enlargement, and the intra-company socio-technical systems view. We have suggested the need to view motivation from the employee viewpoint as well as from that of management. Indeed, in referring to Fig. 5.5 we suggest that such variables as job design and orientation to work will change in emphasis depending upon whether they are seen from the worker or management point of view.

Thus the manager sees job design as an independent variable, something he can change or experiment with in order to affect worker performance or attitude. For him the intervening variables may be such factors as individual needs and orientation to work, over which he has no direct control. On the other hand, for the employee, orientation to work and individual needs are in the nature of independent variables (i.e. they may be changed), whilst changes in job design are intervening variables over

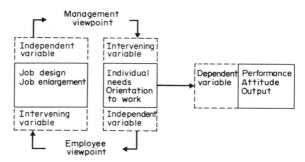

Fig. 5.5. Motivation strategy – which is the independent variable?

which the employee may or may not have some direct control.

The implications of this way of looking at motivation are important for the planner in a number of ways. Firstly, any changes made in job design should not be made on the assumption that the intervening variable of orientation to work remains static. As we have pointed out already, this may be affected by factors outside the work environment and change over time. However, such changes that are made in job design may themselves affect the orientation to work particularly where these involve greater participation in decision making. This may be particularly helpful where employees now are involved in planning for the future operation of the business.

Secondly, the model given in Fig. 5.5 can be used by the planner to generate pertinent questions on the nature of employee motivation and its likely effects on the planning process. Indeed, consideration of the needs and orientation of employees is paramount if the results of the planning process are to reach fruition.

Thirdly, it is suggested that corporate planning as a dynamic multi-variate activity can take account of the dynamic nature of motivation by considering cause and effect of changes between individuals, the organisation, and the environment within which both exist.

In this chapter we have attempted to build up to the present-day complex picture of motivation, recognising that the planner neither seeks nor would accept an oversimplified approach or a "set of answers". Instead we have sought to review that theory and research, into motivation at work, which offers the best questioning and predictive utility, understanding that whilst we can obtain very few (if any) absolute answers, we can nevertheless make planning less of a process of chance by considering the available evidence and asking the right questions about human behaviour at work.

References Chapter 5

1. H. Behrend (1961) A fair day's work, *Scottish Journal of Political Economy*, No. 8, June.
2. F. B. Gilbreth (1911) *Motion Study*, Van Nostrand, New York.
3. F. W. Taylor (1947) *Scientific Management*, Harper, New York.
4. J. Munro Fraser (1963) *Psychology General/Industrial/Social*, Pitman, London.
5. F. J. Roethlisberger & W. J. Dickson (1939) *Management and the Worker*, Harvard University Press.
6. J. A. C. Brown (1954) *The Social Psychology of Industry*, Penguin, London, pp. 71–75.
7. A. Zaleznick *et al.* (1958) *The Motivation, Productivity and Satisfaction of Workers*, Harvard, Boston.
8. A. H. Maslow (1954) *Motivation and Personality*, Harper, New York.
9. A. H. Maslow (1971) *The Further Reaches of Human Nature*, Penguin/Pelican.
10. D. McGregor (1960) *The Human Side of Enterprise*, McGraw-Hill, pp. 33–34 and 47–48.
11. E. Schein (1965) *Organisational Psychology*, Prentice-Hall, chapter 4.
12. F. Hertzberg *et al.* (1959) *The Motivation to Work*, Wiley, p. 17.
13. F. Hertzberg (1968) *Work and the Nature of Man*, Staples Press, London.
14. R. J. House & L. A. Wigdor (1967) Hertzberg's dual-factor theory of job satisfaction and motivation: a review of the evidence and a criticism, *Personnel Psychology*, Vol. 20, pp. 369–89.
15. V. Vroom (1964), *Work and Motivation*, Wiley, New York.
16. E. L. Trist *et al.* (1963) *Organisational Choice*, Tavistock, London.
17. L. E. Davis and J. C. Taylor (eds.) (1972) *Design of Jobs*, Penguin.
18. A. S. Tannenbaum (1966) The group in organisations, in *Management and Motivation* (V. H. Vroom, editor): (1970) Penguin, chapter 15.
19. J. H. Goldthorpe, D. Lockwood, F. Bechhofer, and J. Platt (1968): *The Affluent Worker in the Class Structure*, Cambridge University Press.
20. G. Ingham (1967) Organisation size, orientation to work and industrial behaviour, *Sociology*, Vol. 1, pp. 239–58.
21. R. Evendon (1970) Roffey Park Management College, Horsham, Sussex; based on the work of H. Behrend.
22. R. Evendon (1969) Roffey Park Management College, Horsham, Sussex, course notes.

CHAPTER 6

Organisational and Management Style

In the previous chapters we have looked at the complex area of motivation and found that behaviour at work is affected by a range of different factors over a varying time span. A significant factor, and one which appears in much of the motivational research, is concerned with the climate of the organisation. The term is used here in a broad sense to cover a number of considerations ranging from the quality and type of interpersonal relationships between manager and subordinate and aspects of "management style" through to such issues as company policy/administration and the overall communication and management style adopted by the organisation. When we consider the process of corporate planning we inevitably find ourselves looking at the structure of the organisation and the manner in which planning policy can be formulated and communicated within the existing structure of communication channels and relationships. Inevitably such channels and relationships will both affect and be affected by the corporate plan. As we shall see later, the planning process means change, and it is important to understand the effects of that change.

We need, then, to consider the effects of organisational style on both management and staff and the effects of manager style on the managing process. It may be helpful to begin by considering the organisation as an entity before going on to discuss the variations in individual manager style.

Organisational Style

The total organisation can be viewed in a communication sense by contrasting different networks available for use. Leavitt (1951)[1] in experimental work has considered four possible systems, which are given in Fig. 6.1.

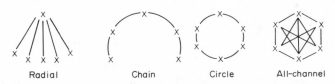

Fig. 6.1. Communication networks. (From Leavitt, 1951[1].)

Of these four systems the radial is closest to the hierarchical system of organisation put forward by the early management theorists (Taylor, 1947,[2] Brech, 1957[3]), where all communications go via the leader or manager of the group. In the all-channel system no such leadership function is apparent. These networks are simplified patterns of organisational communication and we should accept that in complex organisations all four networks may function simultaneously. Nevertheless, it is suggested that most organisations can be characterised by one predominant network since the nature of the structure will predetermine the type of network which can most readily be used. In order to pursue a comparison let us suppose that we set up a situation where four groups of people are formed to test the effectiveness of the four networks outlined. These groups are given a problem-solving task to complete with identical briefing but are then further briefed to work in either the radial, chain, circle, or all-channel network. At the end of the exercise we shall find an interesting comparison between the four groups in terms of some of the determinants of organisational effectiveness, such as speed of decision making, accuracy, efficiency, morale, and response to need for flexibility and creativity. For example, the radial network is generally fast with a good degree of accuracy and efficiency, but morale is seen to be poor and response to need for flexibility and creativity is very slow. In contrast to this the all-channel network is usually slower, has fair accuracy, low efficiency with very high morale, and a fast response to need for flexibility and

TABLE 6.1
Comparison of networks

	Radial	Chain	Circle	All-channel
Speed	Fast	Fast	Slow	Slow
Accuracy (i.e. errors, mis- understandings)	Good	Good	Poor	Fair
Efficiency (i.e. effort expended in achieving results)	High	High	Low	Low
Morale	Poor	Moderate/poor	High	Very high
Response to need for flexibility and creativity	Very slow	Slow	Fast	Very fast

(*Source*: Findings from Roffey Park Management College, Horsham, Sussex reproduced with permission).

creativity. The comparisons of all four networks are given in Table 6.1.

We could argue on the basis of these results that the radial system should work best where the task is straightforward and routine, calling for little need for creativity. In so doing we are aware that the indicated low morale would still be a problem demanding attention. On the other hand, where the task is more complex and the need for creativity and problem solving high, then the all-channel system is likely to be more appropriate.

The comparison exercise outlined has been carried out by Langham and colleagues at the Roffey Park Management College as a learning experience with more than 500 managers. In a straight comparison between the radial and all-channel situations the results outlined in Table 6.1 are almost always confirmed.

It is, of course, too large a leap to suggest that findings from a learning exercise can be related directly to organisational functioning although managers participating in the exercise can usually relate the experience to their own back at work situation. However, important confirmation of the experimental findings is provided in the work of Burns and Stalker (1961)[4] and Croome (1960)[5] carried out in the electronics industry in England and Scotland. This research was concerned with the effects of rapid technological development on a number of electronics firms and particularly with the difficulties encountered in fitting a newly expanded or newly recruited research and development function into the managerial structure. The research contrasted the operations of a number of organisations (twenty studies in all) with the intention of describing and explaining the effects of placing new and unfamiliar tasks upon industrial concerns which are organised for relatively stable conditions. There emerged from these studies the concept that two polar extremes of management system may exist, both representing a form of organisation which could be said to be deliberately and explicitly created and maintained in order to use the human resources of a firm in a way which is efficient and which best suits the particular circumstances of that firm. The two systems are referred to as mechanistic and organismic and may be defined as follows:

The mechanistic management system is appropriate to stable conditions in respect of internal and external change. It embodies a clear hierarchical organisation where roles are defined and members at each level of the hierarchy carry out a specific part of the problems and tasks facing the concern. The immediate superior of each part of the hierarchy is responsible for co-ordinating the tasks of those reporting to him so as to achieve his part in the main task. The flow of control, authority, and communication is hierarchical in that interaction is generally vertical and operations are governed by instructions and decisions issued by superiors. In addition the "whole picture" in terms of corporate objectives is maintained at the top of the concern with those lower down the hierarchy pursuing sub-goals. These sub-goals may be perceived by those at the top of the hierarchy as means to an end but by those lower down as ends in themselves. The mechanistic system therefore follows the "formal" pattern suggested by the management theorists mentioned earlier.

The organismic system of management is seen to be more appropriate to changing circumstances and is characterised by the value and use of special knowledge and expertise in the common task of the concern. It involves defining and redefining individual tasks through interaction with others in relation to the particular problems facing the firm. The flow of control, authority, and communication is through a network of relationships, i.e. upwards, downwards, sideways, across, rather than through a vertical hierarchy. This network stresses technical and commercial expertise in locating the centre of authority and control, therefore those in positions of power are not there because of their designated status in the hierarchy. Since communication follows the network pattern it resembles consultation rather than command, although because the network is stratified there remains a differentiation in seniority born out of differential expertise. The authority will be invested in those who are most informed and capable, such factors being decided by consensus.

It will be apparent from these descriptions that the distinction between mechanistic and organismic systems of management equate with that of the radial and all-channel systems.

It is important to note that the mechanistic system exerts commitment through right and as a condition of membership of the organisation; as we have seen in Chapter 5, this can be problematical. On the other hand, the organismic system involves commitment through a sharing of beliefs about the values and objectives of the concern, and moving to this situation can involve difficulties. In reality, whilst both systems may exist and be discernible in organisations, there also exist systems which fall between the two extremes; thus it is possible for an organisation to change in structure over time, avoiding some of the effects of rapid change.

The distinction drawn between the mechanistic and organismic management systems has important considerations for the planner. Theoretically in stable conditions with a mechanistic organisation the formulation and communication of long-range plans should be relatively straightforward. In practice, situations are never that stable and we are unlikely to work in an organisation which operates in a totally mechanistic way. Indeed, there is a great deal of research evidence to show that whilst organisational behaviour may be looked at in a "formal" sense (what should happen in line with the structure), it is important to analyse the "informal" behaviour in organisations (that which actually happens and which may or may not be in line with the structure (see particularly Argyris, 1972)[6] and Chapter 3 earlier). Any planning process must therefore take account of the character of the goals and the manner in which they are sought by individuals and groups inside the organisation. By groups we mean both the formal work groups, e.g. shift, section, department, and the informal groups, e.g. friendship, common interest groups, which form in all organisations. It is insufficient to gain commitment by top management to corporate objectives and the achievement of specific goals if those further down the hierarchy are seeking to achieve their own goals which are in conflict with those of the organisation. The goals being pursued by individuals and groups are a function of their own needs and the manner in which they perceive themselves in relation to the organisation. Argyris (1972)[6] would argue that in order to understand behaviour in organisations a study of the dynamics of individual and group behaviour is required. Examples of such an analysis are provided in Chapter 3, where we consider the individual in respect of both formal and informal behaviour in the firm.

The planner may, then, have to contend with a pluralistic rather than a unitary organisation in terms of commitment to goals. The translation of the strategic plan into a number of operating and corporate development plans has to take into account the extent and depth of commitment by organisation members: in this respect it can be argued that a mechanistic or formal organisational system is likely to generate more problems than an organic system, where there is greater scope for recognising and coping with "informal" behaviour. We shall return to these issues in Chapter 9.

Our discussion of organisational style in terms of the total organisation has so far been from the perspective of an organisation needing to change in order to cope with changes in its external environment. Our thinking leads us to question the validity of viewing "organisational style" and "organisational goals" except in terms of top management, that is those who decide policy. Since organisations do not exist without people we cannot conceive of corporate objectives as being other than humanly conceived (usually by top management) even though further down the hierarchy they may be seen to transcend the individual. The important point to bear in mind is the manner in which organisational members perceive and react to their part in the overall plan, both as individuals and in groups. In order to do this we need to break down the idea of organisational style into some more manageable or definable parts. This will mean looking at an organisation as a closed system, at least for study purposes. We may therefore move from the mechanistic–organismic analysis with its accent on environmental change to the analysis of organisation and individual manager style with the accent on intra-organisational behaviour.

Some of the most useful work in this area is provided by Likert (1961,[7] 1967[8]), who has researched the effects of differing organisation and management styles ultimately on such "end result" variables as productivity, costs, scrap loss, and earnings. Likert identifies four different

TABLE 6.2
Organisational and performance characteristics of different management systems – two variables only
(from Likert, 1967(8))

Organisational variable	System 1 Exploitive–authoritative	System 2 Benevolent and authoritative	System 3 Consultative	System 4 Participative group
1. Character of goal setting or ordering: manner in which usually done	Orders issued	Orders issued: opportunity to comment may or may not exist.	Goals are set or orders issued after discussion with subordinates of problems and planned action	Except in emergencies goals are usually established by means of group participation
Are there forces to accept, resist, or reject goals?	Goals are overtly accepted but are covertly resisted strongly	Goals are overtly accepted but often covertly resisted to at least a moderate degree	Goals are overtly accepted but at times with some covert resistance	Goals are fully accepted both overtly and covertly
2. Character of control processes. Extent to which the review and control functions are concentrated	Highly concentrated in top management	Relatively highly concentrated with some delegated control to middle and lower levels	Moderate downward delegation of review and control processes; lower as well as higher levels feel responsible	Quite widespread responsibility for review and control, with lower units at times imposing more rigorous reviews and tighter controls than top management
3. Extent to which there is an informal organisation present and supporting or opposing goals of formal organisation	Informal organisation present and opposing goals of formal organisation	Informal organisation usually present and partially resisting goals	Informal organisation may be present and may either support or partially resist goals of formal organisation	Informal and formal organisation are one and the same; hence all social forces support efforts to achieve organisation's goals

| Extent to which control data (e.g. accounting, productivity, cost, etc.) are used for self-guidance or group problem solving by managers and non-supervisory employees; or used by superiors in a punitive, policing manner | Used for policing and in punitive manner | Used for policing coupled with reward and punishment sometimes punitively; used somewhat for guidance but in accord with orders | Largely used for policing with emphasis usually on reward but with some punishment; used for guidance in accord with orders; some use also for self-guidance | Used for self-guidance and for co-ordinated problem solving and guidance; not used punitively |

management systems expressed along a continuum and which can be equated to the mechanistic–organismic distinction made earlier. In order to illustrate the different management systems, Table 6.2 shows two of the variables which he uses, and which are pertinent to the planning process.

The perception of many hundreds of managers is that high-producing departments are seen as operating towards the right of each scale and low-producing departments fall generally to the left. Yet the systems described on the left of the scale (systems 1 and 2), are more often seen to be used, particularly in times when more stringent control is needed over output and costs.

From the planning point of view it is undoubtedly easier and, seemingly, more precise to work on the assumption of system 1 since this offers a more systematic view of organisational functioning. Indeed, one might argue that it is the responsibility of the top management team to plan strategically ahead to ensure the survival of the company. The major question to ask is To what extent should less-senior managers be involved in this process?. It is not sufficient merely to say that corporate planning motivates and obtains the commitment of managers because it makes known what the company is trying to achieve and provides all the company with a common purpose. This may be partly true, but from our discussions so far we know that, without initial involvement in the planning process, commitment to the effects of these plans is likely to be problematical. As Hussey (1974)[9] has pointed out, one of the reasons why planning sometimes fails is that managers refuse to accept planning and respond to planning efforts either with passive resistance or by failing to help overcome obstacles to effective long-range planning. Commitment to planning is therefore very much a function of organisation style as examplified by the chief executive and senior management team. It may also be said that whilst planning under system 1 may be neater in theory, in practice a move towards system 4 is desirable.

We are not just concerned, however, with the effects of organisational style on commitment *per se*, the wider issue is the extent to which the design of the formal planning system will need to embody an analysis of the predominant style of the company and where necessary incorporate changes in that style to ensure involvement on the part of all company employees.

This means that the assessment of the organisational climate, prior to the introduction of corporate planning, cannot be left to chance, since the climate will be related to the style and structure of the company it is necessary for data such as organisation charts, spans of control, and reporting procedures to be related to some specific data on climate. Such specific data may be obtained by using a climate survey (Table 6.2 is an example), or by semi-structured interview. We are not suggesting here that the introduction of formal planning means going through a process of organisational development (see Chapter 7) but that particular regard should be paid to the effects of the planning process in relation to organisational style and the behaviour of employees. In Chapter 12 we deal more specifically with the impact of organisational style on corporate planning.

Individual Management Style

The analysis of organisational style and climate inevitably leads us to consider the effects of individual manager and supervisor style on organisational functioning. The particular style adopted by "an organisation" (i.e. those at the top), whether it be explorative–authoritative (system 1) or participative group (system 4), will affect the style which individual managers can adopt. Most managers will suggest that they are constrained in the way in which they manage by the style of their superior, his superior, and so on up the hierarchy. Thus it is often difficult, for example, for a manager working in a formal, exploitative–authoritative organisation to adopt anything but that type of management style. Nevertheless, it should be pointed out that an individual manager is only constrained to the extent that he himself perceives and interprets those constraints. Managers do adopt styles of management different from those prevailing in the organisation, and do this successfully. In our experience the planner will find, in his discussions at unit or departmental level, managers adopting different styles either consciously by using that approach which best suits prevailing conditions or unconsciously out of experience. The planner may therefore gauge the climate of the unit or department (as distinct from the organisation as a whole) by identifying the predominant style of the manager.

A number of researchers have written at the level of individual manager leadership style. We provide a synthesis of some of this work (Tannenbaum and Schmidt, 1973;[10] Fieldler, 1967;[11] Blake and Mouton, 1964[12]) by identifying those continua which concentrate on the major issues facing the manager.

TABLE 6.3
Manager style-communication

DIRECTIVE	CONSULTATIVE	PARTICIPANT	*LAISSEZ-FAIRE*
Formal	Decides most	Defines	No steering
Dominant	Hears views	Limits/constraints	Monitors feedback
Own way	Then:	Takes suggestions	Group decides
Compliance	Tells/persuades	Influenced by	
Power retention		expertise	
		Concensus sharing	

Source: R. Evendon (1970–3), Roffey Park Management College, based on research and teaching notes. Used with permission.

In Table 6.3 we focus on the styles or approaches which can be adopted by a manager in communicating and decision making. The four points on the scale are indicators rather than precise descriptions, but it is usual to find that managers can identify one of these styles as being predominant in their own behaviour and that of their superior. It is usual to find that one of the styles is used more often than the other three; this may be due in part to the manager's psychological make-up (i.e. his need for affiliation and his need for dominance) and in part to the overall style of the organisation for which he works. The communication style adopted is closely related to the manner in which the manager perceives his priorities. Some managers spend much of their time concentrating on the technical, systems, methods aspect of their job, whereas others spend more time focusing on people, attitudes, morale, and motivation issues. As we shall see later, the technology and type of production process involved may have some effect on the need to concentrate on either of these particular concerns. The task–people dimension of style are outlined in Table 6.4.

The distribution of time and energy between task needs and people needs is perhaps the most fundamental dilemma facing the manager. Too much concentration on the task will inevitably lead to attitude and morale problems, leading to a lowering in quality and or quantity of work. On the other hand an over-concentration on people needs can often mean reduced output through a lowering of standards. The balance is really critical since

TABLE 6.4
Manager style — tasks–people

MANAGER'S TIME/ATTENTION/ACTIVITY DISTRIBUTION	
Technical/systems centres	Employee centred

100%	90%	80%	70%	60%	50%	60%	70%	80%	90%	100%

Focus on things

e.g. Analysis, diagnosis, planning,
action related to systems,
operational methods, procedures,
techniques, equipment install-
ing, modifying, maintaining the
above
Monitoring and regulating task/
technical activities (self, others,
subordinates) studying task/
technical information, communicating with a task/technical
focus.
Activity with a "thing" rather than
"people" focus, i.e. financial
sales strategy/tactics, accounts,
engineering, budget planning
and control

Focus on people

e.g. Identifying personal goals, problems,
diagnosing and acting upon
attitudes, morale, motivation
problems
Interviewing, appraisal/target setting
Counselling, discipline, welfare,
selection, grievance handling,
supporting, guiding, training,
developing
Communicating with individual/
group need focus

Source: R. Evendon (1970–3), Roffey Park Management College, based on research and teaching notes. Used with permission.

even the most up-to-date technology may be useless without the commitment and involvement of people in using it.

The description of technical/systems-centred management may suggest
that those with technical jobs such as engineers will of necessity need to
focus more in that area. By the same rule it could be suggested that, for
example, personnel managers having a "people" job would usually operate
at the employee-centred end of the continuum. Neither of these is, however, the case; it is not uncommon to find a works engineer who spends
60% or 70% of his time dealing with people/group problems, and we have
all perhaps met the personnel manager who is so bound up with systems,
routines, and personnel policies that he has little time for dealing with
real people. The idea of style goes beyond pure job function, although, as
Woodward (1958)[13] has pointed out, as technology in manufacturing

advances, the pressure on people at all levels increases; thus the maintenance of good human and industrial relations becomes more difficult.

We have pointed out earlier that a manager's style may be affected by his own need for affiliation, or to be liked by people, and his need for dominance as opposed to dependency. The degree of need may determine the extent to which a manager is task-centred or people-centred. This further variation in style is reflected in Table 6.5, the sociability dimension.

TABLE 6.5
Manager style — sociability

PSYCHOLOGICALLY DISTANT	PSYCHOLOGICALLY CLOSE
Aloof — maintains social distance	Friendship Relationships "One of the boys"

Source: R. Evendon (1970–3), Roffey Park Management College, based on research and teaching notes. Used with permission.

We find that the psychological distance/closeness can be a real dilemma for managers, especially for newly appointed first-time managers who move from being a member of the work group to the position of having to manage that group. Our experience shows that some first-time managers try to remain "one of the boys" whilst others move purposely to the aloof end of the continuum. Often neither style is successful, and only by trial and error is the optimum style found.

It is important for subordinates to be able to recognise the style being adopted by their manager in order that relationships and understanding between them may be maintained. Managers also find that abrupt changes in style can cause confusion; the following experience is indicative:

In a process plane employing 1100 people the works manager, brought in to try and turn a loss-making unit into a profitable plant, used a directive/consultative style (to the left of the three continua). This approach appeared to work initially because, although many managers did not like his style of regular formal meetings, reporting systems, and tight control, the usual comment was "at least we know where we stand even though we do get a 'rocket' from time to time". In fact there is some evidence to show that to avoid getting a "rocket" some managers were deliberately withholding information, or distorting the facts in their favour. Morale, initially high, decreased over time, and in some departments became problematical. The manager was eventually replaced by a new works manager whose style was participant to the point of *laissez faire* in some instances. This change did not result in increased morale, as might have been expected; indeed, the subordinate managers now complained that they were given no direction and that the absence of formal meetings meant that they did not liaise with other departments and functions successfully. Initially, they were unable to cope with the change in style and, as Likert (1967)[8] has shown, time is an important consideration when comparing the effects of changes in manager style. It is possible to accelerate the translation to different styles by using management educational approaches: for example, group discussion with those affected, using the concepts outlined in this and the next chapter.

Although it has been suggested that most managers have a predominant style, and that the style adopted can be influenced by the overall organisation style, many writers argue the need for flexibility of style to meet changing circumstances. The following situational factors may be usefully taken into account when assessing style appropriateness:

The situation. – Dynamic or changing situations may call for, and support, a different management style from situations which are routine and static. We refer to style in relation to change in Chapter 8. An example of a dynamic work situation is the management of firemen at the scene of a fire, where a highly directive style is required and acceptable. However, the same firemen may respond better to a more participant style of management at other times, e.g. in equipment maintenance or fire-prevention activities.

Relationship between roles. – Relationships between manager and subordinate can be influenced by the nature and expectations of the "leader-member" situation. Problems can occur when the manager's style is incompatible with his role as perceived by subordinates. The manager, therefore, should take account of existing relations, attitudes, and behaviour of his subordinates. As we have illustrated earlier, *sharp* changes in style, where the reasons for such changes are not understood, can create problems.

Motivation and morale. — Where there are attitudinal problems affecting motivation and commitment it may be appropriate to adopt a more participant employee-centred style in order to more effectively diagnose the causes and find remedies to these problems.

Requirements of the job. — Evidence suggests (see Fieldler, 1967,[11] and Fig. 6.2) that the structure and requirements of the job can influence the choice of style which may be adopted. Jobs which are routine, largely prescribed, and repetitive, may require a different style from those which are complex, non-routine, and have a high degree of freedom to act.

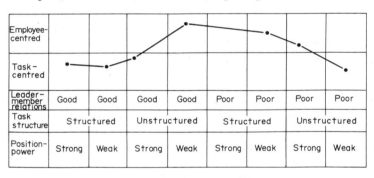

Employee-centred								
Task-centred								
Leader-member relations	Good	Good	Good	Good	Poor	Poor	Poor	Poor
Task structure	Structured		Unstructured		Structured		Unstructured	
Position-power	Strong	Weak	Strong	Weak	Strong	Weak	Strong	Weak

Fig. 6.2. How the style of effective leadership varies with the situation.
(Adapted from Fieldler, 1967[11].)

We have suggested that it is possible for the manager to modify his style and behaviour to suit different circumstances, although the need to avoid abrupt changes has been pointed out. It could also be suggested that manager style is related to individual personality, e.g. in terms of the individual's need for dominance as opposed to dependency and high affiliation as opposed to low affiliation. Therefore, whilst it is possible for the manager to modify his approach, for him to sustain a style which is obviously out of character is likely to prove counter-productive. More permanent changes in style demand a fundamental reassessment of attitudes and values on the part of the manager.

The degree of appropriateness of a particular manager style to different circumstances has been usefully extended by Fieldler (1967)[11] in his "contingency theory of leadership effectiveness". Three principal variables forming the major determinants of effective leadership behaviour are distinguished; these are leader–member relations, task structure, and position/power. We can briefly describe these variables:

Leader–Member relations. The extent to which the leader is liked by his subordinates and they are willing to follow his advice.

Task structure. The extent to which tasks are routined and formalised or nebulous and undefined.

Position/power. The power ascribed to the leader position by the organisation and the extent to which he can reward or punish.

Using these determinants, Fieldler is able to suggest which style of leadership might best operate under particular conditions. Figure 6.2 shows the variations, and from this diagram it can be seen that, for example, where position/power is strong, the task highly structured, and leader–member relations good, a more directive/controlling style can be used. In comparison, where position/power is weak, task unstructured, and leader–member relations poor, a more participative leadership style should work best.

It should be pointed out that the use of leader–member relations as an independent variable in this way is somewhat problematic because these relationships can both affect and be affected by the manager's style.

Conclusions

We have reviewed some of the current work into organisation and manager style, seeking rather to point-up thoughts and considerations for the planning process than to make a deep exploration. Perhaps the most pertinent of the issues is the implied suggestion of this chapter that the corporate planner needs to find means of obtaining information on the style and climate predominant in the organisation and to assess this in relation to its effect on his work. In some situations the prevailing climate may cause such difficulties that it is impossible to begin meaningful planning without first effecting changes in the organisation structure.

We could hypothesise that a very formal, bureaucratic organisation should, on the face of it, be an ideal situation for planning only an inflexible, bureaucratic type of approach. In such a case participative planning may be impossible, and we would advise the planner to look closely at the informal organisation where lower down the line his procedures may be perceived in a very different light from the way senior management see them. The planner's role is very much a persuading/convincing role, taking account of the very real and powerful pressure which groups can exert on the managing process. In some cases groups of middle and junior management can be very strategic in their behaviour (we suggest how this force can be harnessed in Chapter 11), and it is important to determine how they see their objectives in relation to the objectives of top management. We could go so far as to say that since we live in an increasingly pluralistic society the job of the planner will increasingly be to attempt to weld many different objectives into one common set, or at least a set which can be interpreted from a common base. There is no doubt that this can be a problem at senior management level, the first persuasion hurdle for the planner, but while achievement of unitary goals at this level is a precondition for successful long-range planning, it cannot be assumed that the unitary commitment will automatically permeate to lower levels of the concern. The planning process may also be more difficult in a highly participant company where, by the use of task groups, informal behaviour has been formalised. These "expertise" task groups may change membership from time to time according to the nature of the work and problems faced. It is helpful therefore to view the leaders or managers of such groups as having a "linking-pin" function as Likert suggests (see Fig. 6.3), the achievement of sub-objectives then becomes the task of the group with the manager relating the efforts of his group and managing the interface between his own and other groups.

The planning manager may also care to check his own style against the continua discussed earlier; but, more importantly, he should check the perceptions of his own subordinates and those to whom he relates (which probably means all the company management). Frequently subordinates will perceive a manager's style quite differently from the way he sees himself. Where the planner is relying on the commitment and involvement

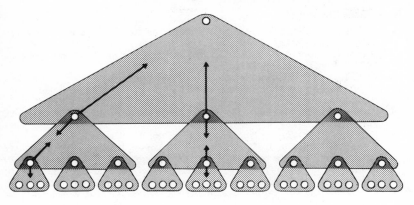

Fig. 6.3. The linking pin. (From Likert, 1961[7].)

of managers and supervisors who are his partners in the planning process it is important that his style is seen to be in keeping with the demands he is making upon them. This is not just a question of being liked and accepted; we have all come across the manager who is seen both as a "really nice guy" and as an ineffectual manager because he cannot modify his style or select the right style for prevailing conditions. The planner may find himself under subtle pressure to accept the approach of a manager — "this is how I get things done around here, it's the only way". Where he feels the approach to be incompatible with his planning objectives then he may have to find some working compromise. This will mean recognising his own style as a planning manager and the limitations on the use of his structural authority (that authority he has by virtue of his position in the company and the extent of commitment to planning by top management). The ability to be flexible in style and approach is therefore axiomatic.

The view of the corporate planner as a manager and a change agent raises important issues in respect of organisation climate and style; these effects are far reaching enough for us to suggest that the planner should consider his role as a change agent and the effects of developing and changing organisation structures in more detail. These are the subjects of the following two chapters.

References Chapter 6

1. M. J. Leavitt (1951) Some effects of certain communication patterns on performance, *Journal of Abnormal and Social Psychology*, Vol. 46, pp. 38–50. (See also V. H. Vroom and E. L. Deci (eds.), *Management and Motivation*, Penguin 1972 edition, Ch. 25, pp. 341–3.
2. F. W. Taylor (1947) *Scientific Management*, Harper, New York.
3. E. F. L. Brech (1957) *Organisation – The Framework of Management*, Longmans, London.
4. T. Burns and G. M. Stalker (1961) *The Management of Innovation*, Tavistock Publ., London.
5. H. Croom (1960) *Human Problems of Innovation*, HMSO, London.
6. C. Argyris (1972) In B. Salaman and K. Thompson (eds.) (1973), *People and Organisations*, Longmans, pp. 76–90.
7. R. Likert (1961) *New Patterns of Management*, McGraw-Hill, London.
8. R. Likert (1967) *The Human Organisation*, McGraw-Hill, London.
9. D. E. Hussey (1974) *Corporate Planning Theory and Practice*, Pergamon Press, Oxford, p. 302.
10. R. Tannenbaum and W. H. Schmidt (1973) How to choose a leadership pattern, *Harvard Business Review*, May–June 1973, pp. 162–80.
11. F. E. Fielder (1967) *A Theory of Leadership Effectiveness*, McGraw-Hill, London.
12. R. R. Blake and J. S. Mouton (1964) *The Managerial Grid*, Gulf Publ. Co., Houston, Texas.
13. J. Woodward (1958) *Management and Technology*, HMSO, London.

CHAPTER 7

Organisation Development

In the previous chapter we looked at the effects of manager and organisation style on the business enterprise, and this has led us to begin to consider changes which may be required in the structure and relationships inside the organisation. In using the work of Likert we opened up the analysis of organisation systems and we shall further develop that analysis in this chapter. The process of corporate planning will, almost inevitably, raise questions of organisation structuring in the form of roles and role descriptions, procedures and responsibilities, but such question may be more far-reaching than simply publishing changes in procedures or formal structure. The need for long-range strategies for business operations, the concept of tactical plans involving such areas as resource development planning, and operations planning cannot be divorced from the need to consider organisation planning in terms of developing work climates, relationships, and communication systems. Hence the need to be aware of the type of work being carried out under the term "organisation development" (OD) is pertinent to the corporate planner. In fact the concept of OD is closely linked to the planning process, and there are similarities in both efforts as we shall see. Although corporate planning is concerned with economical and mathematical analysis like organisational development it is also concerned directly with human variables. As we see it the two are necessarily complementary.

There are a number of definitions of OD put forward by different workers in the field (see Thakur, 1974),[1] and because OD is a human effort involving the behaviour and perceptions of groups of people, perhaps this is to be expected. One of the most comprehensive definitions is provided by Beckhart (1969),[2] p. 9: "Organisation development is an effort planned, organisation wide, and managed from the top, to increase organisation effectiveness and health through planned interventions in the organisation's 'processes' using behavioural science knowledge."

This definition is similar in a number of ways to the definition of corporate planning given by Hussey (1974),[3] particularly the "planned", "organisation wide", and "managed from the top" aspects. Indeed, there are some who would suggest that where a company has a personnel function which can attend to problems of resourcing and be involved in corporate planning there is no need for an OD specialist.

But the fact of life is that all resourcing and planning is dependent for success upon the prevailing climate of the organisation, the way people relate to each other, differing perceptions of management and subordinate levels, and the manner in which information and feedback on performance filters throughout the organisation. Organisation development is very much about the analysis of these processes and the means whereby relationships can become more effective. With increasing social and technological change there is an increasing need to consider the effects of such change on organisation structure and operation.

The description of OD given by Beckhart should be explained further. Organisational development is seen as a planned change involving a systematic diagnosis of the organistion and the development of a strategic plan for improvement. In this respect OD becomes very much associated with the corporate planning process in terms of setting objectives, organising the work, people, and system to enable these objectives to be attained. But OD is chiefly concerned, as we have mentioned, with the "process" inherent in setting objectives, organising the work, and so on, rather than with the *systems* or *procedures* devised for the achievement of objectives. To make this distinction in a simpler way, we can look at the setting of a small team of managers met to resolve a particular organisational problem (Fig. 7.1).

The objective of the group is to move from starting point *A* where all the facts are marshalled to the end point *B* which signifies a solution to the problem. There are three simultaneous streams of activity. (1) The *content* or words, information, facts, etc., available to the group. (2) The *procedure* or problem-solving sequence, which includes consideration of how the group is to be organised, who is to be chairman, secretary, what rules or norms need to be established, what techniques the group should use and so on. (3) The *process*, which is the interactions (conscious and

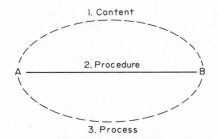

Fig. 7.1. Activities of a problem-solving group.

unconscious) between these present and includes answers to such questions as, how members feel about the way the meeting is going, who has the most influence on the group and why, who speaks to whom and why, how much commitment is there to the solutions being offered. It is important that the three activities of *content*, *procedure*, and *process* are adequately handled if the group is to function successfully. The most often neglected area is that of *process*; very often a problem-solving group will have considerable information and a clear procedure for working but will ignore the *process* to the extent that commitment to the task in hand and the eventual outcome is reduced to a low level. At this point it is usual to hear people complaining about ineffective and time-wasting meetings. If it is possible for a small group of people to become so disenchanted with a meeting that they lose commitment, then it is apparent that such a phenomenon organisation-wide can lead to problems of motivation and morale. It is the *process* activity inside organisations which forms the major focus for OD planned change. The concern is to improve the quality and openness of relationships between people so that "common aims" really are accepted as "common" to all. It is principles such as these which we believe are equally critical to the success of corporate planning.

Organisation development involves the total *system* that means it can only work successfully on the total organisation or a relatively autonomous part of the organisation. The term *system* therefore refers to an entity which can be distinguished as such by relatively clear boundaries and which is responsible in itself for the achievement of certain objectives. Thus a system could be a single organisation or a sub-unit of a larger organisation provided that the sub-unit has reasonable autonomy. Coupled with this is the need for the top management of the system to be committed to and actively encourage the change effort involved in OD.

The final part of Beckhart's definition relates OD to increasing organisation effectiveness and health. It may be useful to quote his own description of an effective organisation.

"An effective organisation is one in which:
(a) The total organisation, the significant sub-parts, and individuals, manage their work against *goals* and *plans* for achievement of these goals.
(b) Form follows function (the problem, or task, or project, determines how the human resources are organised).
(c) Decisions are made by and near the sources of information regardless of where these sources are located on the Organisation Chart.
(d) The reward system is such that managers and supervisors are rewarded (and punished) comparably for:
  — short-term profit or production performance;
  — growth and development of their subordinates;
  — creating a viable working group.
(e) Communication laterally and vertically is *relatively* understood. People are generally open and confronting. They share all the relative facts including feelings.
(f) There is a minimum amount of inappropriate win/lose activities between individuals and groups. Constant effort exists at all levels to treat conflict and conflict situations as *problems* subject to problem solving methods.
(g) There is high 'conflict' (clash of ideas) about tasks and projects, and relatively little energy spent in clashing over *interpersonal* difficulties because they have been generally worked through.
(h) The organisation and its parts see themselves as interacting with each other *and* with the *larger* environment. The organisation is an open system.
(i) There is a shared value, and management strategy to support it, of trying to help each person (or unit) in the organisation maintain his (or its) integrity and uniqueness in an interdependent environment.

(j)   The organisation and its members operate in an 'action research' way. General practice is to build *feedback mechanisms* so that individuals and groups can learn from their own experience." [Beckhart, 1969,[2] pp. 10-11.]

The OD specialist will therefore work inside an organisation to attempt to increase effectiveness by promoting open and honest feedback between members and suggesting ways in which the energy in the organisation can be put to constructive rather than destructive use. An important feature of OD, which is pertinent to corporate planning, is the accent on building and working towards unitary goals with the commitment of all rather than, as is so often the case, having a pluralistic system of goals, many of which are opposed to the stated objectives of the company. Often the barriers and blocks to achieving organisational goals are interpersonal or intergroup based where individual managers or functional units jealously guard their own procedures and objectives, maintaining a distorted perception of their own value and indispensability to the organisation in comparison with other managers or functional units. Many "games" are played between managers with the purpose of increasing individual or functional power positions or for some other purpose, very often in direct competition with and to the detriment of the aims of the total organisation. Organisation development is about finding ways and means of reducing such "recalcitrant" activity. Organisation development efforts may also be used to overcome problems of change in manager and organisational style (see Chapter 6), change in organisational structure, the installation of motivation techniques such as job enrichment (see Chapter 5), the stimulation of creativity (see Chapter 4), and to help open up communication networks and channels in the organisation. A further need for OD is in the design and implementation of better planning particularly since the planning process is rarely the lonely task of the chief executive or main board, but entails the involvement of people throughout the organiation who may need help in the planning and goal-setting process.

What Does OD Entail?

One way of describing the kind of work carried out by an OD consultant or "process consultant" is to take one area of concern to most

organisations — that of communciation — and outline some of the phenomena associated with communication issues and the manner in which these
issues can be overcome. It may be particularly pertinent to focus on communication since we are probably all familiar with the ubiquitous "failure
in communication" reason or excuse for something going wrong in the
organisation. However, in concentrating on communication we are aware
that this is only one of the many areas in which the OD specialist may get
involved, and the particular issues which he may decide to confront and
work on will be dependent upon his diagnosis of a particular organisational
situation. The areas of communication that we shall look at do, however,
often feature in the planned changes suggested in an OD programme.

We need, firstly, to reduce the term "communication" to some
meaningful parts. To simply define the word may not be of great help, but
what we can suggest is that communication in the organisation can be
looked at in a number of ways: (1) communication processing inside the
individual (intra-personal); (2) communication between individuals (interpersonal); (3) communication within groups (intra-group); and (4) between different groups (inter-group). These divisions are not usually
discrete but it will help, for the moment, to think of them as such.

Intra- and Inter-personal Communication

One of the distinct differences between human and other animals is
the ability of human beings to "interpret" or "define" what other people
say or do before responding. An individual's response is not made directly
to what someone else says, but, rather, is based on the *meaning* he or she
attributes to what has been said. Thus it is not a question of reacting to a
statement (or stimulus) intuitively or through training but of interpreting that statement before responding. Figure 7.2 illustrates this point.

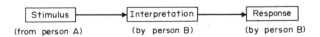

Fig. 7.2. Communication process (1).

In a sense the receiver (person B) is decoding the message sent by person
A and to do this he will use his own set of "interpreting standards". These

will relate to his experience, beliefs, aspirations, motives, needs, attitudes, values and expectations, and his perception of such organisational factors as his role, the organisational hierarchy, norms, and formal/informal procedures. Since each of us has a unique set of interpreting standards it is easy to see why misunderstandings so often arise in communication. By and large, however, there are sufficient common "referents" and understandings between people for meaningful conversation to take place. The difficulties usually arise where emotions and feelings cause blocks to understanding between people. As Fig. 7.3 shows, every message sent

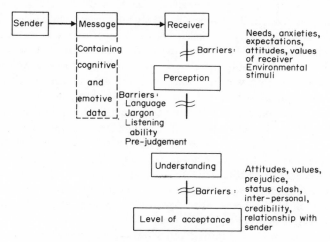

Fig. 7.3. Communication process (2).

contains both cognitive *and* emotive data, and the emotive content particularly can give rise to barriers which affect the process of understanding and level of acceptance. Our unique interpreting standards give rise to a predisposition to hear what we want to hear and vice versa. There is a good deal of research evidence to suggest that we "filter" messages we receive and that we select carefully what we say and how we say it on the basis of our need to support our self-image, the way we perceive ourselves, and the manner in which we would prefer to be seen by others. In this process we also take account of our image of the other person(s) and our definition of the situation of which we are a part. This "filtering" process can give rise to stereotyping and the use of favourable and unfavourable prejudices. We are all aware of the loose and firm handshake or "shifty eyes" assessments made by "knowing" individuals and, perhaps, of the common stricture that it is unwise to judge by first impression. But we do use first impression including both verbal and non-verbal cues in order to make assessments which may then be modified and changed in later encounters. The process of filtering and stereotyping can give rise to self-fulfilling situations where it becomes possible for one person to so stereotype another that the stereotyped person becomes locked into a role from which he cannot escape, at least in the eyes of the stereotyper. An example may explain this process. A newly appointed production manager was unsure of his ability to manage his department in both a technical and managerial sense. Unable or unwilling to share his doubts with anyone, he decided to adopt a highly directive style of management, suggesting to his colleagues that this was necessary due to the low grade of worker employed in his department. This style of management and explanation for it was in the nature of a "mental defence mechanism" since it enabled the manager to rationalise his own fears and inadequacies. The so called low-grade workers quickly perceived how they were seen by the manager and reacted to his style of management with such behaviour as limiting output, waiting to be told what to do, and adopting a sullen approach to the job. The manager was ultimately able to point to these behaviours as indicative of his problems with low-grade workers and his need to be highly directive in order to get the work done.

In this example the filtering and stereotyping process had turned full circle creating a self-fulfilling situation which was then very difficult to break. This phenomenon is not uncommon in organisations between both individuals and groups and can often be the source of considerable friction and communication distortion. The mental defence mechanism adopted by the manager is an example of the "hidden" part of ourselves, that part of which we are aware but which we do not easily share with others. Luft (1963)[4] has provided a model of the individual in four parts relating to interaction with others (Fig. 7.4).

There is a part of us which we know of and which we are prepared to share with others. This is the open self used in everyday relationships and which is bounded by the particular facade we might like to erect in order to maintain our self-image. The extent of openness in our behaviour will

	Behaviour known to self	Behaviour unknown to self
Behaviour known to others	Open	Blind
Behaviour unknown to others	Hidden	Dark

Fig. 7.4. Four parts of the person – the Johari window. (From Luft, 1963[4].)

depend upon a number of factors unique to the relationship we have with the other person; these may include role, expectations, perceived status in relation to the other, our needs and goals in the social situation, and so on. Kelly (1955)[5] has suggested that we anticipate or "construe" the other person on the basis of a set of bipolar personal constructs, i.e. good–bad, honest–dishonest, like me–not like me, using such constructs to predict how the other person will behave and modifying our own behaviour against the predictions (see Langham and Jukes, 1976[6]). It has also been suggested that we always view other people in a totally holistic sense, i.e., we make judgements about a person as a total person (we may here be using our stereotypes) right from first meeting, and that although judgements are modified as we receive further information about the person, we still describe the person as being "this or that sort of individual".

In addition to the open area, which is really the effective communication channel, there are things about ourselves of which we know but which we are unlikely to share with others – the hidden part; even in our most intimate relationships we probably hold something of ourselves back. It is true also that other people can give us feedback on certain aspects of our behaviour about which we have been unaware – the blind area. Finally, there is that subconscious part of ourselves about which both we and others are unaware.

Luft suggests that an increase in the "open" quadrant should bring about a corresponding decrease in the other three quadrants and thus the scope for effective communication is increased. Quite often in OD work the need for more open communication and greater honesty of feedback is seen to be required particularly where blocks caused by role differences and expectations and status differences occur. The OD process consultant may use learning devices in order to open up the possibility for better communication and decreased inter-personal misunderstandings. An example of such a device is based on the Johari window (Fig. 7.4) and involves the participants in assessing the major assets and liabilities of their personality and their perceptions of the assets and liabilities of others in the group. This information is shared in the form of self-disclosure and feedback to others, one effect being to increase the open area of the self and facilitate constructive and open feedback (Pfiffer and Jones 1974[7]).

Person to person communication is one area which may demand the attentions of the OD process consultant, but generally this will be analysed in a group setting since it is most usual to find the process consultant working with groups inside organisations.

Intra- and Inter-Group Communication

The behaviour of both formal and informal groups in organisations has for long been the subject of study by behaviour scientists. The OD consultant is concerned to analyse the effectiveness of formal groups such as meetings, sections, shifts, and more informal groupings at work such as "soviet" or less-formal meetings, friendship and common interest groups. A number of writers have pointed to the "structuring" of relationships arising out of group membership. We referred in Chapter 3 to the work of Strauss *et al.* (1963),[8] and the idea of a "negotiated order" arising from the manner in which organisational members break, stretch, modify, or re-define rules and policies in order to make them acceptable and workable. This is done through a process of informal negotiation with others resulting in relatively short-term understandings or agreements establishing norms to structure acceptable behaviour. These norms are dependent upon the amount of trust developed between the parties concerned. It can be suggested that whilst trust may be high between negotiating parties (who are seeking to satisfy certain specific aims), such a high level of trust is not generally found throughout an organisation, hence the need for negotiation over issues rather than an approach such as joint problem solving between parties. A number of other writers have pointed to the quite delicate balance of exchange and reciprocation present in relationships between people of differential status in organisations (see Chapter 3 for a full account of these concepts). Many of these accounts show how individuals attempt to cope with the system of administration, which they perceive, imposed upon them, in a sense how the individual may pursue his own ends either within or despite the system.

In OD there is a concern to bring into the open the personal issues which face people in coping with their own needs, their role, and the organisational constraints. This is particularly true when one analyses the behaviour of individuals in groups. As Schein (1969)[9] has pointed out, a number of issues may face the individual as a member of a group whether it be a work group, friendship group, or management group, and often — although we refer to such groups as teams, e.g. the management team — so many personal issues remain unconfronted that the group does not function effectively as a team in the accepted sense.

Some of these issues are:

Identity. Where there is a concern to find a role or identity which will be both compatible with the self-image and acceptable to the group. The individual may seek to answer such questions as How shall I behave in this group? How do the others see me? What is the best way in which I can use my expertise and resources to further my own and the group's aims? There is a large body of research existing which purports to show different roles adopted in group or meeting situations, and the role of leader or chairman may often be much less clear-cut than is imagined. Group members tend to use a range of resources and ploys to further their interests so that influence is often widely rather than narrowly spread throughout the group. This exercise of *influence or control* is a further concern facing the individual. In the early stages of a group forming (e.g. a project planning group) there may be internal in-fighting defensive, offensive behaviour between members which is often the way of establishing where the power and influence is located and some norms for the future operation of the group. During this time there can be dangers in having a chairman or leader who operates according to a tight structure for procedure (see Fig. 7.1) since this may force a lot of the necessary levelling behaviour under the surface and create unresolved concerns which will be manifest later in the life of the group.

A third issue concerning the individual is his need to be accepted by the group and the extent to which he is able to achieve a comfortable level of intimacy with other members. The *acceptance* needs may vary depending upon the type of group and the length of time available for the group to operate, but the acceptance process can be a source of tension whilst group members are attempting to work as a cohesive team.

Schutz (1966)[10] defines these major concerns of inclusion, control, and affection, and suggests that they may be recurring, underlying issues facing a group. Indeed, the needs which individuals bring to a group are only part of the underlying process found in working groups. In addition there are concerns that the group will have for the "task" or the work it has met to accomplish and for the maintenance of the group as a viable entity. In terms of both of these concerns an over-emphasis on individual needs can be disruptive; thus it is often suggested that an effective group needs to balance the needs from these three areas (Fig. 7.5).

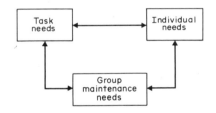

Fig. 7.5. Major concerns of a working group.

The task and group maintenance functions are equally important in an effective group; indeed, as we have already pointed out, the importance of the task is often so over-emphasised that group maintenance and individual needs are reduced to the level where internal friction between individuals and subgroups can threaten the life of the group. The OD consultant may use forms of analysis of group behaviour which can highlight these processes and bring into the open some of the unresolved under-the-surface issues facing the group. The following example of such a mode of analysis has been compiled from a modification of the work of Schein (1969)[9] and other practitioners.

Task Behaviour

1. *Initiating*: proposing tasks or goals; defining problem; suggesting procedure; contributing ideas.
2. *Seeking information or opinions*: requesting facts; seeking relevant information about group concern; asking for opinions; seeking suggestions and ideas.
3. *Giving information or opinions*: offering facts; providing relevant information about group concern; stating opinions or belief about a matter before the group; giving suggestions and ideas.
4. *Clarifying and elaborating*: interpreting ideas or suggestions; clearing up confusion; defining terms; indicating alternatives and issues before the group.
5. *Summarising*: putting together related ideas; restating suggestions after the group has discussed them; offering a decision or conclusion for the group to accept or reject.
6. *Seeking decision*: testing for readiness to make decision; seeking decision-making procedure.
7. *Taking decisions*: stating group's feelings in terms of a group decision; invoking the decision-making process.

Group Maintenance Behaviours

1. *Harmonising*: attempting to reconcile disagreements; reducing tensions; getting people to explore their differences.
2. *Gatekeeping*: helping to keep communication channels open; facilitating participation of others; suggesting procedures which permit sharing remarks.
3. *Encouraging*: being friendly, warm, responsive; indicating by facial expression or remark acceptance of other contributions.
4. *Compromising*: modifying in the interests of group cohesion or growth; yielding status in conflict situations.
5. *Standard setting*: expressing or suggesting standards for the group to attempt to achieve.
6. *Standard testing*: attempting to evaluate the quality of the decision-making process in the group; testing whether the group is satisfied with its procedures.

Individual Needs Behaviour

1. *Dominating*: trying to assert authority or superiority in manipulating the group or certain members of it.
2. *Aggressing and blocking*: attacking group members or group ideas and suggestions; stubborness beyond "reason".
3. *Recognition or help seeking*: drawing attention to oneself in various ways; attempting to call forth sympathy response through expressions of insecurity, personal confusion; deprecating oneself beyond reasonable limits.
4. *Pairing up*: seeking out one or two supporters and forming a kind of emotional subgroup in which the members protect and support each other.
5. *Special interest pleading*: speaking for particular interests (e.g. "engineers", "personnel", "management") as a cover for prejudice or stereotypes which best fit the individual's needs and desires.
6. *Withdrawing*: trying to remove the sources of uncomfortable feelings by psychologically leaving the group.

Further forms for the analysis of group behaviour are given in Langham and Barker (1976).[11] Of particular value is the mode of analysis suggested by Bales (1950,[12] 1970[13]), who distinguishes between the occurrence of task-related and social emotional behaviour, suggesting that successful groups need both a task leader and a social emotional leader. Bales also outlines the phases through which problem-solving groups move, indicating the major preoccupations of the group in each phase, these are: (1) integration, (2) tension management, (3) formulating decisions, (4) control (of members), (5) evaluation (of decisions), (6) orientation (in the form of clarification or summary of decisions reached).

There exists a vast body of on-going research data into the behaviour of formal and informal groups in organisations, and it is from this research that the OD consultant can both draw and add to when operating with groups.

Inter-group Behaviour

In our experience, reinforced by discussions with hundreds of managers in companies and on management courses, the most often-quoted problem area is that of communication between departments, functions, or groups. Such inter-group friction seems to be an area where a great deal of energy is expended, reinforcing the position of a group and its members in opposition to other groups in the organisation. It is quite common to hear of conflict between departments, e.g. production versus sales and between levels of management, e.g. middle management versus supervisors, and the result of this conflict is often a deprecation of total organisation goals in favour of the narrower, more parochial goals of the competing groups.

A useful empirical investigation by Roy (1955)[14] illustrates in a dramatic way both management versus work group conflict, and patterns of relationship and control within the work group itself. In the study a clear contrast is made of inter-group co-operation between work groups united in a common goal of "war" with management. It is often suggested that one way of overcoming inter-group conflict is to establish a common goal, often a superordinate or overriding goal towards which all groups can strive. Roy's account illustrates this process very well, whilst also giving vivid accounts of the perceptual set adopted by the groups in relation to management and examples of stereotyping often found in situations of group conflict.

The problems of inter-group conflict in organisations has been very usefully outlined by Schein (1969),[9] who suggests a range of behaviours typically found within and between groups in competition. Each competing group will become more closely knit and loyal, the group climate changes from relaxation to more intense work, and individual member's problems are deprecated in favour of the task. The group becomes more willing to tolerate autocratic leadership, more highly structured and organised, and demands more conformity from its members. Relationships between groups is affected by changing and distorted perceptions, the other group is now the enemy and is perceived negatively, stereotyping and hostility increases, whilst interaction and communication decreases. Each group perceives only the best parts of itself subsuming its weaknesses and filtering in only those aspects of communication which supports its own image and position. In situations where this win–lose orientation results in a clear outcome, the winning group becomes more cohesive and releases tension, loses its fighting spirit, and behaves in a complacent and playful manner. (Schein calls this the "fat and happy state".) In comparison the losing group tends to splinter and fight, become more tense and ready to work, and scapegoating takes place. The major concern is for recouping the loss, therefore concerns for individuals and intra-group maintenance are low (Schein calls this the "lean and hungry state").

In many situations the outcome of inter-group competition is not clear cut, and in such situations the effect of selective perception, stereotyping, and filtering by each group creates an ambiguous situation which serves to maintain the negative climate between the groups and affects later encounters.

The effects of inter-group conflict and the maintenance of "tribal systems" are quite readily observed in organisations and the OD consultant is often concerned to help group-members better understand these phenomena. Suggestions for overcoming the negative effects of these situations are sometimes put forward, Sheriff (1956)[15] puts forward the idea of "super-ordinate" goals; other suggestions have included creating a third group composed of high status members of the conflicting groups, reforming the groups by the mixing of members based on nominations and individual vote, and establishing negotiations between one representative member of each group.

It is obviously of clear benefit for organisational members to understand the potentially destructive effects of inter-group conflict in relation to attitudes, morale, and communication flow. In Chapter 13 we return again to this issue, and will refer to research that relates to specialist groups, such as the planning department. In addition to the phenomena of organisational behaviour we have just discussed, the process of OD also covers manager and organisation style which, as will be seen from Chapter 6 is closely related to organisational communication and the search for a system of unitary goals.

We have given examples of some of the facets of organisational behaviour with which the OD consultant may be concerned. It should be stressed that an OD programme involves extensive analysis of the organisation with the resultant data being used for further work in team building and intra- and inter-group problem solving and training. In some cases climate surveys may be used (see Table 6.2 and Chapter 17 for examples of a climate survey), or the consultant may interview with a semi-structured questionnaire; but whatever the method of inquiry used, by the very nature of the investigation, the OD process begins with the first piece of data collected. It can also be seen that, in addition to having a behavioural science background, the consultant should also be aware of his own process and the effects of his behaviour on organisational members and groups. In this sense he must be aware of the difficulties of acting as a true catalyst and of the importance of selecting the appropriate consulting style. There are some parallels here for the corporate planner in that he, too, acts as a change agent and will therefore need to be aware of the effects of his behaviour on the "process" inside the organisation. The effects of change and change agents form the subject matter for the following chapter.

References Chapter 7

1. M. Thakur (1974) *O.D. The Search for Identity*, Report No. 16, Institute of Personnel Management.
2. R. Beckhart (1969) *Organisation Development – Strategies and Models*, Addison-Wesley, Reading, Massachusetts.
3. D. E. Hussey (1974) *Corporate Planning – Theory and Practice*, Pergamon Press, Oxford.
4. J. Luft (1963) *Group Processes: an Introduction to Group Dynamics*, National Press, Palo Alto, California.
5. G. Kelly (1955) *The Psychology of Personal Constructs*, Vol. 1, Norton, New York.
6. M. J. Langham and A. Jukes (1976) *Matching Individuals to form Effective Syndicate Groups*, European Industrial Training Vol. 1, No. 3, pp. 30–32.
7. J. W. Pfiffer and J. E. Jones (1974) *Structured Learning Experiences for Human Relations Training*, Vol. 1, No. 13, University Associates, San Diego.
8. A. Strauss *et al.* (1963) The hospital and its negotiated order in E. Friedson (ed.), *The Hospital in Modern Society*, Macmillan, New York.
9. E. Schein (1969) *Process Consultation – Its Role in Organisation Development*, Addison-Wesley, Reading, Massachusetts.
10. W. L. Schutz (1966) *The Interpersonal Underworld*, Science and Behaviour Books, Palo Alto, California.
11. M. J. Langham and D. Barker (1976) The Observation and Measurement of Social Interaction, unpublished manuscript.
12. R. F. Bales (1950) *Interaction Process Analysis: A Method for the Study of Small Groups*, Addison-Wesley, Cambridge, Massachusetts.
13. R. F. Bales (1970) *Personality and Interpersonal Behaviour*, Holt, Rinehart & Winston, New York.
14. D. Roy (1955) Making-out: a counter-system workers' control of work situation and relationships, in *Understanding Society* (1970) Social Science Course Team (eds.), Macmillan for the Open University Press, pp. 235–45.
15. M. Sheriff (1956) Experiments in group conflict, *Scientific America*, November.

CHAPTER 8

Coping with Change

As we have so far seen, the planning process involves change, and the planner both effects and is affected by changes in the business environment. With other specialists such as management development and managers, organisation development specialists, the planner can be viewed as a change-agent. In such a role the planner clearly has to cope with the actions and reactions of people affected by change. It is important, therefore, to look at the process of change and to find some means of analysing change situations in such a way that the likely effects of changes on people can be partly, if not wholly, foreseen and taken account of. In later chapters, particularly Chapter 10, we look at environmental and other factors in planning change; in this chapter we are concerned specifically with the human factor in change situations, the effects of change on individuals, and groups within organisations.

In order to examine the effects of change on people we need first to consider some of the characteristics of organisations and the way in which these characteristics impinge on the individual.

Miller and Rice (1967)[1] view an organisation as an open system of activities involving import-conversion and export processes both within the concern and between the concern and its environment. Taking this open-system approach we can analyse the behaviour of an organisation in terms of operating and maintenance activities and the regulation of the organisation in its interface with the environment. This means that we can delineate a boundary around the organisation which separates it from the environment and examine the interface between the two. In taking this view we can suggest that the corporate planner as a change-agent is, at this interface, mainly coping with the effects of change in the environment, actual or potential, on the performance of the business (Fig. 8.1).

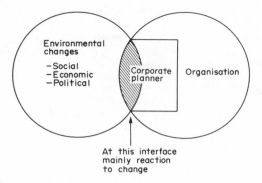

Fig. 8.1 The corporate planner as a change-agent (1).

The organisation, of which the planner is a member, will incorporate both human and physical resources used to achieve the main task or function of the business. Within the organisation the planner is closely involved in planning and implementing change, therefore can be seen as much more proactive in change. The effects of planning decisions and actions will frequently cause changes in the way in which the physical and human resources are used in the organisation as a system.

The work of Woodward (1958)[2] suggests that the technical complexity employed in a firm can, to a large extent, predetermine the organisation structure and therefore the possible relationships in the firm. Thus there occurs clear differences between such organisation features as: (1) span of control (i.e. number of subordinates reporting directly to a supervisor or manager), (2) number of levels in the hierarchy, (3) relationships between specialists functions and production or line functions, (4) flexibility of the structure and the type of manufacturing technology, i.e. mass production, batch, process production employed by the firm. Figure 8.2 illustrates these comparisons.

The Tavistock studies of coal mining (1963)[3] and subsequent studies (1967)[1] have examined the effects of changing technology on social groups suggesting that the worker and the workplace constitute what might be referred to as a psycho-socio-technical system. Thus in change situations there is a need to consider the individual in relation to the workplace as a member of a formal group, e.g. shift or section or

System of production ⟶		Unit production	Mass production	Process production
Median number of levels of authority in management hierarchy	(1)	3 levels	4 levels	6 levels
Span of control of first line supervision	(2)·	21–30 people	41–50 people	11–20 people
(3) Ratio of managers and supervisory staff to other personnel	Size of firm ⟶			
	400/500 employees	1:22	1:37	1:25
	850/1000 employees	1:14	1:15	1:18
	3000/4600 employees	1:8	1:7	1:7

Fig. 8.2. Relationships between (1) number of levels in hierarchy, (2) span of control, and (3) ratio of managers/supervisors to other personnel — and the technology employed in the firm. (From Woodward, 1958[2].)

department, and as a member of an informal group, e.g. "social" or friendship group. In addition there is a need to look at the technical functions and processes employed in the firm.

We have a model here which will assist the planner in predicting the likely effects of change or, at least, will provide the basis of some useful questions to ask about change situations. We see the planner to some extent managing the interface between planning process and plans and the rest of the organisation viewed as a psycho-socio-technical system.

As Fig. 8.3 suggests, there are three major and related subsystems to be considered.

The *technical system* refers to the technology and technical methods employed in the organisation, the practices, procedures, systems, and techniques used to get work done. Clearly there are differences in manufacturing ranging from individual "one-off" production methods through to highly automated mass production and including advanced technology

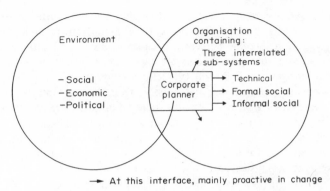

Fig. 8.3. The corporate planner as a change-agent (2).

process production. Similarly, in commercial organisations the methods of work may vary from individual clerical operations to sophisticated computer systems. It could be said that most of the changes taking place in organisation originate in the technical system; indeed, many companies employ specialists such as work-study engineers or organisation and methods to devise improvements and implement changes in work methods which are embraced by the technical system.

The *formal social system* refers to the formal reporting structure of the company as expressed in "organisational charts" or described by the pattern or shape of the company including the number of levels in the hierarchy, spans of control, range of expertise and roles, and the communication networks employed. The style of management (see Chapter 6) habitually adopted by the executive management of the organisation or its subunits is also a feature of the formal social system. It is possible for changes to take place in the formal social system, e.g. appointment of a new manager, rationalisation of a reporting system, or the addition of another "layer" in the hierarchy, and such changes will have repercussions on the other two systems.

The *informal social system* refers to the attitudes and behaviour of individuals and groups including an analysis of the morale conflict, motivation, and relationships both real and apparent in times of change. Most change situations, it is true to say, do not originate in the informal social system, but all changes will have an effect on this system, and it is wise firstly to recognise and accept that fact and, secondly, to plan in order to anticipate the likely effects of change on this system. Significant to such planning is a consideration of the perceptions of individuals and groups and the realisation that such perceptions are based on a "frame of reference" or personal viewpoint which will typically include past and present experience motives, expectations, and beliefs. Thus the perceptions of a work group facing a change in shift roster may be quite different from those of management, the former perceiving such a change as designed to get them to work harder or to break up traditional friendship groups, the latter as the best way to improve a service to the customer whilst maintaining full employment of physical and human resources.

Coupled with the idea of differing perceptions is the concept of relative deprivation, where individual or group comparisons give rise to feelings of being deprived not in an absolute sense but in relation to the situation of other groups or individuals. It is apparent that the strength of feeling involved in relative deprivation is as great as that for absolute deprivation, occurrences of industrial conflict centred around, for example, the perceived erosion of differentials, or calls for parity with other groups frequently occur at national level through to minor local issues.

It is as well to remember that people will feel themselves to be relatively deprived and may in some cases be absolutely deprived, of information even before any planned changes take place, particularly where an organisation's communication is ineffective and badly timed.

The concepts of "perception" and "relative deprivation" are just two, albeit important, ways of considering behaviour in the informal social system.

The model of an organisation as a socio-technical system allows the planner to ask some critical questions about the likely effects of change on people *during the planning stage* and before any change is implemented. The primary question is In which area of the socio-technical system will the change originate. Thereafter, supplementary questions relate to the effect the change will have on the other two areas. Most commonly, changes originate in the technical system and may well be the result of strategic planning decisions based on, for example, growth through increased market share or by new product launching. Such changes will have also a considerable impact on the formal and the informal social systems. Other changes originate in the formal social system, e.g.

acquisition, centralisation, decentralisation, and have repercussions in the technical and informal social system. Fewer changes originate in the informal social system, which is perhaps just as well since such changes cannot easily be *planned* by management. However, since all changes will affect the informal social system, and since this is an area where prediction of effects is most difficult, it is not unusual to find attitudes, morale, and behaviour influencing strongly, and even causing modification to planned changes originating in the other two systems.

In Chapter 11 we discuss some practical approaches to involvement of more junior managers in the strategic planning process, and in Chapter 17 we look more deeply at participation. Clearly, the greater the involvement of people in planned change the more possible it is not only to predict and understand the likely effects of a change process on the informal social system. It is interesting to examine the application of the socio/technical systems model in a real change situation. The example of the change situation is real, although modified here to simplify and to preserve the anonymity of the company.

The company concerned operates a countrywide network of departmental stores with a centralised buying function and a regional store organisation. Originally each store, average floor area of 12,000 square feet, carried its own supporting warehouse, and established procedures existed for the planned ordering and stocking of merchandise so that replacements to counters could be effected immediately from warehouse stock. This meant that each store, in addition to a sales and administrative staff, employed warehousemen under the control of a warehouse manager who reported to the store manager. The company's long-term strategy called for a doubling of turnover over five years by increasing the product range and increasing the selling area of each store. This was to be done through centralising the warehousing operation in each region and converting the warehouse at each store into sales floors. The region selected for a pilot study was small in comparison with other regions, but generally representative. The geographical layout of the region, including the proposed location of the regional warehouse, is given in Fig. 8.4. The three stores A, B, and C were to be served from a regional warehouse D situated roughly equidistant from each store. This was, clearly, a change originating in the technical system in that established methods of stocking and replacing the sales area were changed together with changes in the warehousing systems,

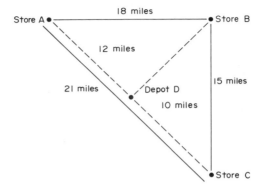

Fig. 8.4. Geographical location of regional stores.

not the least of which was the installation of new techniques in the central warehouse to handle a stock level more than three times the size of that previously held at individual stores. These new requirements could be planned well in advance of installation, including the computerisation of stock with sophisticated terminals including visual display units at each of the stores.

The changes planned within the technical system affected both the formal and informal social system. In the formal social system it was possible to anticipate and plan for the changes required in organisation, roles, and expertise to operate the new warehouse set-up. A great deal of planning and thought was given to the organisation design and selection and training of staff to ensure that the regional warehouse could offer an efficient service to the stores.

To some extent, the effects of the changes on the informal social system were taken into account by management in that communication was planned and effective and consultation with groups of employees took place during the planning phases. In this way the worst effects of uncertainty and low morale was avoided. However, as is so often the case, less time and effort was spent researching and assessing the likely effects of the change on the informal social system than on the other two systems. A number of problems and issues only came to light after the central warehousing function had been set up. For example, it had not been recognised just how closely sales assistants and warehouse staff had worked as a team in order to maintain full counters and cope with reordering requirements. This unofficial or informal system developed over the years was destroyed by the change, and warehouse and stores now became not only physically but also psychologically remote from each other. This factor added considerably to the difficulty in training and motivating staff to use the computer terminals. The former stores warehouse, now changed into a large central complex, no longer reflected the particular needs of a store, and it was some time before sales assistants adjusted to a situation where replacement counter stock was no longer immediately available. In fact a system of requisitioning at specified times, to allow for delivery from the warehouse by van, was installed which meant that sales assistants had to plan counter stock very accurately. Typically the assistants attempted to counteract errors or forgetfulness in ordering by establishing "under the counter" stocks of merchandise, and it was not long before the stores contained a whole series of these "buffer" stocks, unknown to management, but serving to protect the interests of particular sales assistants. Of course, some assistants were not able to establish such reserve stocks because of the size or bulk of the merchandise sold on their counters; this only served to create rifts between groups of assistants when comparisons of work situations were made.

A further interesting effect occurring within the informal social system was concerned with inter-store comparisons. Before the change, a friendly rivalry existed between the three stores with comparisons being made on sales turnover, range of goods sold and particularly, such issues as the quality of shopper attracted into one store as opposed to another. Such rivalry was maintained with perceptions being fed by inter-store deliveries and the occasional exchange of staff between stores, but was constructive in that it helped to maintain the motivation and commitment of sales staff, and it facilitated mutual assistance in that the staff in one store were prepared to help another store at times of staff shortage or by the exchange of merchandise between stores.

After the change this co-operation turned to conflict; the situation now was that the three stores were all making demands on the same warehouse, which in theory should have held no problems, but in practice when the particular store failed to receive merchandise ordered, the tendency was to blame not only the warehouse but the other stores, and very quickly the perceptions of staff in one store were that the other stores were receiving more attention and better service from the warehouse. Such perceptions were fed by the information gleaned from van drivers to deliveries to other stores and the occasional forage by a member of staff of one store into one of the other stores in the region. The co-operation previously existing between the stores degenerated into conflict and expressions of mistrust.

A systems analysis of the change situation might well have predicted these, and other effects not outlined here, on the informal social system. Clearly the situation existing before the change was one of three self-sufficient and discrete stores operating in a given region with links to each other as part of a larger company and links with the environment — specifically the market-place (Fig. 8.5A). After the change the boundaries of each store merged, in part, into the common warehouse, and problems began to occur at the interface of these boundaries (Fig. 8.5B). The authors' experience shows that this is so often the case, particularly where previously discrete boundaries have become blurred. The management of these interfaces is crucial to the smooth implementation of planned change. Hence the value of the socio/technical system model and mode of analysis.

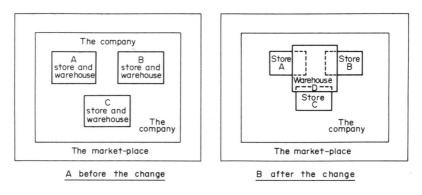

Fig. 8.5. A systems representation of the change situation.

We have already suggested that different models can be applied to each of the three systems in socio-technical analysis, for example, a range of mathematical and scientific analysis will increase the chances of predictable success of the technical system. The potential of formal social system analysis can be enhanced through the use of theories of human behaviour such as "relative deprivation" and "perception" already outlined.

Many of the human problems in change situations stem from the uncertainty and insecurity felt by individuals and groups often due to lack of information, though affected by individual personality and emotional differences. Thus in a recent newspaper merger situation the reporters from one of the papers conducted a sit-in of the boardroom which lasted until the directors were obliged to explain the possible merger conditions. This was, perhaps, a highly predictable piece of action in the face of the mounting uncertainty about their jobs and future. Individuals and groups will often hold differing viewpoints about a particular change from those of management or planners.

Consider the following:

1. The introduction of budgets, standards, or targets perceived by management as a necessary means of controlling activities towards some common business aims. Such a move may be seen by employees as an attempt to pin them down more closely to the job, to extract more work from them, or to provide management with the means to pressurise and punish those who do not make the grade. In our experience, one of the major hurdles facing the installation of a system of performance management is the resistance by staff who see objectives and standards as constraining their freedom in the job and providing management with the means to punish poor performance. Resistance of this type is usually indicative of their perception of the prevailing style of organisations or the specific management style adopted by their boss.

2. The recruitment of a new manager seen by management as necessary to inject new life and better leadership so as to raise the standard of an ailing department. Employees are quite likely to view this situation as a threat, uncertain of the changes that the new manager may make, uncertain of their ability to cope with such changes, and wary of any change in the style of management. These fears are not usually verbalised. The overt behaviour of employees may take the form of passive resistance or only partial co-operation with the new manager until they are satisfied that their job and/or self-esteem is no longer threatened.

3. The introduction of a job evaluation wage structure seen by management as necessary to establish a common system of payment and to make consistent internal comparisons between jobs. Employees are likely to be

concerned over the fairness of the system to be adopted, sceptical of the means by which their job can be compared with other jobs, and worried about losing money or perceived status when comparisons are made.

These issues tend to be highly emotive and need careful handling.

Resistance to change is often emotionally based and is not easily overcome by rational logical argument. The resistance may be based on such feelings as: loss of status; implied criticism of present competence; fear of failure in the new situation; annoyance at not being consulted; lack of understanding of the need for the change or insecurity in changing from well-known and fixed methods. It is necessary, therefore, to overcome such resistance by creating situations of participation and full explanation (with a two-way dialogue) when changes are envisaged.

Clearly, the timing of change and the communication plan need to be carefully thought out, balancing the needs of the company and the demands for confidentiality against the effects of the change and possible change rumours, on the employees. But change in an organisation is a process rather than an event since it takes time to recognise that changes in present or future business activities are required and further time for such changes to be developed and planned. The planner is at the heart of such changes, and, as we have suggested, is, in a sense, a change-agent. We have also recognised that people need time to change their viewpoints and working habits.

The distinguishing stages in the process of change are, firstly, the recognition of the need, secondly, decision to take action, thirdly the provision and use of methods to analyse the situation, and, fourthly, the development of a plan. In these first four stages the planner will take an initiating role, the nature of which is fully outlined in other chapters.

The second group of stages covers decisions on the implementation of the plan, communicating the plan and securing the commitment of those involved. It is as well to appreciate that commitment to a planned change can be seen at one end of a continuum of resistance to change which ranges through co-operation, support, acceptance, indifference, apathy, protests, and slowdowns to sabotage at the other end. It is now widely recognised that commitment to change is most readily obtained where those affected are involved in the planning stage, and we discuss in detail in Chapter 11 the necessity for involving managers "down the line" in the strategic planning process through the use of planning conferences and seminars. However, as we point out in that chapter, certain types of decision which will involve change cannot be disclosed too fully too far ahead, and we therefore will often be faced with a situation where high level confidential planning has to be ultimately communicated to more junior staff and commitment to plans obtained. This will involve a third group of stages in the change process where the explanation of new roles and responsibilities is required, together with the aligning of systems and/or incentives to reinforce the plan and training in new methods to secure effective change behaviour. Therefore the change plan must be monitored and adjusted to take account of on-going requirements since all changes are part of the dynamic and continuous process of survival and growth.

The key elements in any process of change are effective communication and participation, the most critical judgements required being those of timing and depth of involvement. It is becoming increasingly apparent that such judgements cannot be made solely within the organisation since, as we discuss in Chapter 17, increasing social change in the environment calls for consideration by the planner of greater breadth and depth of participation.

One significant approach to initiating change, although it requires a high degree of skill, is to base an in-company training programme around the change. This may introduce those involved to new skills (education) to help them cope, but is equally concerned with getting those involved to work through the change, understand the reasons for it, and to identify the impact on their own jobs. If those attending represent different functions and skills, it is possible for all concerned to understand the interdependence of different parts of the organisation. Such approaches require a participatory style of programme: case studies and group discussion rather than academic lectures.

The corporate planner, in his role of change-agent, must ensure that top management balances the opportunities and benefits of long-term plans against the effect of the changes such plans bring on both individuals and groups in the undertaking. This will invariably mean placing as much emphasis on the human asset as on the other assets employed in the business. To this end, the socio-technical systems analysis of change can be used as a key model for the assessment of the likely costs, in human terms, which will be incurred where significant business gains are sought. The challenge to the planner is to balance effectively both costs and benefits in deter-mining the net advantage to be gained from any process of change in the organisation.

In the next chapter we take the information and approaches, applied so far to organisational behaviour, a further step in outlining the practical considerations of objective setting and achievement.

References Chapter 8

1. E. S. Miller and A. K. Rice (1967) *Systems of Organisation*, Tavistock Publica-tions, London.
2. J. Woodward (1958) *Management and Technology*, HMSO, London.
3. E. L. Trist, G. W. Higgin, H. Murray and A. B. Pollock (1963) *Organisational Choice: Capabilities of Groups at the Coal Face under Changing Technologies*, Tavistock Publications, London.

CHAPTER 9

Objectives

We have used the term "objectives" quite frequently so far and our use has been varied in that we have referred to individual, group, and corporate objectives using objectives to describe the goals or end results which both people and organisations may be intent on achieving. Hussey (1974)[1] has reviewed the concept of objectives quite extensively from a corporate planning point of view, dividing the broad concept of objectives into the following components:

"— The primary, or profit, objective of the business set in advance of strategy.
— The secondary, and mainly narrative objectives, again set in advance of strategy.
— Goals which are time-assigned targets derived from the strategy.
— Standards of performance (often identical with goals) assigned to particular individuals." (Hussey, 1974, p. 104.)

Each of these components of the concept bears some relation to the others.

Since we are seeking to balance the planning process (which includes the use of objectives) against the designed and actual behaviour of employees (which also includes the use of objectives), it would seem necessary in this chapter to review the meaning and value of the concept of objectives from the individual and the organisational point of view. We have, at once, to be aware of the fact that regardless of the manner in which we may seek to match individuals' objectives to those of the total business, in practice the two will not necessarily be synonymous. Indeed, the matching of individual (and group) objectives to those of the organisation is the on-going theme of this book.

A company may be structured and organised in terms of explicit roles and a clear authority system in order to attain its objectives, but within that structure and organisation there exists a range of informal behaviour, informal roles, and authority systems which may mediate against company objectives.

Selznick (1957)[2] has used the term "recalcitrance" to describe the tendency for any part of an organisation to strike off on tasks and goals to achieve objectives of its own. Thus in discussing the matching of individual and group objectives to those of the organisation we can assume that a necessary precondition is the gaining of commitment and involvement of the individuals concerned. We have noted earlier (see Chapter 3) that it is, for example, perfectly possible for a middle management group to undermine and nullify particular edicts or systems imposed by top management where such edicts or systems are perceived to be alien to the group's own objectives.

With this reservation in mind we may look at the concept of objectives from an individual and job point of view in terms of what that individual is expected to achieve in his role as an organisational member.

In theory and in practice, since an organisation has a purpose and objectives, every job in the organisation will also have a purpose and objectives. It is possible for jobs in an organisation to be analysed and described in a systematic way such that the purpose and content of the job is known. Many companies carry out job analysis and produce job descriptions for purposes of selection, appraisal, training, job evaluation, succession planning, safety, or organisation planning. It is arguable that the most valuable statements contained in a job description are the *accountabilities** of the job. The *accountabilities* are defined as the end results expected of that job; they are usually within the jobholder's control; they are usually measurable in some way; and they represent a significant contribution which the job makes in relation to the overall company objectives. In an accurate and well-written job description the list of *principal accountabilities* should express 90 or more per cent of the job in terms of the end results that job is expected to achieve. They are, therefore, action statements. Thus if we look, for example at the job of a production director we might expect to find the following kinds of *accountabilities*:

*The term *accountabilities* and description of this term originate from the HAY-MSL approach to written job descriptions and is used with permission.

1. Co-ordinate the preparation and secure agreement for annual production plans and supporting budgets.
2. Forecast, secure agreement for, and monitor the execution of required capital investment programmes ensuring that expenditure and implementation schedules are controlled.
3. Design and monitor the organisation and resourcing of the manufacturing function to facilitate the achievement of such plans and programmes.
4. Ensure that reporting managers are working to clear objectives and provide for regular review, support, and guidance for achievement of such objectives.
5. Ensure that regular production control information accurately reflects manufacturing performance so that variances from plans and budgets are known and can be acted upon.
6. Motivate and develop subordinates to provide a high level of present job competence and secure future succession for key production posts.
7. Agree and implement employee relations practices which will provide for high morale and a positive industrial relations climate.
8. Provide the leadership and co-ordination to pursue and install cost-saving systems and procedures for production planning and control which will enhance present and future efficiencies.
9. Contribute as an executive director to the formulation of company policies and development plans.

Such a list of principal accountabilities covers both the immediate and longer-term outputs of the job, and in most cases it will be seen that the jobholder can be held primarily responsible for their achievement; in other words if the jobholder does not achieve these *accountabilities* then (in the absence of a substitute jobholder) no one does. These *accountabilities* or end results, although derived from a description of the job, can be seen therefore as the reason for the existence of the job in the company. We may use the *principal accountabilities* as a springboard in the process of agreeing specific work targets with jobholders. This approach offers managers and subordinates a personalised and highly flexible way of achieving a process of performance management.

The manager and subordinate sit down together and attempt to put a time frame and, where possible, numbers on to the *accountabilities* to derive specific targets for a known period of time, say one year. *Accountabilities* can be thought of as representing the on-going long-term objectives of the job. Targets, on the other hand, represent the individual's plan for assuring that the *accountability* is achieved.

Accountabilities are semi-permanent end results and if they change then the nature of the job itself changes. Targets, however, can change in many ways over a period of time, but the fact that they can change need not change the job itself.

Target setting is, therefore, the link between a person and his/her job — and a link between a person and the organisation. A sound target is related (usually) to one or more *principal accountabilities*; is future directed (by definition); is specific rather than general; is measurable in one way or another; and is time limited. In using *accountabilities* as a springboard in the target-setting process it is useful to focus on some specific areas of the job and the person.

(1) *Opportunity or problem areas*. Targets may be agreed in those areas which relate to organisation-wide or unit objectives, problems, or opportunities. These may include new marketing areas, new products, new methods, cost control or reduction, better customer service, and so on. An example of such a situation would be where a personnel manager, having an *accountability* for "the competent staffing of an organisation through effective recruitment, training, and development", was aware that a specific function intended to double its size over three years. Clearly this *accountability* can be turned into three quite specific groups of targets to cover the planning and design of the recruitment/training activities required to keep the company in the "competently staffed" position as the size of the function increases. The ultimate measure of achievement is at the end of the three years but, if targets are agreed over one year cycles, there will be two interim measures of progress on the way.

(2) *Personal strengths*. Those areas where the job incumbent is strong and where this strength may be further capitalised upon, suggest target areas for agreement. There is a tendency for managers to spend more time

doing those things which they are good at and, consequently, like doing. It is useful to harness this strength and motivation to specific work targets.

(3) *Personal deficiencies.* The converse to the above is also true in that most people will leave aside or consider as low priority those aspects of the job they do not do well or are less interested in. Where this means a non-achievement or poor achievement of an *accountability* it may lend itself to the agrement of what is, in effect, an improvement target.

(4) *Development.* Targets may be agreed in personal development areas in relation to obtaining greater expertise or know-how in a job and development for possible future jobs. In our opinion this is a key area for consideration in setting targets, an area where managers and the company as a whole can offer an individual planned experience and learning, and increase the intrinsic interest in the job, thus providing greater motivation.

(5) *Present competent performance.* It should be remembered, that for almost every jobholder some (even most) areas of *accountability* achievement will be competent. In such cases the target agreed may be to maintain that level of achievement. The process of performance management we are outlining does not necessarily call for greater or better achievement of end results but rather an agreement of what is required in the shorter term if longer-term *accountabilities* are to be discharged.

The process of agreeing work targets between a manager and employee demands a high level of mutual trust and open, two-way communication. Managers who operate at the extremes of directiveness or lack of direction (see Chapter 6) may find that their management style is inappropriate for target setting. Such managers may have to change their usual style or accept that the target-setting process may have little impact.

The jobholder should ensure, to the best of his/her ability, that every target is developed, clarified, and evaluated in terms of its relative importance and feasibility within the framework of the individual job and that job's relationship to other jobs.

The degree to which a target can be judged as reasonable depends greatly on the thoroughness of the planning that preceded it. The job-holder should be prepared to outline the plan he/she feels will lead to meeting the target. In order to formulate an adequate plan, the subordinate will find it useful to:

* Analyse previous and present conditions.
* Assess internal and external constraints that will affect target achievement.
* Project available financial, material and human resources required to achieve the objective.
* Evaluate the relative importance of the target as compared to other possible goals which could be established for the same accountability.
* Appraise the target's compatibility with an impact on the successful achievement of organisation, unit or, subunit objectives to which it must contribute.
* Assure that the developed list of objectives corresponds to the major accountabilities.

The manager must, of course, evaluate whether the target is relevant to organisational purposes, and also whether it is challenging enough to stretch the abilities of the subordinate. In developing a list of unit or individual objectives for a given period (usually one year), attention should focus on those *principal accountabilities* which have the highest priority in the coming year – that is, the critical ones.

A manager developing the targets for his own position or the unit he supervises may find the following approach useful:

* Review all the *principal accountabilities* and determine which have shown deficiencies or which should receive priority attention in the coming year.
* Establish the necessary targets as they relate to the selected accountabilities. Note that every accountability will not necessarily require a written target in a given year. Or a given accountability may result in more than one target in the coming year if it is a special problem.
* Review the measurements that will best describe the achievements in the selected *principal accountabilities*.

Every business is forced to operate within certain constraints and on the basis of certain assumptions. These realities are part of management and this is where practical management judgement must be called upon. Targets may be quantified, clearly stated, and appear eminently attainable — but they are still based upon assumptions. Will the economy show a general upturn? How prevalent will unemployment be? What will happen to the rate of inflation? In many cases we cannot answer such questions before the event. We must make assumptions based upon past experience and seasoned management judgement.

The same holds true for the target-setting process. When we say that the chances are a given target will be achieved, we are assuming that conditions will remain as we expect them to. Obviously, if certain key events occur which we did not expect, these can affect the targets we have set. In order to keep on top of this situation, in order to ensure that our target-setting has value in giving purpose and direction to our activities, we must understand the assumptions under which we will be operating.

Assumptions give us the opportunity to make a more objective appraisal of our target achievement. If we fall short of a target we can tell the reason for our failure. We will know whether the failure to achieve the target was the result of unalterable circumstances or stemmed from neglect on our part.

By the same token, unforeseen circumstances can also work in a positive way and provide exceptional benefits. If such a windfall does occur, we are forced to ask ourselves whether our surpassing the target resulted from sheer genius on our part or from good luck. Target-setting should help us organise our activities by allowing us to identify the sources of our strengths and weaknesses. It can do this only if we are willing to evaluate all the reasons for attaining a given level of achievement. If achievement is low, we should identify the causes and take remedial action. If achievement is high, we should know whether it resulted from good fortune and could have been even higher if we had taken maximum advantage of the situation. By understanding the assumptions underlying our targets we can gain that much more objectivity when it comes to evaluating target achievement.

This process of performance management requires the commitment of those concerned and will require skill and knowledge training in areas of agreeing targets and the means of measuring performance objectively or, in some cases, subjectively and in appraising performance against the agreed targets. A number of companies use this process as a means of relating salary increases to work performance in an equitable and known way. In such cases the approach we have outlined will need taking several steps further to consider in more detail the measurement of performance in objective/subjective terms and the means by which performance may be assessed between the manager and subordinate to reach an agreed overall performance appraisal.

Other companies do not tie target setting and appraisal explicitly to pay, but use the results of the approach for the assessment of training need, people development, and succession planning.

The approach we have outlined has, of course, similarities with the more classical forms of management-by-objectives, but we believe the approach offers a number of practical ways of achieving the sustained commitment of employees to the practice of performance management as a natural work process. These may be seen as follows:

(1) The use of well-written *accountabilities* provides an on-going and long-term focus on the end results expected in the job and will therefore include the planning aspects of a job. Providing managers are involved in the planning process, as we have suggested earlier in this book, it is possible for agreement to be reached on work targets at any level in the organisation without a rigid system of target setting being imposed from above. In other words this approach need not be "top-down" it can operate from the bottom or middle upwards.

(2) Bearing the above point in mind it is possible for a manager and his subordinates to adapt and modify the approach to suit their own needs. What is important is that a measure of trust and agreement exists between managers and their staff, and that the manager is quite clear about the end results requirements within his own *accountabilities.*

Obviously, if corporate objectives are to be achieve, then, in theory, the ideal approach to objective management should start with top management agreeing targets with their immediate managers and then follow an approach down the line. What we are saying is that in our experience, even with top management encouragement, the key to successful implementation is commitment to a workable, acceptable form of target setting down the line. This probably means avoiding the worst aspects of a system imposed "from above" and the creation of conditions for a flexible, self-modified approach at the level of the individual manager.

In Chapter 13 we suggest that one of the requirements of good planning is the need to link plans with other management processes such as personal objectives, budgetary controls, and capital budgeting. One approach in securing this linkage is to build in to the *accountabilities* of a manager's job the requirement for formulating, implementing, and achieving longer-term plans to meet overall corporate strategy.

We should not like to position the linkage between personal objectives and corporate objectives as a rigid, unyielding mechanism, nor postulate that corporate objectives equal the sum total of all individual objectives. In fact many jobs for which accountabilities and targets should be agreed are of that semi-routine type which means that the corporate plan assumes continuation of present standards rather than setting something specific. Such jobs will vary from time to time, but many include the chief accountant, the market researcher, and the company's medical office, as well as such stalwarts as the long-service senior clerk, who is considered of little consequence until the day he does not turn up for work and the whole organisation begins to creak.

What we argue for is a framework and compatibility rather than a mathematical logic. The more senior the manager the more resemblance there is likely to be between his accountabilities and targets and the more future-oriented objectives of the corporate plan. At the level of individual performance it is of no importance whether we are dealing with primary objectives, secondary objectives, or goals; or, indeed, an action requirement arising from the observance of a constraint. It is in this area of the flexible link that managers must ensure that the accountabilities and targets of those reporting to them are based not just on the past nor solely on the annual budget, but take account of all the planning initiatives in the company and begin to reflect some of that degree of future change which must accompany the implementation of any corporate plan.

The degree to which managers are involved in the process of planning and the way in which they are involved has great significance here for two reasons: understanding and commitment. Those who participate in the process in the way we suggest elsewhere in the book are likely to have a greater awareness of the corporate plans, and thus the opportunity to synthesise this information when thinking about the parameters of their own specific jobs. Understanding is but one step. What is also needed is commitment: it is not the objective itself which is important to the organisation, but the fact that somebody is setting out to make it happen.

Some of the problems which arise in planning, which are discussed elsewhere, come about because of a conflict between personal and corporate objectives. This may sometimes become evident as actions to achieve company objectives are seen as threats to the individual. Sometimes the threats occur at an unconscious level in that they bear not on defined personal ambitions but on the motivational factors which give the individual satisfaction in his job. In this way he may feel that his reputation or status is under attack, or that his security is diminished, or that some of his power is being taken away. It follows that commitment to personal objectives which have some relationship with corporate objectives is essential if plans are to be translated to action. Failure may mean passive indifference to the corporate plan, or sometimes active sabotage, for we must remember that we are dealing with the perceptions and behaviour of people, not the cold, analytical logic of the chess-board.

At the beginning of this chapter brief reference was made to a classification of corporate objectives into different categories. One element, which is very important is the difference between those objectives established in advance of strategy, which effectively will describe the type of company that the management team is trying to create, and those which are derived from the strategy and provide a series of detailed milestones which indicate the expected results of that strategy. The first type of objective tends to have a longer time-horizon. The second type, for which we use the term "goal", is firmly tied to a specific time benchmark. Thus one of the objectives of the company might be to achieve a certain level of profits within seven years. To this may be added qualifying statements about return on investment and liquidity or such other factors as seem significant. These may also be statements about the general areas of activity seen as significant for the company over this period (What business are we in? What business should we be in?), although the validity of such statements varies greatly with the nature of the individual company. These may be statements about the way the company feels about the other stakeholders in the business, a concept we touched on in Chapter 1.

An explicit strategy may be drawn up to meet these objectives, covering actions in current markets, calling for the development of new products, major investments, production improvements and all the revenue profit, market share, and people implications of this strategy. From this it is possible to single out quantitative and qualitative goals tied to time, which further describe the future shape of the company as it is expected to emerge. These goals have value when performance is ultimately matched to intentions in that they provide a ruler for monitoring and control. They also have value in being part of the bridge that brings the broad objectives of the company closer to the accountabilities of department heads and key specialist managers, and helping to bring about the understanding and commitment we discussed earlier.

There seem to be two basic schools of thought about objectives, whether corporate or individual. One is that objectives should be used to "stretch" the organisation or the person, and should always be ambitious and exciting. The other school says that the objectives should reflect what must be achieved for success, and should be viewed more as budgetary targets than as a measure of ambition. There is some merit in each argument. A company which never reaches forward, never tries to motivate to do that little extra, will run the risk of producing plans and results which are adequate but by no means as good as is possible. These companies aim to do no better than satisfying shareholders and other stakeholders.

On the other hand, a company which always fails to achieve objectives will soon find that its managers conclude that the objectives do not matter. If no one ever attains his objectives clearly the promotion and reward system must disregard them so that not only do managers lose the motivation of success but they also note that management has little concern.

The problem of using objectives to get that little bit extra out of managers is typified by one management by an objective scheme we once came across. Here the original aim was very worthy. It was to get managers to commit to useful actions which were above the normal expected from the job. Thus a marketing man might have no objectives relating to the main part of his job, which he was expected to do anyway, but he was expected to suggest four or five worthwhile things beyond this. Human nature and time killed it. It was not very long before the instructions from the personnel department began to pervert the original intention by specifically telling people that they would be judged only on objectives that had nothing to do with their job. The scheme died.

Our belief is that both corporate and personal objectives should be achievable with effort, but should not be so far away that failure is inevitable. It may make sense to ask a person to pick the apples which are just beyond his grasp, but which he could reach with ingenuity by climbing the tree, using a stick, or standing on something. It may be less sensible to insist that he clears the last apples from the flimsy and very high top branches. Companies and men need success to motivate. Just failing all the time can be more damaging than a massive failure once or twice.

There is research that shows a link between defined objectives and strategies and corporate success. Bowman (1976)[3] analysed the annual reports of various food companies on the theory that those who succeed do so because of their own efforts, while those who fail find something to blame, like the weather. It was found that the dynamic successful companies referred to their objective for this, their plan for that, their diversification strategy, their new product targets, and the like. Those at the bottom of the league, sometimes in the same sector as successful companies, wrote about adverse harvests, bad weather, government policies, and the like. The only people not at fault were top management.

At the corporate level we cannot overemphasise the co-ordinating and motivating impact of well-conceived, clearly communicated objectives. The sense of purpose of all being on the same road headed in the same direction that good objectives bring, does much for the company. But top management must beware. Platitudes, lies, and lack of commitment become quickly apparent. If you do not mean what you say, and do not intend to do it, you are better off with no objectives. At least that leaves you the weather to blame.

References Chapter 9

1. D. E. Hussey (1974) *Corporate Planning – Theory and Practice*, Pergamon Press, Oxford.
2. P. Selznick (1957) In G. Hutton (1969) *Thinking about Organisation*, Tavistock, London in association with Bath University Press.
3. E. H. Bowman (1976) Strategy and the Weather, *Sloan Management Review*, Winter.

CHAPTER 10

Making Sense of the Environment

"No man is an island, entire of itself; every man is a piece of the continent, a part of the main."

(JOHN DONNE, *Devotions*)

No organisation is an island. This is true whether it is a government department, a mighty multi-national, or a two-man business. In some way every organisation is both affected by and has an effect on the environment in which it operates. The smallest organisation may have only a miniscule impact and the largest may modify the environment in a massive way. Both face a complex pattern of constraints, threats, and opportunities which change as the environment changes.

By environment we mean not only the physical factors which influence the organisation but also the entire structure of interwoven issues which affect the climate in which it operates. A business undertaking, for example, operates within an environment made up of a complex interaction of social, political, legal, economic, and technological factors. These are in a constant process of change. Changes also take place in the company itself, in terms of growth or decline, a changing product base, or caused by management actions as a result of either new leadership or a response to some external stimuli.

Figure 10.1 illustrates the way in which different groups which cause environmental change interact upon each other. The diagram, from Solesbury (1974)[1] oversimplifies, but makes the point. The example shows only certain groups which operate in the environment, and classifies all manufacturers and retailers under the term "operators", and all

153

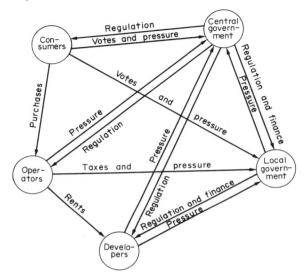

Fig. 10.1. Incentive systems motivating environmental change.
(From Solesbury, 1974[1].)

those who spend capital under the term "developers". Other classifications are possible.

Each group is also made up of numerous subgroups, which are constantly forming and reforming. The strength of the pressure any one group exercises on, for example, the Government, will vary not only with the power of the group applying the pressure but also with the strength of pressure being applied by any other group.

A practical example of this is provided by the actions of the British Government in the personal income tax amendments proposed in the April 1976 budget. Pressure from the left wing led to a feeling that fringe benefits of the higher income earners were insufficiently taxed. A significant increase in the tax liability of a number of these was proposed, among them company cars. Immediately another pressure group swung into action, the car manufacturers, with calculations of the fall in sales which this measure would bring, threats of postponed investment, and projecttions of redundancies. The outcome was that the proposals were modified to something much less stringent. A similar fate befell most of the other proposals to attack fringe benefits, for various reasons all of which involved counter-pressure by one group or another.

Figure 10.1 also omits the complex linkages between any one country and the rest of the world. With the possible exception of the Communist bloc, all countries function within an environment which is partly conditioned by what is going on elsewhere. In addition many businesses function on an international basis and may therefore be group members in many different countries.

Because the relation of an organisation with its environment is a complex mixture of multiple causes and effects of varying degrees of significance, clear thinking about the environment becomes difficult. It seems to us that the environment affects the organisation at two levels: what it is and what it does. This is not a pure distinction, since there is a cause and effect relationship between the nature of an organisation and its activities, but it will serve as a peg on which to hang some thoughts. To simplify, we take as an example the business concern, although a similar analysis could be developed for other types of organisation.

The previous chapter focused attention on corporate objectives, and the discussion of what the company is is an extension of this. Early writers on management have argued that a business's main duties are to its shareholders, and that it exists only to make a profit. If any social factors impinge on the company's profit-making ability, this is as unavoidable constraints. This view is to a greater or lesser extent still held by many.

At the other extreme is the left-wing view, often an academic view, of business. This is that a company is only a small part of a total social system, whose role is to provide employment, serve the community, foster exports, and help people develop and realise their full potential. The extreme view sees profit as a rather nasty concept, and at best acknowledges the need to reward shareholders as a constraint on the company's real purpose.

In modern society neither view of what a company's purpose should be will stand up to practical testing. The first is historic, and the time when this view was relevant has passed. The second exists only in the world of whimsy, although it may become relevant at some future period.

The problem facing the managements of companies in the modern world is different because the environment has changed. Put simply, modern management has to achieve what is effectively a perception of the need to respond to the expectations of the stakeholders in the business (we dealt with this in more detail in Chapter 1). Often the need is perceived intuitively from "soft" data, and is not the result of any explicit analysis.

"Stakeholders" is a phrase which has been coined to cover those groups with an interest in the success of the business; shareholders, employees, customers, suppliers, financial institutions, and the community. In fact, a stakeholder is any group with which the company has transactions and relationships.

Taylor (1976)[2] states:

> "In effect, management is recognising that corporate strategy is concerned not simply with producing a return on the shareholders' capital and delivering satisfactory products to customers, but also achieving social acceptance in the community, ensuring a continuing and uninterrupted supply of key raw materials and components, influencing government policies, and of course ensuring that the work force and the whole management team are motivated and committed to the company and its policies."

Let us not delude ourselves. Profit is important. Without profits the company will become like the starving man who will sacrifice all his higher motives to satisfy his basic biological drives. And even when the company is profitable there are problems, for the expectations of different groups are often conflicting, frequently half-concealed, and always changing.

The company has to adapt its identity to the environment in which it operates. What it is, is conditioned by the expectation of its stakeholders, who in turn are also affected by their environment. Unfortunately, the complexities of modern society are making the task of management more and more difficult. This also is apparent in the effect of the environment on what a company does.

Changes in the environment can bring new patterns of threats and opportunities. Part of the skill of management is to make an appropriate strategic response to these changes to put the company in a better position than it would otherwise be. All companies respond to this sort of stimulus, some because of the almost intuitive decision process of top managers, others when the changes are forced upon them and action is inevitable. The planning approach tries to improve on this situation by forecasting changes and studying their potential strategic impact so that problems can be anticipated and often avoided and competitive advantage can be gained by prompt actions to take advantage of any situations which are emerging.

The environment may affect a company's activity by imposing a constraint or prohibition, which stops it from doing certain things. Most countries, for example, have legislation which restricts the sale of habit-forming drugs and removes this business option from the possible strategies that might be followed. Generally, companies are well aware of the existing pattern of environmental constraints. Occasionally, they are in a position to have them removed, which is particularly justifiable when a new technology hits barriers created to solve problems of an older technology. Concorde provides a striking example of this type of situation, where its promoters have had to work on the removal of existing constraints in order to be able to operate it commercially.

Most companies are broadly aware of the pattern of existing constraints and prohibitions, at least within countries with which they normally do business. We say, broadly, because awareness sometimes lags behind the imposition of the constraint, a number of companies did not appreciate the significance of the United Kingdom's Employee Protection Act of 1975 until it had been in force for some time. The reports of some of the unfair dismissal cases before the Industrial Tribunal suggest that some companies still do not understand it.

Assuming a reasonable degree of awareness at the start, the main issue the company faces is one of response to changes in the environment. (The problem of forecasting and interpreting changes will be returned to later.) Changes can bring two types of threat to the company. The first is a threat of increased constraints, of new things which inhibit the company's freedom of action; examples of this type of action might be new statutory conditions governing employees, changes to the price control system, or a prohibition which means that an existing or planned product may no longer be sold.

The second type of threat is one where the strategy the company is following is not affected by any new constraints but changes take place which will bring reductions to the expected results of that strategy. The company car taxation case mentioned earlier provides a striking example.

Fortunately the impact of environmental changes is not always bad. Opportunities can also arise in two distinct ways. Results of strategies may turn out better than expected because markets may be enlarged or returns from those markets increased. Alternatively, completely new opportunities may be revealed. One significant factor to be remembered is that sometimes threats to one strategy present an opportunity for another. Perhaps the simplest example of benefiting from adversity is provided by the opportunities offered by hyperinflation which is surely one of the worst threats of the modern age. Yet some organisations have been able to seize on opportunities to run management seminars on dealing with the problem, publish books on the topic (which individuals have opportunistically written), or offer consultancy services in inflation accounting.

If a company is aware of the strong likelihood of an environmental change which will affect its interests, it has three main options:

* To apply the type of pressure discussed earlier (either alone, with other organisations, or through the use of public relations to mobilise public opinion) to prevent the offending change from happening.
* To accept the change and live with the results it brings.
* To alter its strategic response so that it ameliorates or avoids the threats and takes maximum gain from the opportunities.

Some indication of the type of environmental factors which affect companies has already been given in general terms in Chapter 2. A more structured approach can aid analysis but should not mislead anyone into thinking that environmental factors are always unrelated. What happens in one area may also cause changes in another — and often does. Thus technology and economics may be intertwined as may fiscal changes and social trends. For analytical purposes it is possible to classify environmental factors under eight main subject headings (Fig. 10.2): in practice they should be studied together so that cross-relationships are taken into account.

1. *Economic factors.* The economy is the only environmental factor which many companies attempt to monitor and forecast, probably because relationships between employement levels, business cycles, gross domestic

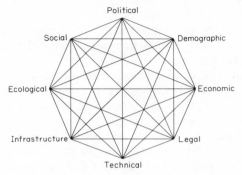

Fig. 10.2. The integrated environment.

product growth rates, and company activities are at least partly understood.

The extent of influence of any one economic factor will vary with the size, scope, and geographical location of the company. For example, in times of high national unemployment it may still be difficult for a London-based company to recruit all the skilled labour it needs.

It is also important for the analyst to understand the meaning of the figures he is studying. For example, Joseph (1976)[3] has demonstrated the numerous difficulties of making economic sense of the British unemployment statistics. Hussey (1976)[4] has dealt with the various definitions of inflation, the ways in which inflation can be measured, and the need for companies to devise their own specific cost and price indices and forecasting mechanism so that they can sensibly calculate what "inflation" means to them. Voss (1975)[5] has developed a similar argument. Berger and Sullivan (1975)[6] show in great detail how such specific indices were created for a hospital.

2. *Social.* The company may be concerned with the way changing social attitudes are affecting the hours which people will spend at work, how they will perform while at work, and what sort of industrial relations climate has to be created for a successful relationship to take place. Changes in social habits (e.g. earlier marriages, different leisure patterns, more working wives, changed values, and priorities) may have

a significant effect on marketing policies.

Social trends may sometimes result from economic factors (hyper-inflation is an example). Just as frequently they will lead to economic, regulatory, and fiscal changes.

What perhaps is of most significance to the company is not so much that social factors will affect products, prices, and distribution, but that it may alter the company's entire approach to management. Marketing aspects are often studied: the other effects are frequently overlooked.

This may in part be due to the absence of commercial social trends forecasting services. Numerous regular services exist for short- and medium-term economic forecasts. Social trends are much more nebulous and difficult to grasp, yet are no less important.

3. *Political.* Political trends are closely related to social trends, and in many cases would be considered with these. Yet there are situations where the two are not always in step, and it is for this reason that they are postulated as a possible area for study.

4. *Legal – fiscal.* The current fiscal environment is usually very well studied by companies, many of which employ outside or inside specialists to advise on fiscal problems, particularly corporation and income tax. Fiscal trends in the short term are also fairly well understood, although there may be occasional surprises. Long-term trends cannot be sensibly considered except in relation to the first three factors in this list.

5. *Legal – regulatory.* Many regulatory changes are announced well in advance, and their introduction becomes a virtual certainty. Both the change to decimal currency and the switch to value-added tax were factors which were known to businesses long before they came into force. All companies are subject to a general pattern of legal restrictions and compulsions. Some face the additional hazard of operating in sectors which invite more than average attention from the regulators, as, for example, the pharmaceutical industry.

All companies have to face up to the possibility that if their activities or the way they go about them are currently considered socially or politically undesirable, there is a strong possibility that they will face a legal restriction at some time in the future.

6. *Technological.* Enough organisations have been concerned with the growth and change of technology for the experts to have developed a bundle of new predictive techniques under the generic term "technological forecasting", although they are by no means in universal use. The technological problem is twofold. Firstly, the development of technology may provide opportunities for new or modified products or pose threats to existing products. The change may be in the entire concept behind the product (e.g. the first motor-car) or merely in the structure of the product (the substitution of plastic for metal down-piping and guttering).

Secondly, the process by which a product is manufactured may be subject to change, threatening the company with obsolescence and an uncompetitive cost structure.

Technological changes are important. They are not all environmental factors since the company may do its own research and development as well as respond to the work of others. There is usually some warning time with technological advance — sufficient for a company to adopt a deliberate strategy of being second in the field rather than being the innovator.

Often it is easier to predict what is technologically possible than what is commercially acceptable. Many textbooks on innovation and change quote the remarks made by distinguished critics of the day arguing that certain developments such as railways and telephones were impossible or unwanted. Unfortunately, the other side of the coin is rarely shown: the remarks of the many distinguished enthusiasts of the day who have waxed lyrical over technological developments which have not come to pass within the predicted time span (electric cars, high-speed tracked hover-trains to replace urban transport, television telephones).

7. *Demographic.* One more tangible feature of the environment is people. Changes in the age/sex structure of populations, the racial/colour structure, and geographical patterns may have a considerable impact on both national and company planning.

8. *Ecology/infrastructure.* In certain cases the physical environment may be significant for company planning. A physical distribution organisation will be affected by changing motorway systems, a chemical company by the pollution problem, and a mining company by its reserves. Physical and regulatory factors frequently tie in more closely together. Pollution control is backed by legislation. Factory location is in many countries controlled by permits which force industry out of congested urban areas; no building of any kind may be erected without authority from the town planners.

Recent publications have stressed the potential raw material problems of an earth of finite size (see Meadows *et al.*, 1972[7]; Ward and Dubos, 1972[8]). These have been emphasised by the energy crises of 1973.

The difficulty of moving from an intuitive interpretation of the impact of the environment on the business by the company's top managers to a more deliberate analytical approach is much greater in practice than it appears in theory. The intuitive approach gains its information from "soft" data: impressions picked up from exposure to press and television reports, supported by gossip and opinion exchange with "contacts". The analytical approach demands an analysis of hard data on a regular basis, and suffers from the difficulty that the human mind can only cope with a certain quantity of data at any one time. There is, thus, a very real danger that environmental analysis will be a paper exercise which will not affect the decisions taken or the way managers read them. This has two implications. One is for the data presented to be screened so that only relevant information with a significant present or probable impact on the company goes before top management, and that, as far as possible, this is given in summary form, stripped of the background support analysis. The background work must still be done and be available if required, but should not be thrown at management unless it is needed.

The second implication is that it is necessary to create a method which encourages the assimilation of the environmental data into the planning and decision-making process. What often happens with corporate planning systems is that managers reach a decision and then manipulate the data in the written plan so that it supports the conclusion they have reached. This is often because the way in which they are asked to contribute to a corporate planning process is frequently alien to the way in which they normally think and operate. The emphasis is placed on making the end result — the plan— look right, rather than on developing a process which contributes to the taking of the decision.

Assimilation of environmental data is facilitated if senior managers are given an opportunity to discuss forecasts of environmental trends before they become firm planning assumptions, both to enable them to compare these with their own judgements of the trends and to allow the planner to demonstrate the potential implications of the trends on the company. Most forecasts include value judgements about subjects on which there may be considerable disagreement. It is important for senior management to have an opportunity to debate their opinions before the company goes firm on the assumption. Failure to do this may leave a situation where a manager finds it difficult to incorporate the factor into his thinking.

Another approach which we have found beneficial in practice enables managers to gain a better appreciation of the impact of an environmental change on the company and to think about the reaction to this. A series of "brainstorming" type meetings are set up, each with about eight managers of mixed seniority and function. The agenda for the meeting is a list of environmental factors, and the aim is to consider each of these in relation to the company. Once tongues have loosened, the cross-fertilisation of ideas from the different functions can get the managers really interested in the topic. This stimulation of thought is often noticeably absent in the type of planning approach which gives managers a list of assumptions and leaves them to incorporate this rather dry and lifeless list into their thinking.

A major variant of both the approaches recommended above is illustrated by a two-day conference organised by consultants Harbridge House Inc., of Boston, for the top forty managers of one of the major multinationals. This focused on trends in government intervention in the United States by giving short presentations on what was happening in a number of other countries, supported by video-tape interviews with ministers and politicians in one of the countries singled out for special study. This brought the issues very much to life. More realism was added when a presentation was made on how the multi-national's own subsidiary was coping under the conditions described. Presentations from leading American authorities brought the issues squarely back to home. This understanding of the way the world was moving (and more detail in written papers and audio-cassettes was provided in the background material for the conference) put those attending in the frame of mind when they were willing to think seriously about scenarios for the future. Six scenarios were provided, each being taken by a syndicate who spent time thinking about the strategic responses they would make under the scenario conditions. The result was that real and deep consideration was made of the issues — a thing which had not been done before, although they were the subject of much current press discussion and were topics of which the managers were generally aware.

The need to ensure that environmental forecasts relate to the realities of management thinking should not detract from the need to ensure that the analytical approach is sound. The business environment in which any organisation operates is dauntingly vast, and some discrimination must be shown in selecting the most significant aspects for study.

It is possible to break down the issues involved in environmental appraisal into a number of tasks: preliminary selection of factors; defining the current state of each factor; forecasting its development; relating the forecasts to the company and screening out the least important factors; stating forecasts in the form of planning assumptions and using these as a basis for the corporate plans. Further work may involve risk and sensitivity analysis and some degree of contingency planning.

Preliminary Selection

A preliminary selection of the factors which are critical to the company can be made on a judgement basis. A pharmaceutical company is obviously affected by changes in drug legislation, trends in drug abuse, and alterations in the nature, organisations, and location of general practitioners. None of these factors need be considered by an airline company, who might be more concerned about international regulations leading to constraints on operations. The danger is that the selection of some factors involves the rejection of others. Inflation, as a factor, was virtually ignored by most companies until 1974, and is still inadequately considered by many. The selection decision should continually be reviewed, and should not be something which is automatically cut in tablets of stone and regarded as immutable.

Current State of Each Factor

It is, perhaps, elementary to suggest that the current situation of each of the factors selected be studied and understood before forecasts are made of trends. In fact an understanding of the present in relation to the company's operations may by itself be a valuable exercise. For example, consideration of inflation may reveal that what the company really needs to do is not forecast movements in the retail prices index (the most common response), but develop specific cost and price forecasts for its purchases, labour, and its prices.

Forecasting the Development of Each Factor

Every planning assumption must be derived from an assessment of the trend each factor is taking. In some cases the forecasts may be quantitative and based on complex mathematics, such as the forecasting model of the national economy. In others they may be judgements based on less-quantitative data: for example, the trend of labour legislation might be derived from a study of political opinion and pattern of legislation in other countries. Some short-term forecasts can be made with a high degree of certainty, others are very uncertain.

The planner is likely to be interested in both medium- and long-term trends, the former to cover the period chosen for the company's corporate plan, the latter because many strategies must ideally be considered against an even longer time frame. The techniques of forecasting for the different periods are very different. The medium-term forecast is likely to be based on conventional forecasting techniques which, although they may include adjustments for new developments, tend to assume an extrapolative relationship with the past. Population structures, size, and distribution are likely to be forecast for periods of up to five years with an acceptable limit of accuracy, barring the discontinuous event such as an unexpected major war or the ravages of a new science fiction type of disease. For the longer term, say ten to twenty-five years, these techniques are likely to become increasingly inappropriate and inaccurate. Population is more likely to be subject to social trends and medical advances, which can considerably alter birth and death rates, for nationalistic feelings to develop (or decline) affecting immigration and emigration, and changes in the relative growth of different economics causing new "brain drains". One might even postulate that if current salary and taxation policies continue, all British middle management will have fled to more financially rewarding havens in Europe.

The longer-term forecast uses a different set of techniques known collectively as "futures" (in earlier writings the term "technological forecasting" was used, but this is less appropriate as the methodology has moved from the technological environment to the general environment). In our opinion the correct use of these techniques is to postulate a number of alternative, or possible futures, and to examine the impact of these on the company's strategies. This is quite different from the medium term, where only one forecast may be necessary as the basis of a firm planning assumption (although others may be developed for risk and sensitivity analysis).

Relating the Forecasts to the Company

Making good environmental forecasts is a difficult process. Assessing what they mean to the company in terms of responses, threats, and opportunities can be even harder. It requires a mixture of intuition, analysis, and the type of behavioural approach discussed earlier. At the first stages the company is more concerned with deciding what is potentially significant than defining the complete strategic answer.

Screening Out the Least Important Factors

Invariably the steps in the analysis will have begun to divide the forecasts into grades of significance. Only those which really matter should go forward to become planning assumptions. The aim is to state only what is highly relevant, and the need is for the planners to avoid the temptation to show how hard they have worked by providing long schedules of forecasts which have little interest to the decision makers.

Making the Assumptions

The final selection of forecasts should be discussed by top management, if possible with some participation from senior management of at least the major subsidiaries. They may then be issued as corporate assumptions on which the company's plans should be based.

The logic behind the definition of corporate assumptions is that it provides a coherent and uniform basis for planning. No one can be sure of the future, but it is possible to construct a logical plan based on assumptions about the future. This, of course, is done all the time by all managers, but the assumptions are seldom explicitly defined or their implications fully understood. Not only are explicit assumptions defined after proper study more likely to be correct, but the fact that they are explicit means that they can be monitored and significant deviations advised promptly so that any necessary changes can be made to the plan. This is a very important part of a good corporate planning process.

Common assumptions are essential for a plan, otherwise the different parts of it may be completely incompatible. It is by no means uncommon to find companies where different divisions have prepared plans based on completely different expectations as the same basic environmental factor. This is not to argue that all environmental assumptions must be set centrally, nor that all assumptions have the same impact on all activities. What is important is for those base assumptions which affect several parts of the company to be issued on a corporate basis and for their impact to be studied by each activity area within the company.

Even the best forecast of any future event is uncertain. Really key important assumptions should be tested by risk and sensitivity analysis to see what significance alterations in the assumption might have on the results. Risk is discussed more fully in Chapter 11. For the moment it is sufficient to observe that a strategy which looks likely to collapse with damaging results to the company under a reasonably probable change in the environmental assumptions should perhaps be avoided.

In some situations contingency planning may assist, e.g. in raw material procurement. Despite the theoretical attraction of contingency planning, the realities are that few companies can afford the time and effort to plan for every possible type of future situation. If contingency plans are prepared they are likely to be restricted to a few key and reasonably concrete areas (what to do in the event of a rail strike, for example). It is not easy for a company to make sense of its environment. It is difficult enough to understand the implications of today's world and immensely difficult to consider the company within the environment which may develop in the future. Management science alone cannot supply the answer, for the science does not always affect the art of management as much as many of its protagonists believe. What is needed is a firm philosophy of corporate planning and a behavioural approach which harnesses the forecasts of the environment to the real process of managerial decision making.

References Chapter 10

1. W. Solesbury (1974) *Policy in Urban Planning*, Pergamon Press, Oxford.
2. B. W. Taylor (1976) New Dimension in Corporate Planning, *Long Range Planning*, August, Vol. 9, No. 6.
3 Sir Keith Joseph (1976) Measuring Unemployment, *Long Range Planning*, August, Vol. 9, No. 3.
4. D. E. Hussey (1976) *Inflation and Business Policy*, Longmans.
5. C. A. Voss (1975) Development of specific indices for measuring inflation, *The Business Quarterly*, Winter.
6. L. B. Berger and P. R. Sullivan (1975) *Measuring Hospital Inflation*, Lexington Books.
7. D. H. Meadows, D. C. Meadows, J. Randers, and W. W. Behrens (1972) *The Limits to Growth*, Earth Island.
8. B. Ward and R. Dubos (1972) *Only One Earth*, Pelican.

CHAPTER 11

Planning Corporate Strategy

Earlier chapters have dealt with the overall concept of corporate planning and the role of strategy within that concept. In broad terms, corporate strategy may be defined as the body of decisions which identifies how the company will use its resources of people, money, and facilities to achieve its perceived objectives. It embraces the decision of what activities the company will follow, how big it will be in each, how fast it will grow, what risks it will take, where it will operate, what methods it will use to grow, and how it will relate to the business environment in which it operates.

In strategic planning the organisation should be looking at these decisions with the future in mind. This is not in an attempt to take all future decisions today, which is patently impossible, but is more akin to the charting of a decision path along which the company may proceed. The longer-term effects of each strategic decision are understood as far as this is possible, but always with the knowledge that the organisation is a dynamic, changing body and that new events may dictate a change in the strategic path.

The concept of a five-year plan that can be made today and will remain valid for five years without modification is now held by few (and by even fewer who have experience in planning). A viewpoint which is increasingly held by practitioners is clarified by Higgins (1976):[1]

"What emerges from this planning interaction process is not a blue print for action for the next five years but rather a clarification of where the company wants to go and where it is able to go. Planning, in this view, is a process which puts present direction into perspective; a process which leads to a continuous affirmation of present course or a change in direction, but not a process which predicts a future state of being for the organisation."

This statement appears as part of an analysis of the problem of separating planning from doing, an issue that is returned to elsewhere in this book. At this point it is sufficient to observe that any attempt to isolate line managers from the planning activity is likely to degenerate rapidly to a minefield of behavioural problems.

One of the most complex of strategic planning issues surrounds the problem of delegation and co-ordination. It is possible for a major, multinational company to be run on the autocratic, entrepreneurial flair, and dynamism of one man. There are many examples of this style of management, and in the past it has often been highly successful.

When the style of management changes to an acceptance that delegation implies a belief that creative and innovative thinking can occur outside the confines of the corporate headquarters building, the difficulty of producing one co-ordinated consolidated corporate plan becomes immeasurably magnified. This may be why some large organisations duck the issue and prepare excellent plans at divisional operating units, but none at corporate level. This abdication ignores the fact that the corporate strategy of an organisation is rarely arrived at by adding up the plans of its component divisions and subsidiaries. The role of a headquarters differs from that of the divisions, and the nature of strategy is not the same at each level.

It is for this reason that the "strategic review" step (see Chapter 2) was formulated by Denning[2] as one of the most important elements of a corporate planning process. This provides for an exchange of ideas between headquarters and divisions at an early stage in the planning process. These exchanges, which should take place in a supportive atmosphere, allow for the exploration of issues, problems, and new initiatives before the organisation gets locked into a tight time-table, firm viewpoints, and complex financial calculations. The free discussion of a strategic review meeting, supported by broad brush figures, can be of great benefit in developing understanding and new ideas.

There are two very distinct elements to strategic planning both of which are of vital importance. One is the development of ideas for strategy, the other in the analysis of those ideas. The former element may lean towards a behavioural approach to management, and the latter to a scientific, quantified philosophy. Both are required, and both must be blended together if good strategic decisions are to be made. One of the disadvantages of modern business life is that the need for expertise in certain areas brings a high degree of specialisation, which in its turn carries the danger of breeding bias. Too many managers, including planners, see strategic planning in only one of its dimensions and neglect the others. Logical analysis, quantification, and the use of the more appropriate techniques are important to good planning. But they are no more important than the human behavioural aspects. Strategic planning is not just operations research, industrial psychology, economics, or finance. It is a compound of many elements, all of which must be balanced within the unique situation of the specific organisation.

Ackoff (1966)[3] distinguishes three broad approaches to strategic planning which are in current use, which he terms satisficing, optimising, and adaptivising.

Satisficing, he claims, is the most common current approach to planning.[4]

"In it the planning process begins with the setting of goals which are believed (though seldom demonstrated) to be both feasible and desirable. Attribution of these properties to the goals is usually based on consensus among the planners. Once these goals are set — and they are usually set independently of other aspects of planning — operating policies are sought which will hopefully attain the goals and are acceptable both to management and the people who must carry them out. . . . Such planning concentrates almost exclusively on obtaining a feasible set of operating policies. It seldom formulates, let alone considers, alternative policies."

This type of planning usually assumes a number of rules. There will be no significant departure from the organisation's present policies and practices; the pattern of resources will not change very much in the future; organisational change will not take place; and no provision will be made for errors in the forecasts and assumptions. Satisficing planning ". . . usually produces a comfortable continuation of most current policies, practices and aspects of the organisations structure, correcting only obvious deficiencies. . . . It also appeals to planners who are unwilling to stick their necks out."

Optimising planning takes a very different course: ". . . an effort is made not to do just well enough, but to do as well as possible." It relies heavily on operational research techniques and mathematical models, which immediately brings one major behavioural problem: it makes it impossible for the non-specialist to do the planning and brings a gulf between planner and doer. It has another defect in that it tends to ignore or under emphasise the non-quantifiable aspects of a problem. In addition, the model can only choose the optimum path from the data fed into it, and the complexities of most aspects of the future affecting most organisations are such that this requires a very high level of skill — almost a superhuman level of skill. Optimising planning tends to undervalue the human aspects, and has a high probability of causing the problem defined by Mintzberg (1975)[6] (which was quoted in Chapter 2), namely producing planning solutions which are alien to the way in which most managers conceptualise and solve their problems.

While it would be wrong to deny the value of operational research techniques in planning, an optimising approach to planning is likely to fall far short of its aims.

Ackoff's third pattern of planning is adaptivising, a word for which he apologises but which sums up what he means. His views are further developed in Ackoff (1970)[5] and see adaptivising as being accompanied by the belief that the main value of planning lies in the process and not the plans themselves. This is not a passive view, for the adaptivising planner believes that one of the main purposes of his plans is to prevent crises from arising, continually adapting the organisation and its systems so that difficulties are avoided and so that management does not have to spend most of its time resolving issues caused by past inadequacies and inefficiencies. This acceptance of organisational change as necessary is very different from the view taken by the satisficer, and brings to the fore many of the behavioural implications discussed in this book, including the "change agent" role of the planner explored in Chapter 8.

One of the adaptiviser's strongest points is that his view of the future distinguishes three distinct types of risk in all future events. Certain things are virtual certainties, for which the best solution is to ensure that the company has adequate plans to exploit the situation. Many more events can only be forecast within varying degrees of probability. Here the adaptiviser will develop contingency plans, and a monitoring approach will allow him to know when things have changed. The third type of risk is the completely unexpected. Here the only answer is to create a flexible organisation that, by using early warning systems that events are changing, can react very quickly.

Risk is a very important part of strategic decision making. Strategic choice is not simply a question of applying creative and innovative ideas. It is also concerned with understanding and balancing risk. Two simple types of risk can be distinguished. One is "project" risk, which is the risk that accompanies anything new; that sales forecasts might not be achieved, costs might be higher than estimated, or external events may adversely affect the project. This sort of risk occurs with all types of business activities. It tends to be greater the less the project is related to the company's current activities. A complete diversification in an area in which the company has no experience thus has more potential for "project" risk than a decision to invest further in the business in which the organisation already operates. (This of course assumes that there is an investment opportunity in that business.)

The second type of risk might be termed "portfolio" risk. This is a development of the argument that advises one not to keep all one's eggs in one basket. Every organisation has a portfolio of current activities, each of which is subject to its own patterns of risk; for example, competitive forces, environmental trends, dependence on few customers, raw material and supply problems, and seasonal influences. A company that trades only in one product has a very high portfolio risk (although it may legitimately decide that the risk is acceptable).

As a generalisation we can postulate that portfolio risk is at its lowest when project risk is at its highest, and vice versa. The strategic judgement that has to be made is on the balance of acceptable risks. The one-product company may feel that it has little option but to diversify, although a multi-product, multi-market company might well think twice.

Good strategic analysis should attempt to evaluate the risks as well as identifying and quantifying the results of the planned action itself.

Strategic decisions may take many forms and be in many dimensions. It is traditional to think of strategy mainly in the dimensions of marketing and acquisition. Equally important are decisions in the areas of manufacturing, finance, industrial relations, and manpower. Although it may be expedient to prepare a manpower plan, for example, which is separate from the main strategic plan, this does not mean that it should be prepared in isolation. The elements of strategy may all have a dynamic relationship with each other: the manpower plan is not simply an expression of the decided strategies in terms of people. It may also modify the marketing strategies which would otherwise be desirable. Similar relationships exist with any other functional strategies.

Strategic planning is an examination and selection of options. Many possible paths face every company. The more creative and innovative the company, the richer will be the selection of projects from which it may make its choice.

The nature of the opportunities facing a company may be broad and varied. The types of actions it may take are relatively few in numbers. Hussey (1974)[7] lists these as:

Divestment. The decision to give up a particular sphere of activity which may vary from the quiet dropping of an uneconomic product, to the closure of a factory, or the sale of an activity as a going concern.

Obtaining licences. This may be a legitimate way of launching a new activity or improving a product range without the company itself having to fund the necessary research or seek the optimum manufacturing methods. Disadvantages are that licences imply a commitment of costs against future market conditions, they can be withdrawn, success may increase the probability of withdrawal, and in some countries legislation acts against them.

Granting licences. One way to reduce the risks of expansion is for the company to license other organisations to manufacture its products. This means that it can obtain an income from royalties without having to make additional investments in production facilities or buying into markets. The disadvantages are the risks of adverse legislation, abuse of the licence agreement by the licensee and the possibility that the granting of a licence might prevent the company from entering that market itself at some later date.

Simple expansion. Expansion of something the company already does may be achieved by applying the necessary resources. Expansion into something new may be carried out the same way, although with greater risk. Key staff with the necessary skills can be acquired, and the appropriate investment made. Sometimes the risks associated with such ventures may be reduced by partnerships or joint venture arrangements with other organisations or people. Other companies' resources may be used to help expansion; for example, contract manufacture, joint distribution activities, or the use of specialist services. The corollary of this is that the company may actively sell its own resources as a contract manufacturer, distributor, or indeed one of its support skills such as the design of computer software.

Research and development. For the science-based companies at least, the development of new products from the company's own research is an essential. Risks of unproductive research and development are, of course, high.

Acquisition and merger. The takeover of an existing organisation already operating in the required business area. It has at last been realised that acquisition is not a simple solution, and brings numerous problems, many of which stem from behavioural issues.

This classification is useful in helping thinking about how a strategy might best be achieved but does not stimulate very much thought about what a company might do. Thus a market opportunity in a food market might be achieved by increasing promotional expenditure (expansion), developing a new product which meets market requirements in a better way (research and development), or buying up a competitor (acquisition). In logical sequence the company should first identify the entrepreneurial opportunity, and only after this decide how best to exploit it. In practice the means is sometimes decided first, not always with the best results. The merger-mania period of the 1960s often appeared to be representative of a drive for corporate power and size rather than the sound economic development of market opportunities.

Modern thinking leans more and more to involvement and participation in strategic planning to the extent that the pressures in some countries are for a style of planning which includes the participation of all employees. The industrial democracy issue, and some of the problems arising from it, are described in greater length in Chapter 16. Methods of achieving participation discussed here refer to work done with managers, although some of the principles are capable of extension further down the organisation chart.

Much of the earlier writing on corporate planning suggested a "pass-the-hat-round" type of approach whereby managers contributed to strategic thinking by writing plans for their own area of operations, discussing and agreeing with their superiors, who in turn repeated the process with the managers to whom they reported. Ultimately the consolidation reached top management, who used it to shape the strategic plans of the organisation, filling in the gaps from their own decisions and analysis. Further involvement might be achieved by linking the process to a management by objectives approach.

There is much of value in this method of approach, although its success depends as much on the style and nature of the discussion meetings as on the quality of the written plans. Some such approach as this is necessary to underpin the other methods which will be discussed later. It is, however, subject to two major limiting factors:

(1) The method is not always suitable for extension very far down the organisational chart, partly because it is liable to become cumbersome and partly because it becomes remote from the jobs people actually do. It may be very logical to ask each product manager in a marketing department to prepare a five-year plan for the products for which they are responsible. It is less logical to ask the depot manager of a transport undertaking to prepare what is in effect a local area version of the company's total corporate plan. Yet both may be the same distance from the managing director on the organisation chart.

(2) Although the method may allow some cross-functional relationships and the style of discussion may widen the scope of its coverage, the degree of involvement is essentially related to areas for which the manager is responsible. He may not be participating in

the planning of the total business despite this narrow involvement with a part of it. Differences of degree to which this statement is true do occur, but in the worst systems it is possible to have plans produced in such narrow, watertight compartments that no participation really occurs at all.

Some of these problems can be partly avoided in the design of the pass-the-hat-round system, and must be if the company wishes to prevent its approach from becoming some annual ritual from which all meaning has drained over the years.

In addition there are some specific approaches that may be adopted. Our opinion is that these should be part of a wider system and should not be seen as attempts to decide the future of the company by referendum. Ideas certainly should flow from them, together with opinions on the company's present policies, strategies, and problems. Leadership is still needed from the top, and the final decisions should in our view be taken by the responsible managers. These decisions will undoubtedly be influenced by the involvement process. However, it is unrealistic to think that the major organisations of the world could develop a participative approach to strategy unless it were within a structured framework. The complexities of decisions faced by the top management of a major multi-national must influence the shape of any approach that creates more participation in strategic decision making.

Two other factors can also be overlooked. One is that top management cannot delegate their responsibility — and in some countries this is a legal responsibility — to manage the company on behalf of its owners. The second is that certain types of strategic decision cannot be disclosed too openly too far in advance. The idea of expanding by acquisition can spring from a participative discussion involving quite low-level managers: the fact that the company intends to put in a bid for a *specific* named company cannot be made public too early in the proceedings.

Getting wider participation is thus not as easy at the strategic level as it is at the operating level. Yet as the world moves more to a situation of management by consensus rather than edict, an acceptable solution has to be found.

One major multi-national has found a reasonable compromise between involvement and the strategic decision-making process. It divides its activities into major groupings, and within that group classifies its world-wide companies into three bands of significance.

Every four to five years it brings together the chief executives of the most significant companies in each group to work on an outline strategy for each group, to examine markets, product development and diversification strategies for the next five years. A number of meetings are held, and in between the chief executives allot investigatory and support work to others in their own companies, thus broadening the extent of involvement in the work. Eventually the outline strategic plan is discussed with top management, and an acceptable strategy emerges. This is then used to set objectives which divide into those that can only be met by head office action and those which are fed into the other companies in the multi-national through their on-going pass-the-hat-round system of planning which operates in parallel.

The approach is not perfect. But it does allow the involvement of many people, applies an easily understood formula to the selection of those involved, and is a declaration by top management that they want other ideas and opinions to help them shape the total company. The main criticism we have is the comparative infrequency of bringing the planning team together.

A better known and more widely practised approach is the planning conference. This may take many forms, and two examples are given.

Morris (1976)[8] describes the method used by a company who, employing 12,000 people, carried out a fundamental review of their plans every three years using a highly participative approach. In the years between these reviews, plans were continuously updated and revised but with a lower level of participation. The fundamental review was treated as an important corporate task.

"Seminars were organised for all the company's managers. Before attending, the managers were asked to prepare individually a report on the company's major internal and external problems and opportunities, and to make proposals for solving the problems and exploiting the opportunities. During the seminars, managers worked in groups which were each composed so as to give the maximum mix of function, work location and status. Using the preliminary work as a basis, each group then prepared a written report which was discussed with the Vice

Chairman. Following an analysis of the 44 group reports, some action was taken immediately whilst longer term proposals were fed into the long term planning committee.

"This long term planning committee consisted of the Vice Chairman and a number of senior line managers who were chosen less for their status than because their particular areas of expertise were relevant to long term planning. Each was asked to put together a small project team which they would use to gather facts, prepare a scenario within a given area and to suggest the course of corporate action which would be most appropriate. Weekly meetings of the planning committee were held and the board was kept informed of developments. The project groups were expected to pay special attention to consulting with other managers who could contribute or who would be affected.

"The outcome of this process was a report which became the subject of a three day conference of the Company's Directors and Senior and Upper-middle managers.

"Before attending the conference the participants were asked to read the report and prepare answers to specific questions. These focused attention on the major strategies and potential problems and invited specific proposals. These proposals were considered first in heterogeneous groups and then in specialist groups.

"On the basis of this conference the final plan was prepared and communicated through line management so far as security allowed. Short-term objectives were agreed in line with the long term plan, and these were then passed down through the levels of the hierarchy following as far as possible the basic principles:

(i) that objectives would be set within the working group and not between individual bosses and subordinates.

(ii) that at each stage managers and supervisors should be left maximum freedom to determine how they would achieve the agreed results."

A similar approach, but with participation mainly restricted to senior managers, has been used by consultants Harbridge House Inc.,[9] in helping a number of American financial organisations to take a new approach to planning:

"A properly structured top management planning conference can lead to:

* Candid assessment of the firm's strengths and weaknesses.
* Agreement as to the firm's mission.
* Definition of the firm's objectives.
* Consideration (and at least the first steps towards the resolution) of any serious actual or political problems facing the firm.
* Development of a plan to meet these problems and opportunities.

"The success of such a planning conference is based upon the premise that the best plan will emerge when all of the firm's top executives are assembled in one place where, undisturbed, they can devote their total ingenuity and energy in a structured format to the single task of business planning. However, it is not enough simply to plan and hold such a conference for, like most meetings, it can fail unless certain critical requirements are met:

* *The conference must have and adhere to a clear-cut agenda.* Without this guide the conference can easily turn into a 'Bull session'.
* *The conference must focus on the firm's actual priority problems.* Thus, advance research is recommended so that a structure for the consideration of key issues can be developed and used.
* *The conference must have effective leadership.*"

The two examples given have a number of points in common, one of the most important being that the final conference starts from a base of information and analysis. Although in one case this work is carried out by participative work groups and in the other by a consultant/client team, the need for a structured approach to the conference is very real. Both of the approaches described (and the Harbridge House approach could be modified to involve lower levels of management) may require some measure of control to ensure that the conference becomes a tool for strategic as well as operational planning (see the definitions given in Chapter 2).

Davous and Deas (undated)[10] draw a distinction between strategic planning and strategic management, and see the latter as a behavioural problem which concerns several levels in the organisation and requires a cultural change if it is to be successful. This view is compared with the traditional conception of strategic planning as something which only concerns top management. The key points in their approach are:

(1) The process cascades down the organisation and progressively involves more people and to a greater degree of sophistication.
(2) Some quick results are sought, which provide flashes of analysis and decision on major issues.
(3) The process is "pedalogical" to bypass the psychological obstacles.
(4) The process concentrates on real problems.

The procedure is for the style of the organisation to be studied before any planning initiative is started so that the way in which the work is carried out can be adjusted to the nature of the problem. At the same time the organisation's emotive response to words like "plan" and "objective" is established so that a vocabulary can be chosen which avoids provoking an unnecessarily negative approach.

The method always involves the use of an outside consultant who is trained in the psychological aspects of group behaviour so that he can monitor the *process* and make intervention necessary to facilitate constructive behaviour.

Planning meetings are tailored to the level of sophistication of those attending, and one of the aims is to gradually raise this level. The writers estimate that the first meeting of a particular group consists of about 80% training and 20% planning, the second splits roughly equally between the two, and by the third the emphasis has changed to 20% training and 80% planning. The two kinds of output sought from each meeting are thus an improvement in skills and decisions on issues. Meetings proceed on a little-and-often basis, and do not seek to achieve too much in too concentrated a time. Normally a meeting is succeeded by a period when individuals carry out some investigatory or analytical tasks in preparation for the next meeting.

Meetings are initially set up at a high level, sometimes including the chief executive but frequently excluding him. One of the first tasks of the meeting is to define the business areas the company is in. Subsequent groups are set up for each business area. Each of the additional groups is made up of what might be termed a diagonal slice down the organisation, so that its membership is made up of several layers in the hierarchy, but with proportionately more people as one moves up the organisational layers. Characteristically, meetings generate work which involves more junior levels, and involvement cascades down the organisation.

An important point is that meetings are structured. Each series of meetings consists of a number of predetermined modules: that is, the purpose and structure of the meetings is predetermined, not the output. A number of specially developed matrix methods of analysis are used (although these are not described in detail by the authors). A general structure to the meetings is provided by working through an analytical "model" which includes familiar phrases such as opportunities and threats, strengths, and weaknesses.

What results from the process is a definition and agreement of objectives, and a strategy which may not only be different from the one which would have been decided by top management alone, but which also carries with it the enthusiasm and commitment of the entire management hierarchy. In addition the company has at the end a very different culture and style of management.

Although some quick results may come out of the process, it is generally a long time before all the cycles are completed. It also requires a continuing commitment of senior management time.

This method has been used within the Philips Group and its use in this context is described by van Ham (1976).[11]

Behavioural approaches to the definition of corporate strategy may also use the techniques for stimulating creativity which were discussed in Chapter 4. They are also akin to the various participative approaches to profit improvement practised by Union Carbide and Procter and Gamble described in Hussey (1974).[12]

Whether the company wishes to delve as far into the behavioural approach is a matter for individual decision. Young and Hussey (1977)[13] describe the development of a more moderate acceptance of the behavioural principles closely allied to the "strategic review" concept discussed in Chapter 2. The problem was to change from a system of extended budgeting within which participation of managers was widespread but on a "watertight-compartment" principle with little departmental discussion and no cross-functional involvement, based on a form filling, numbers only approach, and which assumed that both the business and organisational parameters were virtual constants. The change was brought about by a system that required a different type of planning input, set up participative discussions on strategy between head office and business units, and established a series of overlapping planning groups within the business units. Each group helped to develop the plans of its component managers and draw on the skills of other functions to assist in this. One or more major groups was established by each director for his area of responsibility, consisting of the managers who reported to him, plus invited specialists from and representatives of other departments. Each manager in a group established a subgroup of the people reporting to him as a communication medium, a work task force, and a channel for ideas. The main groups were made aware of the total strategy within which they were planning, and were given the opportunity to contribute to this strategy as well as participating in the development of detailed plans for their own area.

Great care was taken in setting up the groups. All managers in the company were briefed in the new approach and the shape of the total planning process, and help was given to directors to establish the first groups on the right lines and to conduct the meetings in a constructive way. At the strategic review series of meetings the group contributed to strategic planning; at the corporate planning meetings, which succeeded the strategic review in each cycle, the concentration was on operational planning.

Any organised group work, in any of the methods discussed, should give due consideration to the principles of organisational development outlined in Chapter 7. In addition the required objectives of each meeting should be clearly defined and the structure of it established. It is noticeable that all the above methods have a very clear conception of the desired inputs and outputs from each meeting (or series of meetings), all meetings include a high degree of preparation and preplanning, and many use analytical techniques to help discussion. None of them attempts to plan in a vacuum. One of the key features for success is to make participants feel that the meetings are worthwhile and have achieved something: this requires conscious effort on the part of the organisers.

So far in this chapter we have looked very broadly at the nature of corporate strategy and at various behavioural approaches to developing a strategy. The need for sound analysis to complement, and in some cases be an integral part of, the behavioural approaches has been stressed.

The analytical side of strategic planning is vitally important and cannot be over-emphasised. Final decisions should only be made after the appropriate analysis of likely results (including risks). This means that many good ideas will fail to pass the final test or may fall in priority after complete examination. Many useful techniques are available to aid and assist strategic analysis and decision making, and few of these have their application restricted to corporate planners. Some techniques are relatively simple in concept and are aids to ordering thought as much as the quantifying of options (although all techniques should be used in a numerate manner). Others require a more advanced level of mathematical knowledge, and frequently need computer assistance if they are to be employed.

Many of the simpler techniques are ideal for use in the types of group activity discussed in this chapter, either for providing a framework for a particular meeting or for use in blackboard analysis of the points made by the group. These techniques are discussed in some depth in the remainder of this chapter. The more complex analytical tools are described in less detail since each of them requires a book of its own to do it justice.

Strengths and Weaknesses

A simple approach is to analyse strengths, weaknesses, opportunities, and threats in relation to the internal and external factors affecting the company. This checklist is perhaps deceptively simple, since following it is likely to lead into an appreciation of some very complex situations as well as an awareness of many information needs and much detailed mathematical analysis.

Opportunities can be linked to another concept, that of synergy. Often crudely described as the $2 + 2 = 5$ effect, synergy is the mystical quality which means that the whole is sometimes greater than the sum of the parts if they remained isolated and individual. It usually comes about because of some dimension of economy of scale, either in production, marketing, research and development, or management. A proposal to gain a new market for an existing product (which may lead to decreased average unit costs because of higher production levels), is patently more synergistic than a scheme to acquire a company which operates in a completely different industry. Synergy is a desirable attribute and is worth identifying during analysis.

A variant of the strengths and weakness approach is used in the methods of Davous and Deas discussed earlier in the chapter.

Another variation is the critical skills and capability profile approach developed by Denning (1971).[14] Here analysis is made of the skills considered to be essential for success in particular industries or activities. The company can also analyse its own profile and by comparing one with the other will gain some insight into the changes it must make if it wishes to pursue some of the ideas which may have been suggested for its development. It may also be used to explore ways of improving performance in current activities or to examine the reason for the success or failure of competition.

Gap Analysis

The gap-analysis technique attempts to explore the "gap" between objectives and extrapolated performance to help identify both the extent of the strategic task and the ways in which the gap might be closed. The technique is illustrated in Fig. 11.1. The particular example shows profit as the factor considered. Turnover, market share or return on investment

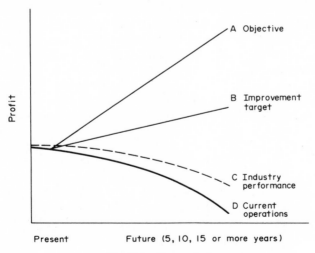

Fig. 11.1. Gap analysis.

ratios are other possible choices which might be selected.

Line *D* gives a forecast of the way in which company results are expected to come about if current activities are simply extrapolated and no new developments are undertaken. Usually this will postulate some decline in performance unless the company has a large number of products about to enter the take-off stage of their product life cycles.

An attempt is made in line *C* to compare this to expected industry performance. The purpose of this line is to try to see whether the company is expected to change its performance comparative to the industry as a whole, as an analytical question to stimulate thought about why any change may be likely.

Line *B* is a form of objective which is based on intentions to improve. It may postulate improved productivity or the implementation of new projects which are already planned by the company. This line should be used to stimulate thought on how the targets might be met, and any obstacles to improvement removed.

Finally, there is line *A*, which shows the company's overall profit target (it need not, of course, take the straight line progression shown in the diagram). This is used to illustrate the size of the task facing the company, and to develop thinking on what might be done to close the gap. The diagram can also be used to chart the expected results of actions postulated, so that its probable impact on the "gap" can be better understood.

Matrix methods

There are numerous matrix methods of analysis. One of the simplest approaches is shown in Fig. 11.2. In the form shown this examines

Market Product	Current	New
Current		
New		

Fig. 11.2. Analysis of strategic options.

products in relation to markets. Similar simple matrices can be developed to analyse other parameters; for example, suppliers/raw materials and supplies, types of finance/sources of finance, human resource skills/source of skills.

The matrix is used to explore the possibilities in front of the company, to categorise ideas, and to serve as a stimulus for new ideas. In group work, for example, the participants might be invited to focus attention on developing ideas for each of the boxes in the matrix in turn.

A more complex technique, the Directional Policy Matrix (DPM) has been developed by Shell Chemicals and is described by Thomson (1975).[15] This uses a nine-box matrix (Fig. 11.3) which measures three

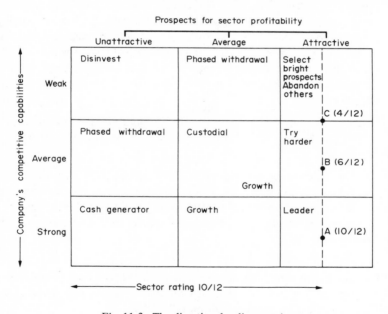

Fig. 11.3. The directional policy matrix.

dimensions of industry sector prospects against three dimensions of the present position of the company within that sector and relative to competition.

"How does one judge the attractiveness of a particular business sector and the position of any particular company in that sector? The DPM method involves a panel of experts from those with knowledge of and responsible for some functional aspects of the business — marketing, manufacturing, product application and so on — with a planning adviser acting as moderator to the panel.

"The experts on the panel must first define the boundaries of the analysis by market segment (for example, resins in general or phenol formaldehyde resins specifically?) by geographic area (Europe or the whole world?) and by time horizon.

"They will then assign a score to the industry sector, expressed in stars, like a Michelin guide or a consumer association's best buy guide. Using four criteria: (1) Growth; (2) Market Quality; (3) Feedstock/Raw Material Availability and Sufficiency; (4) Environmental Factors.

"Similarly, turning to the company's competitive position within that market sector, they will similarly assign stars, using the following three criteria: (1) Market Share; (2) Production Efficiency; (3) R & D Capacity."

House rules were defined for the interpretation of the star ratings. Shell (1975)[16] provide an example of the development of ratings for the matrix.

"The working of the system is illustrated by the following hypothetical example in which the results of the matrix analysis are summarised in highly abbreviated form (it has in general been found desirable to record the arguments and supporting data in considerably greater detail):

Hypothetical example
Product sector. Product X, a semi mature thermoplastic suitable for engineering industry applications with two existing producers in W. Europe and a third producer currently building.

"A.   Sector Prospects Analysis (W. Europe 1975-80)

			Ratings	
			Stars	Points
A.1.	Market growth	15-20% p.a. forecast	+++++	4
A.2.	Market quality			
2.1.	Sector profitability record?	Above average		
2.2.	Margins maintained in over-capacity? ⎱	Some price cutting has taken place but product has not reached commodity		
2.3.	Susceptible to commodity pricing? ⎰	status		
2.4.	Customer to producer ratio?	Favourable; numerous customers; only two producers so far		
2.5.	High added value to customer?	Yes; the product is used in small scale high value engineering applications		
2.6.	Ultimate market limited in size?	Yes; unlikely to be large enough to support more than 3-4 producers		
2.7.	Substitutability by other products?	Very limited. Product has unique properties		
2.8.	Technology of production restricted?	Moderately. Process is available under licence from E. Europe		
		Overall market quality rating. above average	++++	3
A.3.	Industry feedstock situation	Product is manufactured from an intermediate which itself requires sophisticated technology and has no other outlets	++++	3
A.4.	Environmental aspects	Not relevant — not rated		
		Overall sector prospects rating:		10/12

B.   Companies' competitive capabilities analysis

Competitor	'A'	'B'	'C'	Ratings		
				'A'	'B'	'C'
B.1. Market Position						
Market share W. Eur.	65%	25%	10%	+++++	+++	++
B.2. Production capability						
2.1. Process economics	Both A and B have own 'first generation' processes supported by moderate process R&D capability		C is licensing second generation process ex E. Europe			
2.2. Hardware	A and B each have one plant sufficient to sustain their resp. mkt. shares		None as yet. Markets imported product ex E. Europe			
2.3. Feedstock	Manufactures feedstock by slightly outdated process from bought in precursors	Has own precursors. Feedstock manuf. by third party under process deal	Basic position in precursors. Has own second generation process for feedstock			
			Overall production capability ratings	++++	+++	**(+)
B.3. Product R & D (in relation to market position)						
	Marginally weaker	comparable	stronger	++++	+++	++(+)
				'A'	'B'	'C'
			Overall Competitors' Ratings:	10/12	6/12	4/12"

These ratings are plotted on the matrix in Fig. 11.3, along a dotted line raised in the matrix at right angles to the "sector rating score". Thus the sector rating affects the boxes of the matrix in which the company ratings are plotted.

The keywords in the matrix are designed to indicate the directional policy appropriate for the company which finds itself falling in any particular box.

Decision Trees

Decision trees can be used with varying degrees of sophistication. In their simplest form they may chart the options available to solve a particular problem with the supplementary ranges of options that become necessary once the first decision is taken branching out like a tree. More usefully, they will also plot the impact of chance events on each decision, with the resultant decision option which will then become necessary.

In this way it is possible to examine the causal relationships of a whole chain of options and chance events, and to analyse the future results of a decision in considerable depth. The decision tree itself aids analysis, stimulates thought, and acts as a means of communicating a complex series of relationships. In use with groups it can be a tool to be developed from discussion within the group or as a mechanism for explaining a major series of decisions.

More complex analysis with decision trees would include the assigning of probabilities to the chance events, and the quantifying of the likely results of each strategy. Brown and Hussey (1973)[17] provide an example of the use of decision trees in relation to an ICL Prosper model of the project. Magee (1964)[18] gives one of the best general introductions to the technique.

Figure 11.4 provides a simple illustration of the technique. The normal use of the technique would be in more complex situations.

More Complex Techniques

Reference should be made to a few of the many valuable, sophisticated techniques available to the planner. Heading the list in terms of usefulness

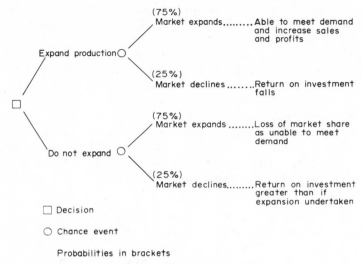

(75%)
Market expands.........Able to meet demand
                       and increase sales
                       and profits

Expand production○

(25%)
Market declines........Return on investment
                       falls

(75%)
Market expands ....Loss of market share
                       as unable to meet
                       demand

Do not expand ○

(25%)
Market declines.........Return on investment
                        greater than if
                        expansion undertaken

□ Decision

○ Chance event

Probabilities in brackets

Fig. 11.4. Simple example of a decision tree.

is the computerised corporate model, which enables the company to explore the implications of alternative strategies and chance events in a depth
that is, for practical reasons, a virtual impossibility by any other means.
There are numerous modelling systems commercially available. Power
(1974)[19] gives a check list of questions which should be considered
before choosing a model.

One of the major decisions to be made is whether to choose an optimising or a stimulation model. In fact careful choice of appropriate "what if"
questions can bring the planner very close to an optimising answer even
where simulation models are chosen.

Some skill is needed in the setting up of a model. Many are designed to
be operated, once set up, by normally intelligent and numerate managers
without systems skills, and are a very powerful tool in strategic decision
making.

Hussey (1974)[20] provides examples of a number of commercially
available models.

Financial methods of investment analysis, such as discounted cash flow,
are essential to thorough analysis. A basic introduction is provided by

Hazell (1975).[21] The use of these techniques is to provide a means of measuring and comparing various decisions, and a discipline within which a common standard of analysis can be carried out.

Certain "subscription" analysis techniques are also available. One of the most significant is the PIMS (Profit Impact of Market Strategy) service, which collects information from its subscribers to provide a data base of experience in different business activity areas. Some thirty-seven factors are investigated and analysed, including market share, total marketing expenditure, product quality, R&D expenditures, and investment intensity. From the data provided PIMS staff are able to derive general "laws" which help determine what business strategy in what kind of competitive environment will produce what results. Answers are provided to questions such as:

What profit rate is "normal" for a particular business?

If the business continues on its present path what are its future operating results likely to be?

What strategic changes in the business have the best chance of improving results?

What will be the impact of the future strategy on cash flow and profitability in the short and long terms?

The PIMS programme has as its members some sixty corporations covering 620 diverse businesses, and enables lessons to be drawn from the collective experience of these businesses.

This short description leaves many techniques unmentioned. Those that wish to know more should turn to the specialist literature, particularly that in the operational research field. Enough has been stated to demonstrate the importance and range of the analytical methods available to the planner and to demonstrate that good strategic planning can be a careful balancing of the behavioural approaches against the analytical. Both have their place and are essential in modern business planning.

References Chapter 11

1. R. B. Higgins (1976) Re-unite management and planning, *Long Range Planning*, Vol. 9, No. 4, August 1976.
2. B. W. Denning. Unpublished manuscript.

3. R. L. Ackoff (1966) The meaning of strategic planning, *McKinsey Quarterly*, Summer 1966; reproduced in *Essentials of Corporate Planning* (S. Jain and S. Singhui (eds.)) Planning Executives Institute, 1973.
4. R. L. Ackoff (1966) op. cit., page 142.
5. R. L. Ackoff (1970) *A Concept of Corporate Planning*, Wiley Interscience.
6. H. Mintzberg (1975) The Manager's job: folklore and fact, *Harvard Business Review*, July–August 1975.
7. D. E. Hussey (1974) *Corporate Planning: Theory and Practice*, Pergamon Press, Chap. 11.
8. G. Morris (1976) Participative approaches to corporate planning, paper presented at the *Realities of Planning Workshop*, Meeting 2, Administrative Staff College, Henley on Thames.
9. Harbridge House (1974) *The Planning Conference in the Financial Community*. Harbridge House, Boston, USA.
10. P. Davous and J. Deas (undated) Design of a consulting intervention for strategic management, Conference paper.
11. K. van Ham (1976) Strategic planning and organisational development, paper presented at *Realities of Planning Workshop*, Meeting 2, Administrative, Staff College, Henley on Thames.
12. D. E. Hussey (1974) op. cit., Chap. 17.
13. R. Young and D. E. Hussey (1977) Corporate planning at Rolls-Royce Motors Ltd., *Long Range Planning*. Vol. 10, No. 2.
14. B. W. Denning (1971) *Corporate Planning: Selected Concepts*. McGraw-Hill, P. 14.
15. W. C. Thomson (1975) A rational approach to corporate strategy in the chemical industry, an address given to a group of the Verband der Chemischen Industry, Rotterdam, November 1975.
16. Shell Chemicals (1975) *The Directional Policy Matrix on a new Aid to Corporate Planning*, Chemical Economics and Planning, Shell International Chemical Co. Ltd. London.
17. G. C. Brown and D. E. Hussey (1973) New product planning and marketing, in *Case Studies in Corporate Planning* (P. Baynes (ed.), Pitman, Ch. 6.)
18. J. F. Magee (1964) Decision trees for decision making and how to use decision trees, *Harvard Business Review*, July–August and September–October.
19. P. Power (1974) The selection of a computerised planning model, in *The Corporate Planner's Yearbook 1974/5* D. E. Hussey (ed.), Pergamon Press, Oxford, p. 132.
20. D. E. Hussey (1974) op. cit., p. 310.
21. P. F. Hazell (1975) *Investment Appraisal: Accountants Digest*, No. 23, Autumn. Institute of Chartered Accountants in England and Wales.

CHAPTER 12

Getting the Right Approach to Planning

By now it should have become apparent that there is a difference between an organisation's ability to make a plan and its ability to sustain a process of corporate planning, which has much broader management and behavioural implications. The preparation of an isolated plan can be an individual analytical exercise performed by the managing director with little reference to anyone else in the organisation. If, as is likely, he possesses a sound sense of strategic judgement, it may be a good plan and in some situations be just what the organisation needs.

A process of corporate planning is a much more difficult thing to bring about. It may not result in a better plan than could be produced by the managing director alone, although on balance it should. What it should do is make the good plan more effective and more likely to be implemented. It also seeks wider results by giving managers a better understanding of the organisation and what it is trying to do, a feeling of belonging to the organisation and a measure of enthusiasm.

Preceding chapters in this book have discussed the overall framework of corporate planning, some of the approaches and philosophies which might be used in a planning process, and those aspects of human behavioural theory which are most relevant to the introduction of a process of planning. In a way these may be likened to the provision of architect's plans and bricks, cement, tiles, and other materials which a builder will need to construct a house. Everything he needs may be on site, but he will not have a house until he has applied a measure of skill which will change his heaps of sand and piles of bricks into something quite different.

This chapter will attempt to supply something like the builders' skill and craftmanship, and will try to present some principles, drawn from the issues so far discussed, in a way that helps the company actually implement a process of planning. It sets out to show the top management team the steps that are necessary if they wish to create a worthwhile process.

The issue is viewed from two sides. In this chapter we will try to give positive guidance on what should be done. In the next chapter we take a position based on published research and experiences, on the things that can go wrong in planning, so that mistakes can be avoided.

The chief executive who contemplates the introduction of corporate planning into his organisation has to take a number of positive steps. The first is a very personal one. It is to examine his own knowledge of corporate planning, his motivation for wanting to introduce it, and to accept the fact that planning may call for changes in his own style of management, and almost certainly will demand a commitment of some of his time. It is important to realise that his enthusiasm and personal example will do more for the success of his planning effort than all the professional skills which he almost certainly will have to hire to help him.

There is only one good piece of advice for the chief executive who is approaching planning as a fashionable technique which need not disturb his personal time-table in any way. That advice is to leave it alone. The benefits of planning will only come when it is applied well, and a half-hearted effort can be dangerous to the company.

Assuming that the chief executive passes the first test, he should next seek answers to three questions:

What is the organisational style of his organisation?
What planning mechanisms does the organisation currently possess?
What are his expectations/objectives in relation to his planning initiative?

Organisational Style

The question of organisational style is significant because the answer will shape the organisation's approach to corporate planning and may indicate a need for a change in style in parallel with the introduction of the planning process. It is not difficult to see how managers who commonly practised a directive style of management (to use the analysis of Chapter 6) would feel uncomfortable with a widely participative approach to planning which encouraged the questioning of current strategies. Similarly, the managers involved in the planning process may find it difficult to work with a boss who adapts one apparent style for planning and quite another for day-to-day management.

Answers to this question will certainly influence the way in which the planning process is introduced to the organisation, the amount of effort spent on training and developing the right sort of interaction between functions and groups, and the degree of personal attention and counselling which has to be given to certain key managers who might otherwise find it difficult to adjust to the new requirements.

It should also be remembered that organisational style may vary between the divisions and subsidiaries of any large group, and is more likely to vary if there is a diversity of geographic or industry operations. These differences, and the extent to which it is important that they remain, should be understood from the outset. A corporate planning process can be an agent for the unification of organisational style within an organisation, but even within the principles of corporate planning it is possible to establish a number of variants to accommodate desirable differences.

It may be possible for the chief executive to make his own assessment of the organisational style of his enterprise. If he feels that he is too close to the problem to be objective, or if he lacks the time to look at the full breadth of the problem, he may feel that it is worthwhile seeking help from his professional personnel staff or from outside experts.

Existing Planning Mechanisms

All organisations possess mechanisms which relate to planning in at least a broad sense. It is important that the nature of these is fully understood so that their strengths and weaknesses can be identified. The reason for this is that it makes no sense to re-invent the wheel. If a system is working well and is understood by the organisation, the new planning process should try to build on to it. This does not mean that all existing systems should be considered sacred, but it does mean that any necessary changes to integrate them into the new planning process should be made with care.

The sorts of planning mechanisms which organisations are likely to possess include a system of budgetary control, a method of evaluating capital expenditure projects, and possibly a personal objectives or targeting system linked to a regular performance review. There may be a particularly good style of budgetary performance review meeting which could be readily used as a model for some of the planning meetings. The organisation may make a habit of holding regular top management conferences to review problems and strategies: possibly these can be integrated into the planning process. Some parts of the organisation might make a particularly effective use of forecasts of events of the environment; others might be especially skilled in the use of operational research or highly sophisticated forecasting methods.

These examples are given only to make the point. There may be many other good things in the organisation which are worth preserving or developing. Equally likely is the probability that many of the mechanisms examined will be found to be inadequate or incompatible with the new planning process and will have to be changed.

It is fairly easy to identify the mechanisms in use in any organisation with only a moderate amount of probing. Once this has been done it is possible to define the objectives of each of the mechanisms and to assess whether the reality of the performance is close to what was sought. More detailed probing may be needed to uncover some of the less obvious strengths and weaknesses. For example, in one such examination (reported more fully in Young and Hussey (1977)[1]) structured interviews were carried out with about 25% of all the managers directly involved in the company's planning and budgeting mechanisms to establish the way in which they were involved, their opinions of the mechanism, and the actions they took to fulfil their part. This led to the construction of an inventory of good and bad points which was of help in designing the new process. At the same time the widespread discussion of planning issues at a practical level enabled managers to feel a measure of involvement in the shape of the new process. (This aspect was later reinforced when the new process was discussed with all senior managers in groups of 5-8 at a time.)

What is Expected from Planning?

In Chapter 2 we identified the main reasons for and features of a corporate planning process. At the level of a general book this analysis is valid and helpful. At the level of the individual organisation such statements can easily become generalisations unless thought is given to them in the context of that organisation. A planning process should be seen by the organisation as a response to either a perceived problem or a perceived opportunity. If this is done the expectations of the new planning initiative can be defined and priorities assigned to each expectation.

This analysis serves two purposes. The first is that it should help the chief executive to ensure that he really is introducing planning for valid reasons. If his expectations are all generalisations, unrelated to real issues within his organisation, the chances are that either he has not thought deeply about the subject or that he does not really need planning. In either case, possibly, he should think again before committing the company to the corporate planning path.

The second purpose is concerned with the effectiveness of the process. If the main issue faced by the company is inability to attain forecasts, it might be that the initial thrust of the process should be on improving forecasting technique and obtaining a greater degree of personnel commitment to forecasts. This may be a very different solution to the company whose main difficulty is to develop a corporate identity from a number of diverse operations. Here the answer might be to expand more effort on the communication and co-ordination aspects of planning.

Another useful approach is to look at the problem from two viewpoints. What does the corporate body need or expect and what do its subsidiaries need or expect if they are to play their parts in the process? In some instances these are mirror images of each other, although this is not always true. Table 12.1 shows how these views might work out.

By this point the chief executive should be able to move from a consideration of his expectations to a decision about how to try to realise them. It is unlikely that he will be able to introduce a process of planning without some help, and, indeed, many have already had to seek this to answer these first three questions. If help is needed he has three possible ways to obtain it: outside consultants, a planning committee, or the appointment of a corporate planner.

TABLE 12.1
Corporate planning needs/expectations

Corporate level	Divisional/subsidiary level
1. *"Portfolio" management*: to balance risks, returns, and cash flows with corporate objectives, strategies and resources	1. *Strategy*: acceptability to headquarters and compatability with the organisation as a whole
2. *Financial planning*: the use of the financial resources in the best interests of the organisation	2. *Knowledge of financial objectives*: what does the head office require (profit growth, return on assets, cash flows)?
3. *Strategy gaps*: managing the overall shape of the organisation so that objectives can be met (this recognises that strategy may be more than the sum of the divisional plans)	3. What financial resources are available to the unit?
4. Reconciliation of conflicting divisional interests	4. *A positive reaction*: plans should be properly discussed with and approval (or otherwise) communicated by head office.
5. *Soundness and compatibility of plans*: to be sure that the plans of units of the business are sound and compatible (e.g. common assumptions, performance/promise analysis)	5. What are the company's corporate objectives?
	6. What is the planning style? Guidance on approach and methods
6. Overall objectives of the corporation in response to "stakeholders"	7. The desire to participate by providing ideas and advice which will help to shape the whole organisation.
7. Style of corporate planning	8. Knowledge of any corporate assumptions about external events and an opportunity to discuss these.
8. *Control*: making sure the organisation is on course	
9. To ensure that the company as a whole is responding to changes caused by external stimuli	9. A process of planning which fits divisional management needs and is an integral part of total management – rather than an annual paper exercise conducted solely for head office.
10. *Creativity*: ideas and help from the units which will assist the shaping of corporate objectives and strategy.	

Outside Consultants

Specialist help on a temporary basis may be what is needed: partly because a high level of skill is required to introduce a planning process, and this is not always easy to find from other sources; and partly because the nature of the tasks is different and the manpower requirement heavier during the early stages of introduction. A consultant can bring an objective viewpoint and — if chosen wisely — a high degree of personal skill to the company.

But there are consultants and consultants. Quite separate from the fact that some are better than others is the question of their own approach to the problem. Some consultancies specialising in corporate planning are strategists rather than process consultants. This means that they can do an excellent job in helping a company define its strategies and can help produce a first-class top-level plan. They may not, however, have the skills to develop an on-going process of planning for the organisation. Then there are consultants who will design a process of planning for a client and pass it over to him as if it were a piece of software for the computer. Possibly of more use for the type of approach discussed in this book are consultants who apply a "process" rather than a "task" concept. These will work with the client's managers to help them design and implement the new process: assisting organisations to do their own planning rather than attempting to do it for them. This type of consultancy carries a high degree of training with it, and the aim is not only to solve the problem but to develop the client's own people so that the solution is implemented. Such consultants will be well aware of the impact that corporate planning can have on the organisation of the enterprise, and will take account of the behavioural implications in all aspects of their work.

A Planning Committee

Some organisations have used a planning committee to introduce a process of planning. Our opinion is that this is unlikely to be an appropriate move because many of the tasks which have to be carried out are not suitable for committee action. There may be good reasons for setting up a committee to work with the consultant or the organisation's own corporate planning manager. Similarly, the chief executive may find it advantageous to appoint a top-level planning committee to help him evaluate plans before they are presented to the main board.

There are two main reasons why a committee will fail if it is the only means the company is using to implement planning. The first is that the infinite variety of tasks which have to be carried out to implement any planning process will defeat any committee which does not have at least one full-time top-level executive assigned to the task, in other words, which does not have a planner. The second is that a committee itself consists of a network of interpersonal relationships. Much of the work of introducing planning is of an interpersonal nature. It is difficult for any executive who is not on the committee itself to develop a relationship with the "committee". His difficulties must be dealt with on a person-to-person basis. When such tasks are split up among the members of the committee, two more problems arise: Do all committee members understand and respond to the issues in a compatible way? Will each committee member have the ability to get the relationship he has negotiated accepted by the other members?

Few committees, for any purpose, give complete satisfaction to those using or participating in them. They are notoriously difficult to manage, and can easily become talking shops or paper generators.

A Company Planning Manager

From the discussion so far it will be seen that we do not see committees as a sensible alternative to the use of an outside consultant. The appointment of a company planner is a genuine option (although this may also be additional to using a consultant). A company corporate planning manager may be recruited from outside the organisation, in which case the selection process should ensure that he really is an expert and a better choice than anyone who might be appointed from inside. It must be a senior appointment, since it operates at top management level, and the person in the function has to be able to both discuss and criticise planning decisions made at all levels in the company. Although rightly described by some experts as an extension of the chief executive, he must be an extension with his own critical faculty of judgement: this rules out all yes-men or people too junior to have any credibility.

The personal characteristics required for a good corporate planner are numerous. It is important that he possesses strong leadership capabilities, is a first-class communicator, is seen as an expert in his field, and has good intellectual qualities. Expertise is the most difficult thing to acquire since he will need not only knowledge of the process but must also be skilled in some of the techniques. Few, if any, managers can hope to gain expert knowledge of all the techniques a planner might need. However, not all companies will need all the techniques, which means that expertise will be judged on his knowledge of those that are relevant to the organisation. Certainly he must be a broad man, and not one who sees planning as dominated by his basic functional skill. Good experienced planners are still hard to find if only because most of them have qualities which put them in line for other key jobs in the organisation.

One further point not always recognised is that the nature of the planning task is very different at early and late stages of an organisation's adoption of corporate planning. It can be very stimulating for a planner to move into a company to help it design and implement a process of planning and to help it define its strategy for the first time. In a very dynamic organisation with an ambitious growth objective, this stimulation may continue indefinitely. Most companies are not in this category, and once the process is working properly the planner's task may become more repetitive and less exciting. This is in direct contrast to the qualities sought in the planner, and it is not therefore surprising that the average corporate planner will change his job every three or four years either because of an internal promotion or because he leaves to take on a more stimulating assignment in a new organisation. Those who wish to retain their planner for their organisation should be aware of this change in the planning job, and take action either to transfer him or do something to enlarge his responsibilities.

There is another problem about the corporate planning job. Not only is the good planner trying to work himself out of the job but he is unlikely to see it as his ultimate ambition in any company. It is certainly senior enough: to do his job he should be at board level, but there is a feeling that it is a younger man's job. While a planner might see himself functioning well in this position at 35, 45, or even 55, there is a nagging doubt that beyond this he may run into some sort of age barrier. Few can conceive the planning function as an immediate pre-retirement-at-65 type of job. Another reason why the planner has to move on in the organisation and why few can contemplate being a planner for all their board-level working life.

The alternative to outside recruitment is an internal appointment, and this has many attractions. Provided a careful choice is made, it is possible to obtain a planner who already has an established position in the organisation and is acceptable to his colleagues. Some companies have used planning as a regular two-three year posting for senior managers who are scheduled to move on to another senior management post at the end of the period. The dangers to avoid in internal selection are:

*The appointment of a senior manager already regarded by his colleagues as over the hill. This can be a severe temptation as an attempt to remove a senior, poor-performing, long-service employee to a position with considerable prestige. Planning cannot be treated in this way, and although the intentions behind the action may be humane, the damage that can be done to the organisation (and to the self-confidence of an inadequate planner) is enormous.

*Giving the appointment to the bright young MBA as "good training". It may succeed in developing the manager, but has the potential to wreck the organisation. To make planning work the corporate planner must be able to talk on equal terms with all senior managers. He must be a member of the top management team, not a junior with potential. (However this can work if the junior is very much an assistant to the chief executive and spends his time on analytical rather than motivational tasks and if supported by outside consultancy or internal skills.)

*To appoint a good man of appropriate skills and seniority and to expect him to immediately know everything about planning is a recipe for failure. He must be given the opportunity to learn the philosophy and concepts, either outside the organisation in an academic institution or by providing appropriate training and counselling inside the company. (This may be where a firm of outside consultants can help.)

*To force an unwilling manager into the job. The role of corporate planner is a demanding one, which calls for a measure of dedication and dynamism. The unwilling planner may not be enthusiastic enough to be able to carry others with him. Worse is if the planning role becomes equated with an unpleasant but necessary task, which is only undertaken because somebody has to do it.

Designing a Planning Process

Published case histories and books on corporate planning can be of considerable help to the organisation embarking on planning for the first time. Few of the published planning systems can be lifted from the printed page and dropped neatly into the organisation without effort. Considerable work has to be carried out with skill to match the process to the organisation and its needs.

The questions asked by the chief executive before he embarked on the process should provide much of the data needed for the specialist to design the process. Fundamentally, the planning process must:

* Be compatible with the organisational style.
* Fit the structure of the organisation (which means reinforcing reporting relationships).
* Meet the major needs facing the organisation and be sensitive to its problems.
* Fit in with other corporate time tables (e.g., budget, personal appraisals, review of management objectives).
* Gain widespread management support, which means among other things that it must be perceived as relevant.

It is easy to underestimate the amount of work that should go into the design of a planning process. One of the biggest problems is to match the formality of the system with a need to avoid unnecessary paper work. Many planning processes resemble computers in their ability to generate a mountain of paper. Care must be exercised to see that only the right level of detail is passed on to the next higher level of management, so that the chief executive of a multi-divisional company is not, for example, showered with all the operational detail needed by the managers of his subsidiaries.

As planning should be a process function rather than a mechanistic analysis, opportunities should be provided for planning meetings and reviews to take place. The temptation to ask every manager of every function to produce a mini-corporate plan should be avoided where the same ends can be served by building in a formal discussion.

Just as the plans themselves must be flexible to survive, so must the process itself be flexible enough to cope with adverse circumstances such as upset time tables, the disparate qualities of different managers, and the varieties of management style within the organisation. Rigid, doctrinaire solutions are unlikely to work, since they ignore the important behavioural issues.

Implementing the Planning Process

Many organisations have thought they were practising corporate planning because the chief executive said they were. Unfortunately, because so much of corporate planning lies in the field of human behaviour, a simple edict is unlikely to bring much in results. Corporate planning without the overt support of the chief executive is also likely to fail, but support alone is insufficient.

What is needed is a programme to help each involved manager to understand the concepts of planning, the overall process as it will work in the organisation and his own role within the process. In addition each manager has to be persuaded to give the process a fair try and to change any adverse attitudes which he might have. This combined educational and attitude change initiative becomes a problem of major proportions in any organisation of size.

One of the first steps should be to write the planning process into a short guide or manual. This is partly to ensure that it has been logically conceived and partly to aid communication and understanding. Most companies that practise corporate planning, including many who do it badly, have planning guides of this type and, as the data they contain is not usually confidential, are often willing to show the guide to outsiders. A published example may be found in Hussey (1974).[2]

The guide itself is only a small step in a major task. Just how the total task will be undertaken is a matter requiring careful consideration in relation to an assessment of the organisation's specific needs. Although indications of possible approaches can be given, no universal solution can be postulated. Factors such as the variations in management and organisational styles, the general level of education of managers, the age/seniority structure of managers, the state of awareness of managers to planning theories, any crises or changes facing the organisation, and the number and geographical spread of managers involved will affect the final solution, and should be taken into account in working out the programme.

The methods which the planner might consider include presentations, personal counselling, educational conferences and courses, and group work. Examples of the practical application of some of these methods has already been given in other contexts, e.g. the previous chapter on strategy.

In order to be more specific we offer a guide to a typical planning situation, that of a newly appointed corporate planner in a company with a number of major divisions, some of which already have planners who have been operating their own concepts independent of head office. It may sound surprising that managing directors of subsidiaries should have developed an approach to planning quite separate from that of the centre, but it is by no means an unusual situation. In our examples we are assuming that our corporate planner has found that some at least of these existing systems have to be modified to fit the new corporate system.

Let us assume that the corporate planner has done a good job of designing the new process, during which he has discussed his ideas and the company needs with a wide spectrum of managers, including those with approaches of their own. If he has done this, those with a proprietary interest in their own systems will have become aware that change is about to take place, will feel that they have been consulted, and should not be actively hostile, although naturally those managers may have a better developed critical faculty than managers to whom the concepts are new. However, human behaviour being what it is, there is at least a possibility that some resentment may be manifested. Equally, those subsidiaries who have never considered a planning process may resent being called upon to change: the more so if their trading results have been consistently good, and possibly better than their fellow subsidiaries who have attempted planning.

Problems of differing organisational style of subsidiaries, internal political relationships, and the almost instinctive human resistance to change, lead to a situation where the planner has to be very careful how he handles the communication, educational, and attitude-change tasks. Fortunately, if the steps we have discussed in this chapter have been considered, the planner will have a good idea of the magnitude of the problem he is facing, and will not be rushing blindly into a minefield of behavioural difficulties.

The planner in the situation described should develop a clear programme of what he intends to do. We suggest the following actions.

(1) Discuss the new process individually with each member of the top team, including the chief executives of major subsidiaries or divisions. In a mammoth organisation spread across the world this may not be a practical step, and other methods may have to be substituted.

(2) Similar discussions should be held with any managers not in the top team who are expected to play a key part in the new process, or with those whose key role under the old system is significantly changed.

(3) In each of these series of discussions care should be taken to explain the way in which the new process will affect the role of the individual. Any ruffled feelings should be smoothed and the planner should handle individual questions and problems with understanding, sympathy, and tact. It is worth remembering that an apparent loss of responsibility (e.g. the budget accountant who is no longer responsible for the five-year projection) may be construed as a threat or a slight by the persons concerned. This must be treated positively.

(4) Once individuals have been counselled, the total process should be presented to the board and any appropriate management committees, to again make sure it is understood, to give opportunity for debate, and to obtain a motion of support.

(5) Set up a series of "workshops" or seminars with any divisional corporate planners to discuss the new process and its implementation into their organisation. In a multi-national with geographical barriers it may be necessary to expand this into a three-to-five-day course to get maximum value out of bringing these managers together. In a one-country organisation it may be convenient to bring the group together for periods of a half-day to a day on a number of occasions. (Indeed, there are situations when considerable benefits can be obtained by bringing this group together at an earlier stage to help with the design work.) Although pimarily a problem-related work session, meetings of this nature provide an opportunity for a straight educational input which can improve the professional capability of the planner as a whole. One important purpose of the workshops in the situation postulated is to make divisional planners aware of the incompatibility of each other's systems, so that there is a growing acceptance of the need to change.

(6) The next step should be to involve the whole of middle

management and to explain the process to them. Some conceptional input should also be provided so that the reasons for the change can be better understood. There are a number of possible ways of dealing with this problem: discuss the issues with each manager individually, hold a series of conferences to explain the process to large numbers of managers at the same time, or hold a series of less formal meetings with groups of up to a dozen managers. In the hypothetical case under discussion a mixture of these methods might be appropriate, supported by similar work by the divisional planners where they exist. The corporate planner has to get the problem down to dimensions which he can solve. In a very large company he may not have the time to hold many small meetings personally, and must either find someone to share the work with him or choose a conference style.

(7) Some managers will require a deeper level of help if they are to play a meaningful role in the planning process. In our example the planner would organise a number of short residential courses to help increase individual skills in planning, which would be designed to cover the needs of selected people. An alternative may be to send people on outside courses. The decisions can be made only after the real needs have been assessed, and the costs and benefits examined.

(8) In Chapter 11 we illustrated a number of approaches to the behavioural aspects of getting people involved in planning; these involved various approaches to group work, usually in real (rather than classroom) situations. In our hypothetical example the corporate planner would realise that there is a wide gap between telling people about a planning process and getting them to implement it in a worthwhile way, and would plan a programme of group work.

(9) Much of the impetus of corporate planning comes from the dynamism of the chief executive and the top management group. The planning process should build in a sufficient number of review meetings, which by their frequency, style, and relevance demonstrate top management concern. Planning will work when it has real meaning to the business, its managers, and the way their performance is judged. Effective reviews form a critical part in making planning "live" in the organisation, and providing a forum for judging planning skills and highlighting areas for improvement.

Analytical Tools

Emphasis in this chapter has been placed on the development of the planning process. As has been stressed so many times in this book, corporate planning is a compound of the behavioural and the analytical. One aspect of the design of any process should, therefore, be concentrated on information input and output, the forecasting methods and techniques which are most relevant, and ways of analysing planning data to arrive at the best solutions.

This aspect of planning process design should take the planner into a study of the critical aspects of the company's business, so that approaches may be selected which help to cope with these issues. Decisions have to be made on the format of plans at different levels in the organisation, how to select and handle environmental data, and what performance criteria should be established.

Many of these impinge on the behavioural aspects of planning. More precise exploration of data, the options open to the company, and their probable outcome is an important part of meaningful planning. The end product of planning should be action, and attention to the human factors which contribute to planning and action is in no way an excuse for mindless meetings and aimless waffle sessions. Emphasis must be on meaningful involvement, which means a measure of discipline must be brought in to blend analytical skills, information, and the behavioural process into a meaningful whole.

The planner has to guard against one thing. This is the development of techniques and analytical methods beyond the level of understanding of the managers in the company. A computerised planning model may be desirable — but only if its use can be explained in terms which managers can understand, so that it becomes a tool and not a barrier. Similarly a sophisticated forecasting technique may be an essential — but only for as long as the experts avoid taking a patronising or superior stance. In other words, there may be many behavioural issues concealed in the analytical aspects of planning as there are in the process itself.

Much of the skill in applying corporate planning lies in the areas covered in this chapter: the application of general and readily definable principles to the specific, individual, and much less readily definable situations. It is usually failures in these skills, rather than the fault of the organisation, which is responsible for disappointments in corporate planning.

References Chapter 12

1. R. Young and D. E. Hussey (1977) Planning at Rolls-Royce Motors, *Long Range Planning*, Vol. No. 2, April 1977.
2. D. E. Hussey (1974) *Corporate Planning: Theory and Practice*, Pergamon Press, Oxford.

CHAPTER 13

Avoiding Mistakes in Planning

Corporate planning is a relatively new concept of management, and it is not surprising that many mistakes have been made in its implementation or that the wrong initial expectations have led to disillusionment in many cases. At the same time some organisations have been successful with their planning efforts. These differences provide a fertile field for research, and in turn add to the general body of knowledge about good planning practice. Fifteen years ago most of the published "do's and don'ts" of planning were based on the personal experience of individuals. Today they are mainly research based.

A significant exception to the earlier writings is provided by Warren (1966),[1] whose careful study remains a classic with findings that are untarnished by time. He argues:[2]

"The major purpose of planning is the development of processes, mechanisms and managerial attitudes which will do two things. First they will make it possible to make commitment decisions today with a greater awareness of future implications, and second they will make it possible to make future decisions more rapidly, more economically, and with less disruption to the ongoing business. More specifically, this emphasis on process and attitudes rather than blue prints is directed to accomplishing the following expectations."

These are a clearer understanding of likely future impacts on present decisions, anticipating areas requiring future decisions, increasing the speed of relevant information flow, and providing for faster and less disruptive implementations of future decisions.

He maintains[3] that executives apply a number of "tests" when planning is introduced into an organisation, and that it is the result of these which determine how seriously they view the initiative, and whether they make any effort to make it work. The tests are:

(1) *Who is chosen as planning director and how is he treated by top management?* A poor calibre or inappropriate person or one on too low a level of seniority can kill corporate planning. If planning is a low-level position, or if it appears to offer a sideways shuffle or demotion for the incompetent, it will certainly fail this first test.

(2) *How much direct backing does the president give longer-range proposals?* This is the old issue of short-term costs positioned against long-term benefits. If the chief executive *talks* about long-term results and the need to plan but establishes investment criteria which prevent anything new happening, or puts all of his real action behind short-term budgeting, managers generally will soon see where his priorities lie. In a way this is a similar problem to the chief executive who exhorts his managers to delegate, and makes demands on them which mean that he expects them to be fully informed and up to date with everything being dealt with in their departments. In effect his behaviour prevents them from delegating, and managers respond to his behaviour rather than his exhortations. If capital to meet a long-term programme has to be justified by short-term pay-back criteria, if all the emphasis is on short-term results, with no discussion of the long term, and if longer-term planning is all platitudes, managers again will act according to behaviour rather than exhortation.

(3) *What is management's response to strong and weak planning effort?* Few managers will take the time and trouble to plan well unless a critical judgement is applied to the plan by the chief executive and his corporate staff. This is not to suggest that managers are incapable of planning well, but simply that when under pressure for current results, few will devote the additional effort and cost needed for good planning if top management greet good and bad plans with the same reaction? Why should they? In these circumstances good planning is not part of the corporate game they are playing. If the rules (by observed behaviour) are that a successful manager throws together some financial predictions which reflect wishful thinking supported by a few pages of wordy platitudes, then this is what all managers will tend to do.

(4) *How much emphasis is given to long-range planning in determining bonuses, promotions, etc?* The acid test in Warren's view is who gets promoted or obtains the biggest bonuses and the best salary increases. If the rewards go mainly to the short-term operators, who may even be damaging the future by their behaviour, the rest of the managers will note the lesson and act accordingly.

A reward system based only on short-term results which relies on retribution for poor planning coming at some future date, will usually mean that corporate planning fails. The retribution usually rebounds on the company, not the individual manager, who by then has probably been promoted and is busy piling up future problems on an even wider scale. For the company "tomorrow always arrives".

What Warren is stressing is that these tests allow managers to assess the depth of the chief executive's commitment to corporate planning. Virtually every case study, most researchers, and all writers on planning stress this need for commitment.

Underlying Warren's message is another: the need to understand the planning process. The empty platitudes which some chief executives use when talking about planning frequently demonstrate their ignorance and lack of involvement and betray to other managers in the organisation their feeling that planning does not matter all that much.

Warren's was one of the earliest research-based contributions to causes of success and failure in corporate planning, and remains valid.

Equally interesting is the work of Steiner (1972),[4] who asked organisations to rank fifty common pitfalls which should be avoided in corporate planning in order of importance. The sample covered 215 organisations. The top ten pitfalls from this survey are discussed below.

1. *Top Management's assumption that it can delegate the planning function to a planner.* Steiner (1972)[5] comments: "Had the respondents to the questionnaire been predominantly chief executive officers of companies with formal planning systems I am certain that this pitfall would not have been named the number one to avoid. Since most of the responses were by corporate planners I am not surprised it was identified as number one." It is a recurring theme in many studies of planning, and

in gatherings of corporate planners. Parts of the planning task can be delegated (otherwise why have a corporate planner?), but the central core of strategic decision making must be retained. And unless the chief executive retains an involvement in the planning process, managers will begin to opt out. It is precisely this that Warren's tests set out to reveal. Pennington (1972)[6] makes a plea for selective involvement of chief executives. They do not have to drown themselves in the administration of the planning process or in reading every document generated. They do have to become involved at the stages where it matters: reviews of plans, major decisions, and follow-up of planning efforts.

2. *Top Management becomes so engrossed in current problems that it spends insufficient time on long range planning, and the process becomes discredited among other managers and staff.* Good planning requires a blend of attention to both the present and the future. Neglect of the future is likely to lead to bad planning. Neglect of the present can mean that the company has no future to plan for. Many writers have stressed that corporate planning is not a solution for a current crisis although it may help a company coming out of a crisis to avoid the next one. When a ship is sinking it may be more effective to man the pumps than to prepare the cargo loading chart for its next scheduled port of call. Yet the introduction of planning is often associated with a major crisis, and because management attention is limited and must be directed at priorities, it is not surprising that disappointment often results.

3. *Failure to develop company goals suitable as a basis for formulating long-range plans.* Steiner (1972)[7] observes that those facing this pitfall fell into a number of categories. Some were in companies where goals were stated in only the vaguest of terms, like "make the best acquisition possible" or our old friend "maximise profits". Platitudes such as these make it harder to plan because they give no guidance. The second category is companies where objectives and goals are always wildly optimistic and can rarely be achieved. This does not even serve the purpose of stimulating greater effort: the stretching effect of well-defined objectives only works when extra effort can put the objective within grasp.

A third, and in our experience very common category, is where the head office gives insufficient guidance to its divisions. In some cases this is because the head office cannot, rather than from wilful neglect, but in either case the result can frustrate good planning.

What this pitfall really is, is a failure of the planning process that the company has developed. Some of the other pitfalls are also of this type, and take us back to the principles developed in earlier chapters. Good corporate planning is hard to do, and is almost certain to fail when critical steps in the planning process are overlooked or deliberately ignored.

4. *Failure to assure the necessary involvement in the planning process of major line personnel.* We have discussed "involvement" from several viewpoints, and stress that our own experiences completely reinforce Steiner's research findings. The way to get bad planning is for all planning activities to be delegated to a staff planner. Not only does this run into the danger of ivory tower plans, another problem against which many authorities give consistent warnings, but even good staff plans tend to be rejected by the line managers who have to implement them and who are responsible for results. In our view this is closely related to pitfall 7, discussed below, and strongly underlines the need for the entire management to be trained in and understand the principles of planning. It is too easy for the line manager who does not understand the principles to try to pass off the work of planning to a staff specialist in order to remove a current work pressure: it is tempting for the planner struggling against deadlines to do the job himself rather than involve a reluctant manager. In either case this is the road to disaster.

5. *Failure to use plans as standards for measuring managerial performance.* This is closely akin to Warren's test 3, and is related to our belief that planning must be seen as having links with other management processes and systems. Figure 2.1 showed links between corporate planning, personal objectives, budgetary control, and capital budgeting. There should be a relationship between personnel systems (such as annual appraisals, training need assessments) and the corporate plan. Where there is no link, corporate plans tend to lose their effectiveness. All processes

should be like cog-wheels which can interact, although sometimes indirectly, with all other processes in the company. Where there is no link it is like a cog which has no teeth. It may rotate very happily on its own axis, but will have no effect whatsoever on any of the other cogs in the system.

6. *Failure to create a climate in the company which is congenial and not resistant to planning.* It is fairly obvious that the wrong climate will kill off planning very successfully. It is significant that this is seen to be a serious pitfall in the opinion of experienced planners. It is equally significant that this is part of Warren's theses, and that it is an issue which appears in many other researches.

This being so, it begs the question of why chief executives try to introduce corporate planning without getting the climate right. The answer, regrettably, is that many do not know enough about planning to understand the importance of this issue.

7. *Assuming that corporate comprehensive planning is something separate from the entire management process.* Planning is a part of the total management process. It contains a cross-section of everything there is to that process. Management in its entirety is more than planning, but is certainly incomplete without it. Those who see corporate planning as a discrete task which has nothing to do with current problems (pitfall 2), line managers (pitfall 4), or other management processes (pitfall 5) will waste any time or money which they invest in corporate planning.

8. *Injecting so much formality into the system that it lacks flexibility, looseness, and simplicity, and restrains creativity.* Formality of planning processes is not the same as rigid form filling, although often the two are confused. A common mistake is to design an approach which fits large units within a group and to impose it willy-nilly on the smaller units for whom it becomes an irrelevant burden. Problems in stimulating creativity and the "little boxes" approach to planning have been discussed in earlier chapters. Steiner (1972)[8] states: "It was my general observation from

around 1955 to about 1965 that formal planning systems were moving toward more rather than less formality. Since the mid-1960s formal planning seems to have been moving towards the loose, flexible and simple."

One of the underlying causes of this simplification is, of course, the growing awareness of the problem brought by over-complicating planning. Another, in our opinion, is an acceptance of the fallibility of planning. In the earlier period there seemed to be a belief that what was planned was almost certain to come true: a forecast once made was bound to be correct. Managers were invited to attend seminars with titles like the "Control of Corporate Destiny". If belief was that strong, it was an act of faith to try to plan in precise detail.

With greater experience has come the understanding that the name of the game is awareness of, and strategic response to, change, and an acceptance of the fact that formal planning is partly about making changes to a defined strategy with some awareness of the various possible outcomes. Ringbakk (1969)[9] pointed to a weakness in many companies' plan: that they were based on one-point forecasts, and gave an impression of inevitability, which was increasingly being seen as unreal. Once the fallibility of planning is perceived, over-rigid formality becomes an unproductive burden. The benefits of planning are released by processes which, in Steiner's words, have "flexibility, looseness, and simplicity".

9. *Failure of top management to review with departmental and divisional heads the long-range plans they have developed.* Here we again see the ghosts of Warren's tests. A failure to review leads to a feeling that top management does not really care about planning. Some divisional managers, who are themselves committed to the concept of planning, would attempt to do a good job of planning despite this. Even so, good attempts can be frustrated by lack of feedback, if for no other reason than that the divisional managers may never learn whether their strategies fit the total corporate strategy, or whether the company as a whole intends to back them. The rejection of a well thought out strategy on which a subsidiary may have spent much time and effort always tends to be demotivating, and is more so when it comes through the post, in a brief letter, without there being the opportunity for proper discussion.

One of the reasons for a planning process is communication. This implies that the receiver should hear the message that the sender is actually transmitting, should respond to it, and in turn his message should be received as he intends it to be.

The way in which plans are reviewed is critical. In earlier chapters we have recommended an approach to the planning process which treats strategy formulation as something preliminary to detailed planning. At the "strategic review" stage there should be a supportive approach to discussing these issues of mutual concern to subsidiary and corporate headquarters. The purpose here is to ensure that the viewpoint of both parties is defined, explored, and understood. In our opinion the chief executive must give adequate time to preparing for this meeting (with staff help) and must run it. At the second stage the review may be more probing and more a question of giving corporate approval than in a mutual exploration of possible strategies, which has already been done. This is the meeting when a hardnosed attitude may be taken to the expected results of plans, the validity of forecasts, and whether the plan provides for adequate performance. Although this meeting may be shorter and have a higher level of analytical input from support staff, it is difficult to conceive of it being carried out in any other way than a top-level discussion between at least the chief executives of the group and each division or subsidiary.

10. *Top Management's consistently rejecting the formal planning mechanism by making intuitive decisions which conflict with formal plans.* Steiner (1972)[10] says of this: "Whenever a company falls into this trap it means that the top manager is, in effect, delegating the planning function to someone else and if plans do not sit well with him they are rejected. It means insufficient involvement of the top manager in the planning process. It also means a lack of understanding of the requirements for successful, formal planning. In such a company the climate for effective planning is absent." In our opinion such a defect may also point to inadequate attention to strategy in the planning process, if for no other reason than that many companies have still to discover how to blend the analytical and behavioural aspects of planning.

As previously mentioned, Steiner's list of pitfalls includes another forty which fell outside the top ten of the survey, although many are potentially lethal. We shall devote the remainder of this chapter to one issue: the internal political aspect of corporate planning. Steiner (1972)[11] refers to aspects of this in two of his other points to avoid pitfalls: (a) "The power structure in the company must not be ignored in the development and operation of the planning process." (b) "The decision-making process in a company is infused with political, social and other considerations. To think that it is a completely rational process, in the sense that any fairminded person would come to the same conclusion with the inputs which were used, is to misunderstand not only the decision-making process but the human mind."

The political aspects of planning have received inadequate attention. We would certainly have included them in the top ten pitfalls had we been producing our own listing rather than reporting research evidence. The fact that it did not feature at the top in the survey could be either that respondents had not encountered the problem or that they had not recognised it.

Irving (1970)[12] found that one-third of his sample had encountered internal political problems in establishing corporate planning. The majority of planners claimed to have encountered no such problems.

Pettigrew (1975)[13] makes a particularly useful contribution to understanding "the political context of the specialist's (or internal consultant's) work by focusing on some of the strategic factors which affect the long term viability of specialist units".

Figure 13.1 shows his classification of the evolution of specialist units (which would include the planning department) into phases.

Conception Phase

All the firms studied by Pettigrew had set up the new specialist unit either because of an "internal political drama in the company, such as the loss and gain of a key director or directors, or a reaction to a major environmental change". That these reasons are usually the basic causes for the introduction of corporate planning with its specialist planning department has been demonstrated by the research of Irving (1970)[12] and Denning and Lehr (1971/2).[14] At the conception phase the specialist group tends to be associated with a successful protagonist in the "political

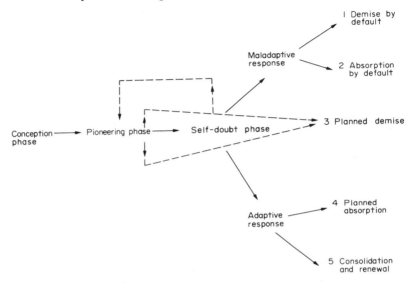

Fig. 13.1. Evolutionary phases of specialist units.
(From Pettigrew, 1975[13].)

drama" or a particular happening. Often this results in the hasty recruitment of a manager for the new unit, who in turn sets out to recruit and manage the first group of professionals that form the new unit. "The essential characteristics of the conception are a sudden unplanned act of creation out of a combination of internal or external change."

Pioneering Phase

At the outset there is apparent clarity about the role of the new group, and it starts doing what it is set up to do with great enthusiasm. The members of the group typically have a high involvement and commitment to the group, its goals and tasks. Often the togetherness of the group leads them to appear increasingly different from the rest of the organisation. Differences may take the form of dress, language, or behaviour, and will be accentuated by the development of the group's identity. Leadership style often consists of the new manager taking on a barrier role to protect his new department from the pressures of the organisation. Lines of tension may also develop within the group.

"The single most pervasive source of tension in the case study specialist units was between the 'talkers' and the 'doers', between those with a long term perspective and those with a short term view of the group, those who wanted to further the long term interests of the group and those who wanted to demonstrate immediate tactical gains."

In our experience this sort of tension often appears in planning departments, between, for example, those who believe an immediate "success" is essential to establish credibility, and those who are more concerned with building a long-term process.

Pettigrew's findings were that this tension aided problem solving in the pioneering phase, but the fact that the pragmatists tended to dominate those concerned with the longer-term strategy of the group helped to develop the later self-doubt phase.

The rest of the organisation, because of the inward-looking nature of the group, tends to "disinterest, lack of awareness and silent acceptisism".

Self-doubt Phase

The self-doubt phase begins to set in once the original task to which the specialist group committed its energies nears completion. Typically this is about eighteen months from conception. The batch of reports and activities generated give the group a new visibility to the rest of the organisation "Because the process of diagnosis has been largely consultant centred and not client centred, with a great deal of the specialists' linkage being with their political sponsor and much of the important synthesising of the diagnostic data going on in the closed walls of the specialist unit, there are many surprises in the initial reports. Some groups in the organisation may suddenly find themselves confronted by specialists of whose existence they had been in virtual ignorance.

The reaction is resistance to change, the feeling of being threatened, with all the problems discussed elsewhere in this book. There may be active or passive hostility to the specialist group, the more so if the original political sponsor moves on or otherwise withdraws support.

Pettigrew found that all the groups he studied tended to over-perceive the degree of threat posed to its existence by the organisation. This may be particularly so if the original heavy work volumes tend to decline, and individuals begin to worry about their role, the value of their work, and their careers. Initial tensions, swamped by the group spirit of the pioneering phase, tend to widen. A leadership crisis may occur in the specialist group.

"The general picture of the self-doubt phase is of a group receiving its first real feedback from its environment, some of it positive and some negative but a great deal more of it confused, and difficult to interpret, of the group overperceiving the degree of threat in its environment and turning in on itself and its leadership system and, in effect, creating more uncertainty for itself rather than managing some of the original causes of doubt."

Re-cycling

Temporary salvation may come from the group being given a new task, which thrusts it back into the pioneering phase. Eventually there will be a tendency to reach the self-doubt phase.

The self-doubt phase may be of little consequence when the group terminates as a "planned demise", such as the disbanding of a task force set up to complete a specific project.

Where planned demise does not take place, Pettigrew's finding is that the group develops either a maladaptive or adaptive response, which in turn changes the group's future.

Maladaptive Response

The maladaptive responses come about because of distinct patterns of human behaviour. Typical maladaptive responses are:

* Reacting to symptoms of problems instead of causes.
* Withdrawing from pressure sources instead of facing up to them.
* Avoidance of risk, and therefore failure to add to the "capital of

credibility" of the group.

*A hardening of lines of association and disassociation within the group, and between the group and the rest of the organisation.

A typical situation which will be familiar to many is the specialist group which begins to turn its energies from constructive activities to destructive carping and criticism. Other people are labelled as ignorant, incompetent, unreliable, power hungry, inefficient, or whatever term comes to mind, and are blamed for the situation in which the group now finds itself. The feeling of isolation increases. "The picture being painted is of a group of people reacting to a doubt by turning in on itself; of being passive, letting the world happen to it rather than trying to create its own world, and when the group tries to initiate, driving it in a unilateral rather than co-operative fashion."

Pettigrew states that the extent to which the maladaptive response occurs is variable. The symptoms described are matters of degree, not absolute. The actions of the group produce secondary effects within the group, and between itself and the organisation "before the group know where it is, it may have engineered a self-fulfilling prophecy; its demise".

Another frequent result of a maladaptive response is the unplanned absorption of the specialist group into another group which is perceived in a more favourable light by the organisation.

Adaptive Responses

Pettigrew maintains that adaptive responses are concerned with building processes and relationships in a way that seeks to understand and confront the causes of self-doubt and rejection. The ways in which response strategies are formulated are more important than the responses themselves.

This contention will strike chords of memory. Many will have heard planners claim that the process of planning is more important than the plan itself. And a major feature of this book has been the emphasis of involvement and human behaviour, rather than relying only on the analytical.

"The central thrust of adaptive strategies are towards the diagnosis of the causes of self-doubt, real and imagined, and the formulation, implementation and continuous monitoring of these strategies in such a way that the specialist unit deals both with problems in its internal makeup and across the boundaries of the unit to the market place of service it hopes to thrive in. The key-notes to this approach to strategy management are diagnosis and anticipation, not carried out unilaterally but in relation to the needs and experiences of its potential and actual clients."

The lesson to be learned by planning departments is that they cannot survive in isolation from the organisation or in a role that is purely a one-way information flow. Contact should be wider than with those who Pettigrew calls "clients" and the (usually) one "political sponsor". One strategy might be for the group to gain access to important policy committees, and this is one reason why we believe the corporate planner should be a board-level appointment on equal terms with other directors. This gives the group access to the most important policy committees in the organisation.

A widespread of linkages should be developed. Pettigrew suggests.

> *Physical movement of the specialist unit.* The aim here is to prevent geographical isolation and encourage informal contact. One of the worst traps is to put a new specialist department in a separate building exclusively for their use. This is often a locational solution which appeals to the organisation and the missionary group. It fosters the "togetherness" of the group but acts against the building of relationships with others. The location of the specialist departments should be checked to ensure that it aids contact between the department and the rest of the company.

> *Planned liaison.* To set up systematic procedures (such as an inter-departmental steering committee) which forces regular contact with a wide range of people.

> *Decentralisation.* Splitting up the work of the specialist department and physically locating some of its personnel in the user department. An alternative to this is the setting up of project teams with joint membership of the specialist and other groups.

> *Personnel policies.* To recruit personnel for the specialist group from inside the company or with company compatibility in mind,

or to arrange secondment of personnel from other areas to the group for short periods.

The results of adaptive rsponses may be either a *planned* absorption of the specialist group with another, or the consolidation and continued renewal of the group, so that its position in the organisation becomes firmly established.

Planning departments have one advantage in that their size is usually small, and frequently is only one or two people. Although lack of numbers makes it harder to maintain regular visibility at all levels, it also means that those in the department are more responsive to the contacts they do have. There is no filter of inter-personal relations or organisational barriers within the group itself.

Wide contact, follow up of processes and plans, and an acute awareness of the political power links must be part of the stock in trade of every successful planner. If he blunders along, producing test-book plans which fit a paper but unreal organisation, offending by accident, and not knowing who or when to involve others, the planner will surely fail.

All this says is that the behavioural aspects of planning are of critical importance: and by now this statement should come as no surprise.

References Chapter 13

1. E. K. Warren (1966) *Long Range Planning: The Executive Viewpoint*, Prentice-Hall.
2. E. K. Warren (1966) op. cit., p. 29.
3. E. K. Warren (1966) op. cit., pp. 51–60.
4. G. A. Steiner (1972) *Pitfalls in Comprehensive Long Range Planning*, Planning Executives Institute.
5. G. A. Steiner (1972) op. cit., p. 13.
6. M. A. Pennington (1972) Why has planning failed?, *Long Range Planning*, March 1972.
7. G. A. Steiner (1972) op. cit., p. 15.
8. G. A. Steiner (1972) op. cit., p. 19.
9. K. A. Ringbakk (1969) Organised planning in major U.S. companies, *Long Range Planning*, Vol. 2, No. 2, December.
10. G. A. Steiner (1972) op. cit., p. 20.
11. G. A. Steiner (1972) op. cit., pp. 23 and 24.
12. P. Irving (1970) Corporate planning in practice: a study of the development of organised planning in major U.K. companies. M.Sc. dissertation, University of Bradford.

13. A. M. Pettigrew (1975) Strategic aspects of the management of specialist activity, *Personnel Review*. Vol. 4, November.
14. B. W. Denning and M. E. Lehr (1971/2) The extent and nature of corporate long range planning in the U.K., Parts 1 and 2, *Journal of Management Studies*, Vol. 8, May 1971; Vol. 9, February 1972.

CHAPTER 14

Monitoring and Controlling

Planning is not an exact science. Time may make a plan inappropriate, and unfortunately for the planners this is the rule rather than the exception. The things that can go wrong with a plan are:

*The assumptions on which the plan was based may prove to be incorrect.
*Implementation may bring results which were not what was forecast nor what management intended.
*Key factors within the organisation may have changed (perhaps the death or resignation of key people or an alteration in the level of internally generated cash flows).
*Actions may not be implemented because of human failings or errors or may be implemented at the wrong time or in a distorted manner.

The best analysis of a situation made today will often prove to be inaccurate tomorrow. Problems may be caused when the results of a plan are better than forecast, e.g. an over trading situation, just as they may result from failure to achieve the forecast. Even when a plan is achieved, a shift in circumstances may suddenly make it the wrong plan. Plans may fail through human error, the sheer difficulty of forecasting events accurately, or the complete impossibility (except by chance alone) of predicting some external environmental changes. Good planning recognises these imperfections, and an effective planning process will incorporate the need to exercise vigilance and be ready to adjust plans to new circumstances.

The aim of all planning activity must be to have actions and the best possible results as the end products. Planning is not an end in itself. The significance of monitoring and controlling is that it helps to ensure that the "right" decisions are implemented, and that the "wrong" ones are altered. Slavish adherence to an inappropriate plan may be more damaging than failure to implement an appropriate one. When actions are inappropriate they should be changed in a coherent and orderly fashion. When they have been overlooked, or turn out badly because of human failing, management has a need to know.

It is important that monitoring and controlling be seen as an integrated part of the planning process. Although each control mechanism may measure only one of the subsystems of the total process, the decisions which result should be made with the total process in mind.

Monitoring is subject to a number of problems, not least of which are those in the field of human behaviour, to which we will return later in this chapter. Sometimes, too, it is hard or impossible to obtain the appropriate data to monitor a plan, and in any case the only results which can be monitored are those which have happened. There is always judgement to be applied over whether a variance is an acceptable temporary departure from the desired trend, or whether it indicates a longer-term change which should be taken into account. The danger is that short-term solutions will be applied, and the issue is complicated by the fact that in some situations even an off-trend result which is almost certain to come "right" may cause short-term effects which the company cannot afford to ignore. Although we may live for the long term, we always die in the present.

Figure 2.1 provides a model from which we can begin to examine the different monitoring and controlling mechanisms and their relationship with each other. If the logic of the process is followed, planning begins with assumptions derived from a study of the business environment in which the organisation operates. This process was described in some detail in Chapter 10. Assumptions at their best are forecasts and assessments made from an intelligent study of the available information: at their worst they are estimates where the organisation lacks any real knowledge of the event. In either situation they are subject to error. The environment provides the first area which should be subjected to monitoring, the control element being a feedback of information to the appropriate level of management so that any necessary corrective action may be taken. This means that the study of the environment must be a continuous process. Under modern conditions it is rarely sufficient for an annual assessment of the environment to be made as a special exercise. Information must be assessed far more frequently than this.

In a few cases issues will be straightforward. An assumption about corporation tax rates next year will in due course prove to be either right or wrong. If wrong, cash flows may be affected and plans may require change. Most issues are less straightforward. Many assumptions are nothing more than the best possible forecast of future events: short-term changes may not "prove" them to be right or wrong but may indicate that the forecast is likely to be unreliable. In these situations a new assumption may be judged necessary, but whether the fresh assessment will come over with sufficient strength to justify changes to the plan is a matter requiring definite decisions.

Sometimes it is not practical for environmental factors to be assessed in detail on a continuous basis. If market surveys are necessary, it is unlikely that they can be carried out more often than once per year and it may be even less frequent. In these cases an attempt, should be made to identify and monitor indicative data, so that potential changes to trends are observed. Even forecasts of the economy may be difficult to make in depth more than once or twice per year. Here economic statistics can be plotted against the forecast to show major departures, or economic forecasts from outside agencies may be used to indicate an apparent need for more detailed work.

The monitoring of assumptions has two prerequisites. The first is that the assumption is defined in a way that can be monitored. For example, there is little value in expressing inflation only in terms of the consumer price index, as this measurement is only published once per year, about a year in arrears, and is subject to retrospective amendment. If this particular definition of inflation is considered to have value for the company, it must be accompanied by some more mundane but more readily available indicators.

The second prerequisite is a clear understanding of who is responsible for monitoring assumptions for the organisation. In all but the smallest of enterprises this task may be divided among activities, levels of management, or geographically. A definition of responsibilities should be attempted to prevent wasteful overlapping of effort, or the dangerous gaps that can occur when everyone assumes that someone else is fulfilling the monitoring function.

Changes in assumptions may lead to alterations of long-range plans, budgets, or project plans.

In earlier chapters we have stressed the need to integrate the annual budget with the total corporate planning process, and have drawn attention to some of the research findings which lend weight to this recommendation. Most organisations already carry out monitoring and controlling through the budgetary process, although there are a few which lack this important but rudimentary management tool, and many who could do much to improve it. The basic methods of budgetary control are outside the scope of this book, and can be found in any publication dealing with basic accounting principles.

What we would argue is that the monitoring of figures against a chart of account headings is not by itself sufficient for the organisation to be sure that it is on course for attaining its longer-term plans. The figures are vitally important but do not tell the whole story: sometimes they give a false picture.

One common happening in any organisation is that budgets may yield the right financial results for the wrong reason. Typically, an organisation may achieve its annual budgeted profit, but may have carried out many actions which are quite different from these originally intended. Indeed, it would be surprising if this were not so since budgetary control is a dynamic exercise, the purpose of which is to stimulate action when things go wrong. The danger is that corrective action may be taken with only the short-term implications in mind, and any deviation from the long-term intentions may lie concealed in the figures.

This is not the only problem. A budgeted expense level may be achieved but without actions necessary for the long-term being undertaken. Research and development effort may be diverted into different projects, essential market planning work may be overlooked, key action in management development or in recruiting people with the skills needed to implement parts of the plan may be forgotten. In each of these situations the normal budgetary control process will indicate that the plan is being performed when in fact it is not. Key actions omitted this year may make it impossible for the sequential actions planned for next year to come about.

The answer to this problem is relatively simple. It is to break down the first twelve to twenty-four months of the long-range plan into a series of actions which should be implemented with assigned responsibilities. These actions should be monitored in a parallel system to the budget, both for performance and the results of that action. For complex, interrelated actions, control may best be performed through some form of critical path analysis. Indeed, many of the actions necessary to implement a particular plan may not be apparent until some such analysis is completed. A corporate plan may demonstrate an action to launch a new product in two years' time. This may conceal several hundred individual tasks and sub-decisions which have to be undertaken if the plan is to be achieved. Failure of even the smallest of these tasks may sometimes put the whole plan in jeopardy.

In effect, the message of the preceding paragraph is one that occurs often in this book: that plans have to be implemented by people and that planning will be an empty exercise unless they are so implemented.

A simple monitoring system might be to appoint co-ordinators whose job is to check and report on progress at frequent intervals. This is what usually happens when sub-programmes are large enough to become projects, and are controlled by critical path networks or similar techniques. Another method is to ensure that the major issues are reported on at the appropriate board or executive committee meetings, with directors taking responsibility for reporting on an exception basis for items under their control. This works well in smaller organisations and provided the programmes do not involve any complex inter-departmental relationships. In larger companies the director would need a reporting system (verbal or written) to ensure that he was in possession of the up-to-date situation for tasks which had been delegated.

There are numerous methods of ensuring regular monitoring of actions, varying from a full, comprehensive MBO system, to regular discussion at committee meetings: from a regular upwards reporting on progress to a system of exception reporting. The right answer is the one which best fits the company, but all require that the plans be treated with seriousness. Perhaps the clearest distinguishing feature between companies where plans are monitored and those where they are not is the degree to which they are seen as an important contributor to the management process.

Yet another area requiring monitoring and controlling action is in the field of major capital expenditure projects. Many companies have a comprehensive approach to the analysis and evaluation of major capital expenditure projects, often using highly sophisticated discounted cash-flow techniques and computer assistance in analysing risk and sensitivity. Auditing these projects is a much less frequent practice, and even where this does take place it is more likely to compare capital expenditure with the project and to ignore the results of that expenditure. An important element of monitoring is to find out whether the expenditure has brought the benefits expected: if it has not, some further action may be required.

This is easier to state than to do, for the reason that the need to monitor is frequently overlooked when the evaluation is made. Most capital expenditures are, in some way, incremental to an established business and are (correctly) evaluated on their marginal effect on that business. Once the project is implemented the results may not be separately distinguishable unless special action is taken because the accounts are not kept on a marginal but on a total basis. In addition, other factors in the business which have nothing to do with the capital project may also have changed. For example, a capital expenditure project to increase yields may give a saving in total raw material costs matched by an unexpected rise of the same proportions. In profit terms the result may look the same, and the accounts may reveal no benefit from the expenditure; yet there has been a benefit. Thought at the time the project is evaluated will enable appropriate standards to be set up which can be measured, and adjustments made to the management information system (not necessarily only in the accounting area) so that the appropriate information is generated.

The only other problem is to decide at which points in time an expenditure project should be monitored. This should be selected in relation to the project itself: capital expenditure by amount and timing is easiest to monitor as it happens, for it requires no special study. Results must be measured fairly close to the start of the project, but after sufficient time has elapsed for them to have begun to happen. Once the new project is fully operational it will become part of corporate life and fit in with normal budgetary procedures: however, it will move in to the annual budgets at its levels of realisation, which may be a long way from management's original intentions and expectations.

The final area which should be monitored is the long-range plan itself. The extent to which successive corporate plans differ from each other, and from the actual outcome as they occur, should be assessed at least once per year. This is partly to examine the accuracy of the various financial forecasts, and partly to monitor the extent to which strategic intentions have been changed. There are many good reasons for following this discipline, not least being the need to ensure that planning is treated as an important issue, and that management as a whole accepts the need to treat changes from the plan with responsibility, and at least to know that they have changed. There will be deviations (and indeed there should be if planning is to be a tool and not a straitjacket), but careful study will reduce irresponsible deviations and lead the company to ways of improving its forecasting.

The human element adds another dimension to the task of monitoring and controlling plans, in particular the fear that many people have that they will be judged and found wanting if the results of their plans are measured and compared with the original promises. Dislike of criticisms (which most of us have to some degree), tied to the corporate system of rewards and sanctions, will frequently drive managers to devise ways of avoiding being monitored, or into a system of pessimistic forecasting, so that results always look better than the expectation. There is always an underlying fear that individuals will be blamed for variances which are outside their control; and there have been enough sacked senior managers from chief executive level downwards to demonstrate that there is often more than a grain of truth in this argument.

There are schools of thought which would argue that a main purpose of monitoring and controlling must be to identify ineffective managers, and that this in turn would ensure implementation and effective forecasting. Our belief is that this view is less constructive than the concept of using the monitoring and control mechanisms to assist corporate and personal learning. (Corporate learning, of course, is no more than the collected business learning of the key individuals within the organisation.)

Drever (1952)[1] defines learning as "modification of a response, following on and resulting from experience of results; must be distinguished from remembering, which involves the recall of previous experience, and is therefore narrower, and learning may take place without remembering, as normally occurs in the learning of a motor skill. . . ."

Stones (1966)[2] states: "We might say, therefore, that learning occurs whenever the activity of an organism brings about a relatively permanent change in its behaviour."

A similar definition is provided by Borger and Seaborne (1966):[3]

". . . any more or less permanent change of behaviour which is the result of experience."

Tiffin (1951)[4] draws attention to the fact that feedback of results brings an improvement in learning, and quotes supporting evidence from the educational field and from industry. This concept is almost self-apparent, and on a personal level needs no explanation. In an industrial or business situation it is complicated by the aura of secrecy which surrounds results of the type most necessary for measuring performance against any corporate plan. In recent years social pressures for more disclosure of information to employees, government and outsiders have changed the traditional board room view of what should be confidential, but nevertheless some top managers still have a miserly instinct when it comes to sharing information.

On an individual basis, feedback will help the manager by allowing him to know his successses and to learn from his mistakes. Management by success is an important concept of motivation, and objectives of any kind are only meaningful if they are attainable but a little difficult to reach.

We believe that the classic work of Coch and French (1949)[5] has some relevance here. Figure 14.1 provides a summarised adaptation of some of the findings of this research. Production is affected by both positive and negative forces. The positive forces which improve output include avoidance factors such as fear of losing one's job, and pro-factors such as a desire for financial rewards, liking the job, and liking one's colleagues. Negative forces which act to prevent output rising might include dislike of one's boss, adherence to the norms of another group, resentment of criticism, or feelings of injustice. The research found that increasing the positive forces could increase production, but that this tended to have only a short-term effect because the actions used to change the positive forces had as a byproduct an increase or reinforcement of the negative. A major long-term effect could only be gained by decreasing the negative forces. In the research this was achieved through involving the affected workers with the development and implementation of the new methods of production.

Our hypothesis is that this model of the impact of positive and negative forces also applies to management behaviour. It is possible to use a monitoring and controlling system only to increase positive forces to improving performance at the management task — a variation of the

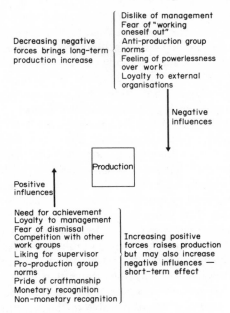

Fig. 14.1. Influences on output

carrot-and-stick approach. We would not rule out completely the desirability of linking good planning and decision making with, for example, promotion. However, we believe that the greater opportunity lies in using the monitoring and control system to reduce negative forces: constructive learning as described above, the identifying of training needs and the provision of appropriate training, and the benefits of involving managers as a whole in the planning process.

Top management is in a better position to counsel those contributing to the planning process and to judge the likely accuracy of the plans of their subordinates if they are aware of their weaknesses and propensity for error. Feedback should help the corporate planner to identify where managers require assistance in developing their planning abilities. Apparent carelessness and lack of consideration of available data in making a forecast may be a symptom of lack of skill rather than lack of interest. Managers may not be aware of the appropriate techniques for forecasting, there may be a lack of co-ordination of data between departments which are interdependent or, and in our experience very frequently, a failure to perceive the underlying logic of the business and therefore an inability to understand the relevance of some of the available information to improve a forecast or influence a decision. In situations like these, the solution may lie in laying on a training course, or personally counselling managers rather than castigating them for inefficiency — an example of how to reduce the negative forces for long-term benefit.

The whole question of control is also tied in with the management style of the organisation (see Chapter 6). Organisations characterised by the exploitive–authoritative (system 1) company will use a much more autocratic approach to control and as Table 6.3 shows, this is likely to be highly concentrated in top management and to be used for policing and in a primitive manner. This style of control brings many behavioural problems to corporate planning. System 4 organisational style (participative-group) is characterised by control for purposes of self-guidance and for co-ordinated problem solving: it is not used punitively. The mechanisms of control are widespread through the organisation, and may well be more rigorous at lower levels of management than at the top. When the plans have the commitment of those responsible for implementation, control is as likely to be as much a self-discipline as something imposed by superiors: when the right sort of participation has been achieved, control becomes part of concensus management. (Monitoring, however, may have to be carried out on a central basis, since this may be the most effective method of collecting the necessary data.)

It is a tendency of human nature which means that plans which are monitored are likely to carry a greater level of management commitment than those which are ignored. The degree to which this tendency is true is partly related to the question of organisational style. Under a system 1 style, managers will tend to react to the things for which they are judged. If an autocratic top management demonstrates that it does not care about its plans by failing to monitor and control, the rest of the organisation will also fail to care. With more participative styles the tendency is less true, since managers play a greater part in selecting their own priorities. Even so, the short term will usually overwhelm the corporate plan unless its importance is demonstrated through the leadership of top management. Even under a participative style, managers have a human tendency to take an interest in those things which top management considers important. The desire for approval and the need to be seen to be effective on whatever scale of measurement is selected by the chief executive, can be an important drive.

The human problems in a monitoring and control system go very deep and cannot be over-stressed. Where the organisation operates a formal management scheme, there is real value in ensuring that this is linked with the corporate planning process. This is important in a psychological sense in that it provides positive proof of the importance of planning and its integration with other management processes. It is also important in that it helps to prevent the development of double standards. Chapter 5 stressed the problem of rewards in the present, while planning is a commitment to the future. Any standard that only judges the present and ignores the future is likely to act against the development of sound planning.

Much of the necessary integration would come about if the approach to monitoring and control already discussed were to be practised, using the plan to identify actions or objectives for which individual managers have responsibility which become part of the personal task on which performance is judged. The integration with personnel mechanisms should be completed by a feedback system from personnel into the planning process, identifying managerial manpower planning issues, such as training needs, management shortages, or unclear lines of responsibility and authority. No plan, whether short, medium, or long term can be implemented unless it is broken down into tasks which are the responsibility of individuals. Action results from what people do.

What we have been saying in this chapter is that monitoring and controlling are essential, but that the different approaches to control will have different behavioural implications. The need to see corporate planning as an integrated part of the management process is very important, but this means that despite the behavioural implications the method of control used for corporate plans must be compatible with the organisational style of the company.

References Chapter 14

1. J. Drever (1952) *A Dictionary of Psychology*, Penguin, p. 152.
2. E. Stones (1966) *An Introduction to Educational Psychology*, Methuen, p. 52.

3. R. Borger and E. M. Seaborne (1966) *The Psychology of Learning*, Pelican, p. 14.
4. J. Tiffin (1951) *Industrial Psychology*, 2nd edn., George Allen & Unwin, pp. 288–90.
5. L. Coch and J. R. P. French (1949) Overcoming resistance to change, *Human Relations*, Vol. 1, pp. 512–33.

CHAPTER 15

The Multi-national
Enterprise

Over the past two decades there has been a significant rise in the growth, organically and by merger and acquisition, of companies which span more than one country, many of which have significant holdings or operations in countries throughout the world. The 1960s were particularly marked by the range and number of mergers resulting in large single-interest companies and multi-interest conglomerates being formed. The growth of the multi-national enterprise (MNE) has not, however, been restricted to manufacturing companies, though these with their generic brand names such as Coca Cola and Ford, are perhaps most readily recognised. Other prominent organisations, either binational or multi-national in operation, have developed. These include professional organisations and banking, insurance, and investment houses. As McMillan (1974)[1] has pointed out, the growth of foreign direct investment (i.e. equity capital involving ownership, in contrast to loan capital) is quite staggering. He quotes Reddaway *et al.* (1967)[2] who points out that in 1929 the basic value of American foreign investment was $7.5 billion, whereas in 1969 it was $70.8 billion with British foreign investment at $30 billion. In Europe this growth has been supported by the EEC and the European free trade area, so that European corporations have in recent times been expanding faster than the larger American corporation.

The growth of the MNE has meant that planning decisions taken by many larger concerns are not related to the country of origin alone but may affect and be affected by the political, social, and economic situation in a number of countries. Furthermore, such countries may have reached different stages in their own industrial development and be adopting different growth policies. In Nigeria, for example, the policy of promoting nationals to key posts in organisations — referred to as Nigerianisation — has required foreign-owned companies to drastically reduce the appointment of expatriate staff and cope with the effects of a political shift in the control of the business in that country. Such situations may have far-reaching effects on the control of the organisation and on long-range plans determined by the company at centre in the "home" country. The reverse of this situation is also apparent in that the MNE, with considerable investment and supporting a range of stakeholders, may be a powerful force in influencing the politics within a country or, at least be able to use sizeable economic muscle in pursuing its own aims. Tugendhat (1973)[3] points out that "companies are usually very careful not to draw attention to the implications of their multi-national production by openly threatening to take reprisals against a government whose policies they do not like. But sometimes the mask drops. In 1969 when the British Government was considering the recommendations of the Sainsbury Committee which it had appointed to advise on the reorganisation of the pharmaceutical industry, Justin Dart, the Chairman and President of the US Rexall Drug and Chemical Company, issued a significant warning indicating that since two-thirds of the British pharmaceutical industry was American controlled and since American companies were responsible for about £50m of the industry's favourable trade balance of £775m, exports would go forward from Canada, the United States, Australia, or the Continent. Thus if the climate in Britain became too unfavourable for American-based companies to develop exports, then invariably they would be bound to re-locate at least a portion of such operations." In the loosely worded pay restraint guidelines in Britain in 1977 it has been observed that the large multi-national company with decisions of new investment and growth in this country may receive more favourable treatment on pay increase decisions than the smaller national organisation with no such investment programme to offer (Aris, 1977).[4] This is not to lay criticism at government, merely to indicate the reality of the influence of the large multi-national enterprise in an economically determined world.

For the planner, then, there are initially two considerations which relate to the degree of control exerted by or upon the MNE at its interface with the political and social milieu in which it operates. In the first consideration, if the planner is to determine the methods and approach whereby long-term business strategy decisions are to be made, he will need to be aware of the corresponding social and economic plans of the host countries in which units of the business operate. It goes without saying that in some countries, particularly in the third world, such social and economic plans may be somewhat tenuous and dependent upon a volatile political situation. It is as well to remember also that the presence of multi-nationals in some countries has generated tensions in the foreign countries in which they appear. Vernon (1971)[5] has suggested that such tension is "a manifestation of powerful psychological and social needs on the part of elite groups in host countries. These needs include the desire for control and status and the desire to avoid a sense of dependence on outsiders." Thus it is not a simple matter of relating the organisation's plans into the political framework of a foreign country, rather the requirement for an analysis of the interactional relationship between the multinational company and the host country.

In this sense the MNE may be acting consciously or otherwise as a change agent. In the second consideration the planner may find himself engaged in proactively influencing change in both the social and economic circumstances of a host nation. In the report by Aris mentioned earlier, which concerned the decision by Ford planners to invest £185m to build a new engine plant, it is apparent that a planning decision covering investment of such magnitude illustrates the control which the MNE can exert on the host nation and the influence which such a company can bring to bear on governments even before the location decision is taken. In the Ford case no less than four governments, viz. the United Kingdom, Germany, Spain, and Ireland were involved in negotiation and lobbying with the company and all were offering substantial incentives for investment in their country.

The MNE may therefore wield considerable power and be in a position to influence government decisions to a significant degree, yet the MNE is usually a far from democratic institution, and, indeed it has been suggested that in the ultimate analysis the MNE need hold allegiance to no specific country. While the MNE offers considerable benefits in economies of scale and division of labour, and contributes to world welfare and economic growth, it is also true that it benefits from bargaining power and experience across countries, and the facility to balance or play-off the trading constraints of one government against the incentives offered by another.

The planning process which adopts a rational calculable approach to business decisions and which ignores the social, emotional and cultural considerations within a country, is likely to result in a number of unintended consequences which may markedly affect planned performance. The MNE of today faces many more problems than did its historical predecessors, and these are things which must be taken into account in the planning of multi-national activity.

Generalising, we can trace the original international strategies of the MNE to two possible causes: the desire to expand the operations of the base company, first through exports, followed by overseas distribution companies, followed by local manufacture; or the need to secure raw material sources to safeguard or improve the operations of the parent company. As with all generalisation, there were many exceptions and combinations, but the picture was true of a significant number of companies, and remains true for many of them. The local manufacture strategy might be secured by acquisition as well as organic growth, and might take the subsidiary company into paths which differed from those of the parent. Substantially, though, the overseas manufacturing operation was a miniature reproduction of the whole or a part of the parent, and its growth was oriented to its own market and assigned export territories.

One of the trends which has recently begun to move the MNE from this pattern has been the realisation that while the subsidiary's market may be local — and must have a local strategy — production, research, and many other operations to supply that market can be examined internationally. Economies of scale, the reduction of cost which comes with the learning curve, and many other advantages may accrue from a manufacturing strategy which is based on a relatively small number of plants. In some industries this may be essential if the company is to compete. Increasingly in those industries, success is seen in world market share terms because only then can the right volumes be achieved to enable the MNE to compete, grow, and profit.

Now for many MNEs the subsidiary is no longer the same unit of strategy which it once was, when it was itself an integrated whole. Most governments may pretend that the local chief executive has effective strategic control, but this is often no longer a real control. The subsidiary in a particular country may have relative freedom in its marketing strategy, subject to certain constraints, and may offer many products to that market. It may have little option where it obtains products: its "own" factory may be the world source for only one of them, or may produce a component or product unrelated to the local market. Research activity may be completely integrated on a worldwide basis and work on problems and priorities which give no consideration to the host country. Whatever the legal shell, such a subsidiary is virtually three or four organisations loosely federated, each with very different objectives.

Consolidations such as this have been facilitated by the closer economic and political unions of countries: the European Economic Community is a notable example.

Management style also changes. Other observers have pointed out that the MNE has tended to have two very different approaches to managing its overseas operations. At the extremes, the approaches are:

*Only the nationals of the parent country are really efficient, honest, and trustworthy: the way to manage is to locate ex-patriates in the really key functions and maintain a tight central-ised control over everything that can be controlled. One Swiss pharmaceutical company is reputed to have taken this to the extent that all managerial expense claims in subsidiaries had to be checked, not by the local chief executive, but by the head office. Many American companies also act on this sort of approach.

*Only nationals of the host country can understand the local market, social environment, and business conditions. The way to manage is to delegate everything except for a modicum of financial control, and leave them alone to get on with it.

Under the first extreme, the MNE will increasingly run foul of another developing trend caused by "the end of the deferential society" in most of the developed countries, particularly Europe, and the growing spirit of nationalism of the third world countries.

Under the second extreme no properly developed integrated world strategy is possible. At best the MNE parent becomes a sort of financial holding company. At worst, and this of course depends on the industry, its local factories will fail to gain the right volumes of throughput, and will be unable to compete with those companies which have a world production strategy. Many multi-nationals have tried for a middle course, frequently delegating control to regional headquarters, and aiming for a truly multi-national management team. There are advantages in genuine multi-national management, and mixed nationality teams can bring a new dimension of experience and knowledge which is beneficial to results. Desatnick and Bennett (1977)[6] state:

"The biggest obstacles to success are *internal* rather than external: they lie within the multinational itself. It is *not* primarily the obstacles of local government bodies, or labour unions per se, or a lack of expatriate management sophistication. It is rather a distrust of foreigners, resistance to 'foreign' ideas and business techniques, poor communications, and a mutual lack of understanding. It is not the responsibility of the host country to attempt to bridge these gaps in understanding and communication, but it is the *first* responsibility of the foreign businessman."

The International Labour Office (1976)[7] draws attention to some of the unique integrated characteristics of the MNE:

"Perhaps even more to the point is the fact that many multinationals tend to live in or create a somewhat special world. Their internal communications are more developed; they must be to operate far flung companies. Their industrial relations functions, especially in the case of United States firms, are often more professionalised. Their fringe benefits and sometimes the wages they pay are often in the lead, compared to surrounding plants in Western Europe. Their systems of personnel training are often more 'modern' and developed and more inward based than is the case with most national companies. . . .

"All of these and other factors often tend to make of the multinational a more integrated enterprise, with personnel more specialised and turned inward."

There is a growing trend of reaction against the power of the MNE. Trade unions frequently devise special strategies to combat the MNE (see Chapter 18 for further details). Industrial democracy legislation in various European countries inhibits the power of the multi-national to take unilateral, centralised decisions, by putting certain rights of consultation and co-determination in the hands of employee directors at board level, or on works councils. The ability of the MNE to take a chess-board approach to world strategy is reduced by the growth of social consciousness in many countries. Much political opinion is against the MNE. For example, the British Labour Party[8] holds:

> "Modern capitalism is increasingly going multi-national. In other words leading national companies are locating factories and jobs abroad rather than exporting from home. This has undermined the sovereignty of national governments in several ways.
>
> "Multi-national companies can blackmail national governments and unions by threatening to locate their next major project abroad or even close down home production if governments do not allow them exceptions to national economic policies . . . less obviously, the financial transactions of multi-nationals can have major effects on monetary policy for individual 'host' nations."

The report suggests that the impact on monetary policy comes about from tax-avoidance measures, avoidance of domestic borrowing restrictions, failure to export because of competing with their own subsidiaries, transfer price policy, and speculating in foreign currency.

Statements such as those by Ford and Rexall quoted earlier in this chapter reinforce public opinion about the adverse effects of the MNE.

It is perhaps not surprising that one of the reactions to these trends has been a call for international controls on multi-national enterprise. At the lowest level there are the attempts by the European Commission[9] to harmonise company law (and industrial participation) in the EEC.

> "The emergence of groups of legally distinct companies and firms which operate according to certain centrally determined policies has been one of the most significant modern developments as regards the structure of large industrial and commercial enterprises in the Community, and indeed throughout the world. However, with a few exceptions, company laws generally take little account of the reality of this situation. The group companies remain legally independent and separate entities, while in practice they act in a co-ordinated fashion. . . .
>
> "The main requirement therefore is the creation of legal systems which recognise the reality of group situations and permit groups to act according to centrally co-ordinated policy, but subject to rules which safeguard the legitimate interests of those concerned, in particular minority shareholders, creditors and employees."

At the highest level there are continuing attempts to control the MNE through the United Nations. The most significant recent development has been the acceptance of guidelines for multi-national enterprises by all members of the Organisation for Economic Co-operation and Development except Turkey. The OECD (1976)[10] state:

"Multinational enterprises now play an important part in the economies of member countries and international economic relations, which is of increasing interest to governments. Through international direct investment, such enterprises can bring substantial benefits to home and host countries by contributing to the efficient utilisation of capital, technology and human resources between countries and can thus fulfil an important role in the promotion of economic and social welfare. But the advances made by multinational enterprises in organising their operations beyond the national framework may lead to abuse of concentration of economic power and to conflicts with national policy objectives. In addition, the complexity of these multinational enterprises in organising their operations beyond the national framework may lead to abuse of concentration of economic power and to conflicts with national policy objectives. In addition, the complexity of these multinational enterprises and the difficulty of clearly perceiving their diverse subsidiaries, operations and policies sometimes give rise to concern.

"The common aim of the member countries is to encourage the positive contributions which multinational enterprise can make to economic and social progress and to minimise and resolve the difficulties to which their various operations may give rise. In view of the transnational structure of such enterprises, this aim will be furthered by cooperation among the OECD countries where the headquarters of most of the multi-national enterprises are established and which are the locations of a substantial part of their operations. . . .

"The guidelines . . . are recommendations jointly addressed by member countries to multinational enterprises operating in their territories. These guidelines, which take into account the problems which can arise because of the international structure of these enterprises, lay down standards for the activities of these enterprises in the different member countries."

The guidelines, which are voluntary but for which governments are pledged to use their influence to bring about observance, impose a number of "good citizenship" general policies, require considerable disclosure of information, provide for moderation in competitive behaviour, and, among other clauses, have a great deal to suggest about employment and industrial relations. Not least is a requirement for union recognition, which runs counter to the real policies of at least a few of the major US-based multinationals.

These trends for increased government intervention, respect of local feelings, equal treatment for all nationalities, the growth of industrial democracy, and the need for worldwide business strategies which jump national borders, mean that top management of a multi-national is becoming an even more demanding task and far too difficult for one man to handle as an autocrat.

Densatnick and Bennett (1977)[11] sum up these new requirements:

"The world is at present in a serious leadership crisis. That this crisis will continue is confirmed by the toppling of various governments and the increased number of business failures within the past two years. Competence is all too scarce a commodity. The day of the technocrat is disappearing. There is an administrative and managerial sclerosis around the world, which breeds mass-suspicion and distrust: the casualties are the leaders themselves and their respective institutions, whether governmental or business.

"There is a new role, particularly in the human dimension, for the chief executive officer. Instead of spending about 10 per cent of his time on matters external to his company, the complex needs of management dictate that he spend 40 per cent or more of his time on these matters. He faces a double dilemma; if he shirks his responsibilities of running the business as a corporate manager, there is dire trouble; and if he shirks his role as a social arbiter, present day assaults against the mega-company could become so intense that they could force a fundamental change in the corporation itself. He must become outcome-minded, whilst maintaining a healthy awareness of profit."

The planning implications, and particularly the human factors in planning, are immense for the modern multi-national. Environmental awareness is critical for success, both in the management sense discussed in Chapter 1 and the understanding sense developed in Chapter 10. Whereas the smaller company may cope with its environment by simply analysing the data, the major MNE may be, as we have suggested, a force for environmental change as well as a unit of business affected by the environment.

What is needed by the MNE as part of its management and planning process is a mechanism for genuine two-way consultation with governments. The growth in the number of new appointments to "Director of corporate affairs" is a manifestation of the fact that some of the MNEs have perceived the significance of this new need. The aims should not be merely to lobby, to bend government policies, nor should they be glorified public relations activity to promote the company. The need is for genuine, frank, and open discussion. A net result of any properly motivated consultation between any two parties is frequently a movement of attitudes by both parties, and this should be the aim.

We have stressed that the planning process cannot ignore the social, emotional, and cultural issues within host countries. This means that the chief executive officer of an MNE and his key staff must firstly be aware that differences do exist, and, secondly, be prepared to take account of them in decision making. It is no longer tenable for MNEs to continue to run roughshod over local differences as if they do not exist. Although such policies may still be successful in some countries in the short term, they feed the fires of emotion which will ensure that the gentle OECD guidelines become translated into stringent, punitive, international controls. The right strategies now can help to stop this happening, and as a byproduct help develop a local management which can contribute more to success of the enterprise as a whole.

Uneven participation laws call for a policy by the MNEs to bring more industrial democracy into those countries whose legal requirements do not yet demand it. There is a need for leadership. Uneven disclosure laws suggest that communication policies should be examined so that all employees are given the right sort of information about the company, and that this information is properly explained. The dangers of many of the disclosure laws lie not in the data which has to be given but in the fact that the laws provide for it to be passed only to a selected few. This means that distortion, either accidental or deliberate, can occur when the information is further communicated along informal channels, and that management is giving away its opportunity to manage the use to which the information is put.

Above all, the process of corporate planning must be designed so that it allows the input of central, worldwide strategic analysis, but still involves local top management. The "pass-the-hat" around system of planning, which we have criticised in earlier pages, becomes a great temptation in multi-nationals where personal discussions take up a great deal of time, large numbers of top managers are involved, and the costs of travel expenses are heavy. Perhaps even more for the MNE than for other business, the vast paper chase of so many planning systems is a luxury that they can no longer afford. Certainly adopt regional, federal styles of management, which reduce the communications aspect of planning to manageable proportions, but ensure that the strategic planning philosophies discussed earlier are employed, and that true top management participation becomes possible. In the long run, only the philosophies of management and planning which take full account of the human factor will suffice. The task is harder for the MNE than for the one or two country firm, but the need is greater. What is at stake is not the success or failure of the corporate planning process, but the survival of the corporation itself. And this seems to us to be rather important.

References Chapter 15

1. C. J. McMillan (1974) In *The Problem of Organisations*, The Open University Press, Milton Keynes, England (Social Sciences: a third level Course, People and Organisations, Unit 2).
2. W. B. Reddaway *et al.* (1967) *The Effects of UK Direct Investment Processes: Interim and Final Report*, Cambridge University Press, Cambridge.
3. C. Tugendhat (1973) *The Multi Nationals*, Penguin, Harmondsworth, Middlesex, England, pp. 137/8.
4. S. Aris (1977) *The Sunday Times*, 9 October, p. 17.
5. R. Vernon (1971) A choice of futures, in R. Vernon, *Sovereignty at Bay*, Longmans, Harlow, England.
6. R. C. Desatnick and M. L. Bennett (1977) *Human Resource Management in the Multinational Company*, Gower, p. 4.
7. ILO (1976) *Multinationals in Western Europe: The Industrial Relations Experience*, p. 65.
8. Labour Party, *The National Enterprise Board*, London, p. 16.
9. European Commission (1975) *Employee Participation and Company Structure*, Bulletin 8/75, Commission of the European Communities, p. 103.
10. OECD (1976) *International Investment and Multinational Enterprise*, p. 11.
11. R. C. Desatnick and M. L. Bennett (1977) op. cit., p. 309.

CHAPTER 16

Manpower Planning

Until now this book has dealt with those aspects of human behaviour which arise from or are intertwined with successful corporate planning. The message has been that the human factor in any planning activity is critically important if the plans are to work. In this chapter we look at the human resources aspect of planning in another light, and examine the ways in which an organisation might plan for its future manpower.

Under modern business conditions it is becoming increasingly important for attention to be given to what has come to be termed "manpower planning". Lack of the right skills and numbers of people can prove to be a critical constraint to an otherwise brilliantly conceived corporate strategy. A surplus of people can be expensive and embarrassing. Social and legal conditions in most countries make it more and more difficult for business to divest itself of excess people. Certainly the days of callous hire and fire have gone forever.

Less obvious, but equally important, is the fact that good manpower planning can lead to a greater cost effectiveness in the utilisation of people, reducing labour turnover, and the consequential hire and training costs, as well as contributing to better productivity and a reduction of industrial relations tensions.

Of course, to do this the organisation must make the right decisions. This brings us to our first point of what manpower planning is really about. It is concerned with strategies, policies, and procedures for the effective utilisation of an organisation's human resources and, like corporate planning, takes a future-oriented view. It is about decisions which enable the company to have people available with the appropriate skills, at the right place, at the time when they are needed. Too many managers equate planning with forecasting, and believe that it is just a

250

numbers game. Forecasts are part of the raw material of manpower planning, just as they are with any other type of planning, but the plan itself is a matter of intentions and actions.

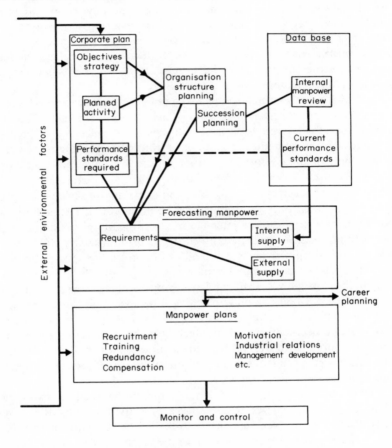

Fig. 16.1. Manpower planning process.

Figure 16.1 provides one way of looking at the manpower planning process in a systematic way. From this it can be seen that the forecasting element is only one of a chain of steps in the process, and that in any case it is split into requirements and supply.

The first thing that the diagram stresses is not forecasting, but the link with the environment in which the company operates. This has an effect on virtually every step in the manpower planning process and, as mentioned earlier, has a major impact on what is possible, practicable, acceptable, and economic in the treatment of human resources. Assessing environmental issues, and taking account of them in planning, was the subject of an earlier chapter which has as much relevance to human resources as it does to corporate planning in general.

No fully effective manpower planning can be undertaken unless there is a corporate or business plan from which the present and proposed corporate activities can be derived. Organisations which try to prepare manpower plans without any attempt at corporate planning must waste a large part of their effort. No corporate plan is perfect, but manpower planning can be worthwhile even though activity can rarely be forecast with pin-point accuracy. So long as a plan exists and the manpower plan is in line with it, coherent decisions can be made even if results turn out not to be in line with those intended in the corporate plan, and progress can be monitored. Where there is no corporate plan, this unity will be lacking, and the manpower plans will tend to drift from one crisis to another until they fall into disuse and disrepute.

Although manpower planning depends on corporate planning, there is another aspect. Good corporate planning also depends on manpower planning. Human resource implications must be fed into the corporate plan so that strategic decisions are taken which help the organisation achieve its human resource objectives. So it is not a one-sided affair. Both corporate and manpower planning should be intertwined and seen as different aspects of the same overall process.

Figure 16.1 illustrates another key relationship between the two types of planning, and explores the interfaces of activity, productivity, and costs. Part of manpower planning is to define the standards of performance which can be achieved in relation to the corporate plan, and to decide how they can be attained. It is important that the organisation do more than simply project the status quo (although the present situation must be known, a point to which we shall return). Equally vital is the need to make realistic assessments of what should be achieved. A numbers exercise which postulates productivity improvements which no one has thought out in terms of health and safety legislation, industrial relations climates, or what realistic policies can achieve, is unlikely to do much good either to the corporate plan or the manpower plan. On the other hand, asking questions such as How can we improve productivity by 20% over two years? may be a good way of beginning an analysis. It is a matter which needs a great deal of careful thought, for the conclusions will affect the forecasts of labour requirements, the estimates of costs and profits, and the actions which spring from the plan. Productivity improvement is a much neglected aspect of corporate planning, at least in the United Kingdom, and should be a conscious part of the manpower plan. Those making the assessments should examine the validity of tasks, the way they are currently performed, issues of poor productivity such as double manning, and whether investment in capital equipment could reduce (or change the nature of) requirements. It will be appreciated that these issues become matters of company decision, and have implications on the planning box of our diagram.

Before manpower needs can be forecast there should be a study of organisational structure. This is shown in Fig. 16.1 together with the closely related task of succession planning.

One thing which is often overlooked is that a change in company strategy will often cause a change in organisational structure. Some of these influences are fairly direct and easy to spot: a new activity may mean a new subsidiary with its own management and supporting structure; a geographical expansion may require a new branch and changes to regional managers' territories. Many changes are more subtle, and less easy to identify, because managements often do not think about them in the right way.

Figure 16.2 shows the interrelationships between three functions: organisational structure, people, and systems. "Structure" covers such items as the formal organisation chart reflecting decisions on job descriptions, authority, span of control, the degree of centralisation/decentralisation, and functional, product, market, or geographical organisation. "People" aspects include personal abilities, background, perceptions, attitudes, feelings, communication patterns, and relationship patterns. "Systems" deal with work flow, information flows, accounting data, and the systems relationships of elements of the structure.

The first point about this diagram is that change in one of the three

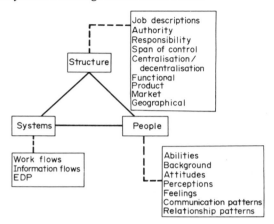

Fig. 16.2. Relationships of change.

factors is likely to have an effect on the other two. One of the commonest actions managements take is to change the organisation chart to solve a problem without giving equal attention to people and systems. Newman (1971)[1] demonstrates the impossibility of running one organisation after a merger, when structure was changed but the old systems were retained, which meant managers had no data with which to manage. This dynamic relationship is, of course, part of the concept of organisational development and change discussed earlier in this book.

From a manpower planning point of view there is more to consider than the relationship of the three elements. This is the impact which strategic environmental or other change factors have on the elements. Figure 16.3 indicates some of this. Pressure from the change factors need be initially on only one of the dynamic elements. For example, in an acquisition situation the initial pressure might be on systems: a new accounting concept, different reporting dates, a fresh approach to corporate planning. In turn this may change people relationships, possibly through the need to recruit additional staff, or possibly because different people are now called upon to supply or use the new data. There may be a need to change organisational structure because of these new "people" situations.

Part of the manpower planning task is to plan the organisation of the

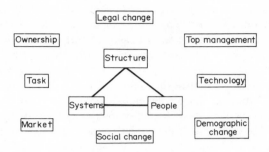

Fig. 16.3. Forces of change.

future. This task is shown in Fig. 16.1 as a prerequisite to forecasting manpower, since it may bring additional or reduced needs quite separate from the productivity ratios (organisational change may be a legitimate method of achieving higher productivity). Implications of organisational change run right through our model and provide a stimulus for new or modified policies.

Closely linked to organisational planning is succession planning. This is an attempt to plan for the right number and quality of managers and key-skilled employees to cover retirements, resignations, death, serious illness, or promotion, plus the new positions which may be defined in the organisation plans. At senior levels, or to a lower depth in large organisations, it makes sense to analyse the organisation to identify potential successors to all present posts and possible occupiers of all new positions. Such a succession plan might indicate people who are ready now, people who could take over in an emergency on at least a short-term basis, and people who would be ready in one or two years time. Such a plan might also show the age of each man named, his length of company service, and the time he has spent in his current job. In addition to demonstrating potential in-house successors, the chart will show up problems. There may be no successors in view for some critical situations. On the other hand, there may be too many, which could mean that promotion will not match the ambitions of men of calibre, and that resignations will increase. This is particularly a problem if those in the senior positions have many years of service ahead of them and no promotion prospects themselves.

Effectively, the succession plan helps to forecast both the demand and supply of managers and key skills, and contributes to the development of policies and actions for resolving the problems revealed. Succession planning is not an easy task and is rarely "right", but it does provide a rational base for taking a view on management and key skill needs in terms of quality, skill areas and experience, rather than by global estimates of total needs which conceal more than they reveal. Key skills are included because sometimes activities are highly dependent on one or two highly skilled technicians or experienced clerks, who are not classed as managers, but whose sudden absence could bring operations to a complete stop.

Another group of activities in Fig. 16.1 is concerned with information about the company which is essential for any planning. This is the personnel data base and includes an internal manpower review and information about current performance ratios (which may be very different from the intentions of the plan).

The review consists of statistics in the form of regular series and a manpower inventory which provides basic information and thereby enables forecasts to be made or policy decisions to be taken. Without a sound statistical understanding of the company, manpower planning is impossible. The sort of information required, where possible with a lengthy run of back data and generally at least on a monthly basis, includes:

Numbers employed	Absenteeism
Age structure of each analysis heading	Incidence of holiday taken
	Reasons for termination
Length of service structure	Performance ratings (from annual
Wastage rate	appraisal)
Stability index	Salary and wage analysis
Hours worked	Training costs
Overtime hours worked	Training activity
Time lost in industrial disputes	

The way in which the data should be analysed will of course vary with the organisation. Normally it would be broken down into logical organisational terms (company, subsidiary, department, group), geographic headings (where applicable), functions, and skills. It is of course possible to take an either broad or fine view of functional and skill analysis. Some companies have very complex manpower inventory systems, which enable breakdowns to be made of skills not being utilised as well as those being used in a current position. Any really detailed analysis needs computer support and a great deal of thought into system design.

Every organisation has to decide itself the degree of detail it wishes to go down to in its skills analysis. An academic approach is rarely practicable, and usually some degree of detail has to be sacrificed on the grounds of cost, virtual irrelevance, or impossibility of regularly collecting the data. One of the problems that a list of requirements glosses over is the unexpected difficulty (at least in the eyes of someone without practical experience) of obtaining many of the statistics. A great deal of thought has to go into the design of the personnel information system, into the definitions and the limitations of available data. For example, the number of people on the payroll in the month may not be the same as the numbers employed at the end of the month.

Knowledge of current performance standards is essential if there is to be an understanding of the relationship of business activity with numbers employed. Figure 16.1 shows the link, already discussed, between current and intended performance. In this context the standards are not the type of data which comes from an annual management appraisal system, and which may measure achievement against the background of the requirements of the job. They are activity or productivity ratios or relationships which relate business volumes to numbers of people. With a little effort, most organisations can, using output figure, works measurement, and similar techniques, develop such ratios for direct workers and certain indirect workers closely associated with production. Few have any real understanding of the relationship of business volumes with most other indirect functions, particularly clerical positions. For some reason business has traditionally closely monitored and developed costing systems to help it understand direct labour, but has tended to regard everything else as overheads, apportioned in costing systems by accounting conventions rather than a real understanding of what people do. There are exceptions, and some firms have studied clerical, accounting, and similar jobs and have been able to break them down into output-related elements. For most companies this is still a pressing need.

The parts of the process we have considered so far have, almost without our trying, taken us into forecasting. A thorough understanding of the organisation in manpower terms, plus knowledge of its business intentions, are the basic ingredients for forecasts of manpower requirements and manpower supply.

There are a number of approaches to forecasting manpower requirements. It is possible to go along the route, outlined above, so that for every group of jobs relationships are established with output, or to deduce elements of the forecast from organisation and succession charts. The ideal is when a ratio can be established with the work unit itself. For example, if it is possible to forecast the number of lines on invoices that will be caused by an expansion of sales, and it is established that every x lines requires the service of one clerk, a fairly accurate forecast can be made of people needed to handle the additional work. Where such detailed data does not exist it may be possible to deduce needs from historical trends, plotting sales on one axis of a graph and numbers of invoice clerks on the other. The weakness of this method is that the relationship is not a direct one — e.g. it is possible that the increase in sales will not cause a corresponding increase in invoice lines, and will not therefore need the same proportionate addition to staff. And this is without getting into problems of over or under-utilised human resources, desirable productivity improvements, or the possibility of producing invoices by alternative means.

In any organisation there are many jobs which are policy decisions, and which may have no direct correlation with current sales or production activities. Examples are market research, research and development, public relations, and corporate planning departments, to name but a few. Some departments which do have a direct relationship with output also have a policy element in their staffing; e.g. the length of delay allowed before replying to a client's request for a quotation will affect the staffing level of an estimating department.

There are other complications in manpower forecasting. The first is work in progress. A builder should not calculate his labour requirements only in relationship to the number of houses he expects to complete in the period. What also affects the calculation is the difference between the labour input on the work in progress brought forward at the beginning of the period and that carried forward at the end. In industries with long lead times, such as shipbuilding, construction, and building, this may be a critical element in forecasting. A similar factor is finished stock levels. So long as inventory levels in any business remain the same from year to year, this may be ignored in manpower forecasting. Once the decision is made to change them, a new set of relationships emerges which will impact on the numbers of people required.

Lead times need to be considered for the impact of a change in, for example, sales bookings on activities in different parts of the organisation. Using the building industry as an example once more, we would postulate that a dramatic fall in sales bookings would have an immediate impact on estimating departments, would take up to a year to be felt by at least some of the trades as they finished the work in progress, and perhaps a year to eighteen months by the credit control section of accounts. A good corporate plan will already have taken note of times, but they are always worth checking.

For certain types of activities, particularly when direct workers are involved, the work requirement may be forecast in terms of hours of work. This has to be converted to people. To do this requires decision about levels of overtime working and forecasts of absenteeism, sickness, and the incidence of paid non-productive time such as holidays, maternity leave, or time off for training and trade union activities. The best base for forecasting is the personnel information system, adjusted for known or expected changes. Although the concept is fairly simple, it is very easy to forget key items, and for this reason we have worked an example in Table 16.1 of the available hours per person per year.

TABLE 16.1
Example of calculation of available work hours per person

	Weeks
Number of weeks	52(a)
Less public holidays = 1.4	
Less annual holidays = 4.0	5.4
	46.6
Less sickness/absence 5% = 2.3	
Less training, etc. 0.5% = .2	2.5
Available weeks	44.1

Available weeks × worked hours per week = time available

e.g. 44.1 × 40 = 1764 hours
44.1 × 50 = 2205 hours

(a)Equate to number of weeks in the accounting year.

The forecast of requirements should be used as an opportunity to question present practice. For example:

* How many of the overtime hours worked are because of custom and practice rather than the need of the organisation?
* How effective is overtime working?
* Does the work need to be done at all?
* Are the manning levels right for the job?
* Has due allowance been made for changes in product mix or geographical spread of activity?
* Could the work be done by alternative methods (work study, investment, new layout of equipment)?
* Is it best done within the company or sub-contracted?

The forecast of requirements should be followed by studies and forecasts of supply. The starting point is internal supply, since this may reveal a problem of shortages which have to be overcome by external supply, or surpluses which have to be dealt with in redeployment, retraining, or redundancy policies. Often the answer may be a shortage of certain skills and a surplus of others, a situation which would remain undiscovered if forecasts were studied on a total headcount basis, and were not broken down into skills and locations.

Part of the study of internal supply can be based on the application of anticipated trends to the present inventory of people and skills. Statistical analysis will frequently provide the best starting point for the evaluation of trends, but forecasts based on the past should be tempered with what is known about factors which might alter the trend. This takes us back to the environmental box, on the one hand, and into the company's own planned actions on the other.

One of the most significant analyses is the age structure analysis of different skills. This may reveal unhealthy situations, such as a predicted loss of skill which is too high due to large numbers of simultaneous retirements. Analysis of this type can frequently give early warning of very severe problems.

The organisation is interested in this analysis for two reasons. One is the problem of maintaining a balanced age-structure in the organisation. The other is that it provides a method of forecasting retirements.

The loss of employees through retirement and other causes is a key element in any supply forecast. Large organisations are in a better position to apply statistical formulae for the calculation of losses other than retirement than are small organisations. Other causes are resignations, incapacitating illness and early retirements, dismissals, deaths, and redundancies. Any organisation can calculate a wastage ratio, a crude index for which is the number of people leaving in the period divided by the average number employed in the period times 100. The weakness of this figure is that it gives the same answer if twenty different jobs become vacant once in the period or if one job is filled and vacated twenty times. There may be very different problems calling for widely different personnel strategies. More detailed analysis on a wastage by length of service basis would reveal the true situation, or alternatively a stability index could be calculated which divides the number of employees with more than a year's service by the total number employed a year ago times 100. This would give very different answers to each of the wastage situations postulated above.

Reasons for terminations are worth studying because they aid interpretation of trends, and direct attention to different situations which might be emerging.

Promotion is the other cause of losses from one skill/function area to another. Movements of apprentices and trainees through the organisation to the completion of their training programmes can be predicted from simple statistical analysis. Other potential promotions may be identified from the organisation's succession analysis. Statistical examinations of past promotion patterns, performance appraisal ratings, and changes in requirements will help the manpower planner make adjustments to his internal supply forecast to allow for this factor.

The comparisons of the internal supply forecast with the requirements forecast leaves a balancing figure, which is either the size of the recruitment problem or a measure of the redundancy/redeployment difficulty the company expects to face. External supply should be examined against the gap and should take account of skills needed, geographic factors, social and educational trends, the national and local skill availability, labour permit problems when ex-patriate staff are involved, and expected local and national unemployment patterns.

None of this work is carried out just as a numbers exercise, although the quantification of the manpower situation will aid strategic and financial understanding. The manpower plan is really about those policies and strategies which attempt to solve the issues revealed in the various steps of the manpower planning process.

Organisations make policy decisions and administer their personnel whether or not they approach the task of manpower planning in the way we describe. The dangers of this are threefold: that policies are not necessarily properly co-ordinated and integrated; they may be directed at solving current problems rather than to the future well-being of the business (fire-fighting instead of fire-avoidance); personnel issues run the risk of being excluded from the factors considered when corporate strategies are planned. We believe there are immense advantages in producing a training plan (policies, procedures, and intended actions) which is part of a manpower plan and prepared with all manpower implications and needs in mind. The same can be said about any of the other issues shown in the penultimate box in Fig. 16.1.

Our model shows a logical step-by-step progression in manpower planning. In fact, issues requiring policy actions are likely to emerge at every stage in the process, and the policy element of planning will therefore have links with each box as well as through the main logic path we have shown.

In addition, we would not argue that the information gained will be adequate for all organisations if they do no more than the bare minimum we have shown. There may be a pressing need to develop more advanced subsystems which support the main process of manpower planning. Examples are management development, training, and salary administration. In each case, the manpower planning process should draw these subsystems together, and ensure that what results is one coherent plan, and not a series of independent plans, separate and uncoordinated, for the various elements of the personnel function.

No plan will be perfect. Figure 16.1 recognises this and provides for a continual process of monitoring and control, which will regularly check progress, provide feedback, and indicate where changes should be made. The concept of monitoring and control were discussed in an earlier chapter, and the issues raised there are as relevant to manpower planning as they are to any other aspects of corporate planning.

Manpower planning is, perhaps, one of the most difficult aspects of corporate planning, which may be why so many organisations do it badly or simply ignore it. One reason why it is difficult is that many organisations still do not give personnel management the voice it should have at top level. Too many people in personnel management are day-to-day administrators: too few are managers in the full sense of the word.

The first step for the company attempting manpower planning might be one not shown in the model: to examine the role given to personnel management in the organisation, its role in corporate strategic decision making, and the skills and calibre of the person filling the personnel manager's job. The result of this study would well be a number of changes which will greatly enhance the probability of success.

People are too important to be ignored.

References Chapter 16

1. W. H. Newman (1971) Strategy and management structure, a paper adapted from the concluding chapter in W. H. Newman, C. E. Summer, and E. K. Warren, *The Process of Management*, 3rd edn., Prentice-Hall.

Further reading

G. McBeath (1969) *Organisation and Manpower Planning*, 2nd edn., Business Books.
J. J. Lynch (1968) *Making Manpower Effective*, Part 1, Pan.
J. Bramham (1975) *Practical Manpower Planning*, Institute of Personnel Management.

CHAPTER 17

Participation: The Social Need

In previous chapters we have referred to the need for the involvement of managers and employees in change situations and planning decisions and we have put forward positive suggestions to create this involvement. In Chapter 3 we postulated the possibility of the individual being manipulated by the "organisation" and looked at the ways in which individuals and groups have an influence on organisational functioning. At present, at least in Europe, there is an ever-increasing interest in the concept and practicability of greater participation by those lower down the organisation hierarchy in the policies and operation of the firm. In this book we have advocated participation in specific changes and plans at the level(s) affected by such plans and at least in a depth sufficient to match the degree to which a particular level will be affected. In some planning situations involvement is centred upon some clear ideas and alternatives, is specific to the functions of those concerned, and is highly connected with what they do now in relation to the future. In other planning situations management involvement can be wider than this as we have suggested in Chapter 11. Such involvement is designed to secure commitment to present and future objectives and an understanding of the effects that commitment will have on the individual's department or function. In other words, the concept of involvement is specific to a particular level in the hierarchy, for a particular purpose, and about particular aspects of the business as they affect that level. This is participation in practice, where individuals and groups are able to influence the decisions taken which affect their function and job. But this is only one of the many different meanings of the term "participation", a term which is used to cover a range of activities from collective bargaining and autonomous work groups through to consultative procedures such as works councils* and worker directors. We have confined ourselves, in this chapter, chiefly to the U.K. experience where participation is a current issue, so as to provide case material which may be related to other countries. A number of companies in the United Kingdom already operate a participative approach of one sort or another to the management of the business. Examples are: the British Steel Corporation which has had a system of worker directors since 1967, the John Lewis Partnership, the Scott Bader Commonwealth, and BP Plastics, where participation is incorporated in productivity bargaining. Much of the current debate on participation including the Bullock Committee Findings (1977)[1] centre upon, what we would term, the structural forms of representation: works advisory councils, works committees, advisory boards, and supervisory boards. The issues being discussed concern the type of representative structure to be used and the manner in which such a representative structure can be related and integrated into existing organisation structures. Macbeath (1973)[2] suggests some of the dangers which might arise if blanket legislation in industrial democracy, making works councils compulsory, was passed. Such legislation would conflict with the British tradition of collective bargaining and could divert managers' attention from the important social issues behind the ideology of participation. The detailed survey carried out by the Coventry and District Engineering Employers Association (1974)[3] into worker participation schemes in eight European countries concludes that it is doubtful whether employees in companies with statutory works councils have any more sense of involvement with their firms than their British counterparts.

The British companies which have embarked on successful participation experiments have done so by starting at the point where workpeople feel they want greater involvement, that is self-control on the factory floor, and moved progressively into representation in decision making at stages removed from the workplace. Examples of such situations are the United Biscuit experience (1974)[4] and the Fred Olsen Organisation (1974).[5] Such approaches allow for a gradual movement towards full board representation ironing out such problems as depth and strength of representation

---

*Note: the works council in most of Europe is a decision-making body with extensive rights and is not much like the usual British works council.

and the position of existing union involvement in relation to greater participation.

In earlier chapters of this book we have advocated the desirability of greater involvement in planning decisions (Chapters 6 and 8) and have suggested practical ways of doing this (Chapter 11). The planner has at once to consider the desirability of participation at the operating level, where decisions reached may have a fairly immediate effect on large groups of people, and at the corporate end of the business where decisions will usually be greater and further reaching over a longer span of time. The situation facing the planner, and indeed the organisation as a whole, is summarised in Fig. 17.1. The identifying letters on the diagram illustrate that participation ranging from *G* (autonomous work groups and vertical job enlargement (which is essentially worker control over the planning and execution of the work itself), to *B*, the supervisory board (where worker directors participate in overall company policy formulation). There are a number of further explanatory points relating to the model:

(1) In certain forms of participation, for example co-determination in West Germany, groups *A* and *B* would appoint a management board which is the equivalent of *C*.

(2) Currently in the United Kingdom, *A* and *C* are, of course, related by law within companies legislation.

(3) Groups *A*, *B*, and *C* would form a three-tier structure which is the form of participation currently in operation in certain companies in West Germany, e.g. production companies in coal, steel and mining (over 1000 employees), parent companies of coal and steel industries and other joint stock companies of more than 500 employees. The EEC Commission fifth directive (Article 2) proposes three ways in which workers should be represented — one of these is the three-tier system.

(4) A unitary structure, as opposed to the three-tier system, would include employee representatives in *C* — the board of directors. This is the system currently in use in the British Steel Corporation (Fig. 17.2 gives the representation with some notes on the arrangements made for employee director involvement).

(5) The advisory board system *D* has a right to information on those aspects of the company pertinent to employee needs, but has no power of decision making or veto in the firm. A number of commentators have suggested that the introduction of an advisory board would provide a

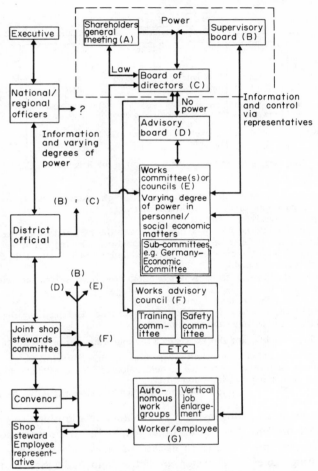

Fig. 17.1. A model illustrating the various forms and combinations of forms which employee participation can take (with an attempt to relate current trade union structure and machinery involved in joint consultation).

suitable *entrée* into employee participation for British companies. It has the advantages of preserving the unity of the main board, keeping power and responsibility together at board level, meeting the information rights

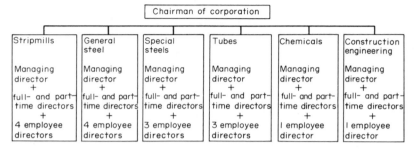

Fig. 17.2. System of employee participation in the British Steel Corporation

Notes:

> Employee directors are part time and paid the same salary and expenses as other part-time directors plus loss of earnings
> Appointment is for 3 years
> Appointment is by BSC in co-operation with the TUC and within the industry
> The Employee Directors serve in a personal capacity and not as Trade Union Representatives, therefore they must relinquish any TU office held during the period of Directorship.
> Appointments are from works grades, non supervisory, supervisory and management.
> Joint TUC/BSC training is given.
> Employee Directors are involved in commercial and planning functions in addition to personnel and social matters.

In March 1972 the BSC and the TUC agreed the following changes.

> More trade union involvement in selection of worker directors.
> Worker directors can continue to hold union office and will have much closer contact than before with union officials.
> Worker directors can now take an active part in joint consultative meetings.

of employees, and allowing for a workable relationship between the employee representatives and all other employees. It allows opportunity for employee representatives to discuss and make views known on key issues, easing the effect of major conflict or industrial action on the role of the employee director, ensuring that speed of decision making and entrepreneurial flair remain unaffected and, finally, it leaves open the possibility for a three-tier board system to be gradually introduced.

(6) Works committees or works councils *E* tend to take various forms and exist in a number of firms at the moment. Such councils, depending upon their terms of reference, may have varying decision-making or veto power and access to information in personnel, social, or economic matters.

It is suggested that there is a need to relate the function of collective bargaining and joint consultation, already existing in the United Kingdom, with the possible function of a works council, although where the former two functions merge to form a single channel for negotiation and consultation there may be little scope for the creation of a works council. However, given that there are limitations and variances in the extent to which existing arrangements for negotiation and/or consultation are developed in the United Kingdom there is scope for the establishment of works councils. It is suggested that frequent changes at middle management level create difficulties in the area of trust and confidence building and that employees may prefer to communicate their views, on wider company questions, via an elected representative rather than through their immediate superiors. The CBI recommends that all companies over a certain size should be required to establish consultative machinery and that such machinery should satisfy the following conditions:

(i) employees would be allowed to participate more fully in decision making throughout the company; and

(ii) such participation operated through the board in such a way that employees could be confident that their views were taken into account.

It is further suggested that works committee members of proven ability might be elected to the Board.

The TUC has stressed the need for continuation and strengthening of collective bargaining. It has further stressed that all ways of extending industrial democracy should be based on trade union machinery. The gradual elimination of the separation of machinery for consultation from that of negotiation is welcomed since this should widen the scope and increase the range of issues which become negotiable. The TUC suggest that the introduction of works councils as a general step in industry would result in one of two things: (1) either they would duplicate existing structures and therefore become superfluous or (2) they would displace or supersede existing trade union arrangements which would be unacceptable to the trade union movement. The TUC suggest that the tendency in the United Kingdom has been for long-established works councils to become part of the trade union machinery. The establishment of works councils can be seen as a first step towards participation at board level although a number of major questions arise concerning such issues as: how and by whom representatives are to be nominated and elected, what form the structure of the works council should take and how it should relate to other procedures and structures in the company, and what rights and powers should be given to company and works councils and any subsidiaries. Such questions beg a further series of questions about relative power and the integration of existing trade union representation.

(7) Works advisory councils F again already exist in many companies in various forms. One of the most common forms is the works safety committee. These are, as the name suggests, advisory bodies having limited access to company information usually specific to their function, e.g. safety policy, and exist to provide a two-way channel of communication between management and work force. In some cases, such as safety, they may have limited power of veto through the support of appropriate legislation. Works advisory councils may be elected from union or non-union members or a mixture of both, this varies both in the United Kingdom and in other EEC countries.

(8) A number of writers (cf. Thomason)[6] have reviewed participation at the level of the work group itself, G. Job-enrichment programmes, management by objectives, work group productivity bargaining, and autonomous work groups have been described as forms of participation in that they offer the employee greater control of decision making within the job itself. A number of studies have outlined attempts by companies to integrate employee participation into existing trade union representation in which there can be varying degrees of employee involvement depending upon the approach adopted. Since, by nature, employees are likely to take most interest in company decisions which affect their specific job and working arrangements, it seems sensible for firms to look at the degree of participation and decision making allowed on the shop floor or in the office as a first step, with greater involvement in company affairs arising naturally from this situation. In analysing strikes, Turner (1970)[7] points to the increase in the proportion of strikes about "wage questions" other than demands for increases, questions related to working arrangements, rules and discipline. He suggests that three types of demand can be isolated:

(i) An "effort bargain", i.e. the amount of work to be done for a given wage to be as explicitly negotiable as the wage itself.

(ii) Changes in working arrangements, methods, and the use of labour to be subject to agreement or agreed rules.

(iii) Demands concerning the treatment of individuals or groups by managers and supervisors.

Turner concludes by suggesting that these disputes all involve attempts to submit managerial discretion and authority to agreed — or failing that — customary rules; alternatively that they reflect an implicit pressure for more democracy and individual rights in industry. It is further suggested that this current feeling has not, so far, been satisfied by the limited development of joint consultation.

The organisation has, then, to face an entire range of possibilities for the introduction of greater participation. In addition the firm faces pressure of impending legislation via the EEC 5th directive and strong argument from the unions that structural or formal forms of participation should be based on existing trade union representative machinery. The most recent government-sponsored study, the Bullock Report, is in favour of this tie in with existing trade union representation, although the minority report of that committee favours a form of supervisory board.

It seems likely that some variation of the German system of co-determination will ultimately be introduced into the United Kingdom. However, there are considerable dangers in trying to transplant a system which is effective in one culture into another country. For example, in Germany the introduction of co-determination was related to a trade union system geared more overtly to profitability, a situation which exists to a lesser extent in the United Kingdom. In addition, whilst German unions play a national wage-bargaining role, they have no effective shop-floor base; also the German system does not cater for the full and active involvement of shop stewards as the British system does. It is valuable, therefore, for those involved in the introduction of worker participation to carry out some preparatory analyses of the organisation and employees before attempting to introduce any participative scheme.

Walker (1967)[8] has used the concept of "propensity to participate" to cover all those factors in an organisation which determine the willing-ness and ability of employees to participate, and the concept "participation potential" to describe all those factors which determine the organisa-tion's ability to promote employee participation, e.g. the cultural setting, size, location, and technology. These two concepts clearly interact with one another in determining the need for and possible extent of participation in the firm. Kilcourse (1976)[9] has extended the use of these concepts in producing a diagnostic model for determining the extent and degree of readiness for employee participation. This model isolates some of the elements which may feature in both *propensity to participate*, examples are the degree of identity which employees have with different organisational levels, stability of the work force, expressed union concerns, and *participation potential*, examples are the technology employed in the organisation, the diversity of the organisation's activities and locations, the management style and expectations. These elements are then related to the three definitive variables of (1) level in the organisation, (2) degree of power in participation, and (3) the subject areas with which participation will be concerned. The use of matrices relating propensity and potential to each of these variables will then allow questions to be asked about the requirement and readiness in the organisation for participation, about what subjects, with what depth of involvement, and at what levels. Figure 17.3 illustrates one matrix relating to the "subject area" variable in participation where a range of subjects from rewards (remuneration) policy to the process of objective setting are considered. This is a particularly useful method of analysis since it highlights the extent to which management and employees may begin to approach jointly the problems of increasing participation in company affairs.

The planner may be in the position of wanting to increase involvement, at all levels, in the planning process but be unsure of the propensity of employees to be involved in forward plans. In addition the planner is in a unique position to answer many of the questions posed when considering the organisation's potential need for participation. One of the "subject" areas considered within the model may of course be forward planning or objective setting.

A further model has been put forward by Globerson (1970),[10] which breaks down participation in terms of five dimensions ranging from institutionalisation through decision making, subject matter, personal participation to material gain. The various levels of participation can then be related to each of these dimensions. For example, against the dimension "decision making" which has a range of five levels: (1) general information to personnel, (2) joint consultation, (3) passive participation in

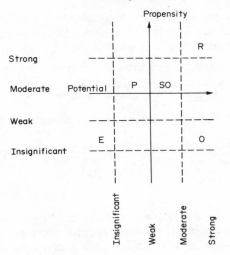

Propensity

Subject
R = Rewards
E = Environment
P = Personnel policies
O = Operations
SO = Setting objectives

Fig. 17.3. Propensity/potential matrix related to "subject".
(From Kilcourse, 1976[9].)

management, (4) active participation in management, (5) self-management. This model is another useful attempt to put an analytical framework around the many variables in the concept of participation.

Useful though these models may be, however, in directing attention to specific questions which require to be asked of the organisation, it is necessary to find acceptable means of asking and eliciting answers to such questions from stakeholders.

An approach for measuring the "climate" of an organisation used by HAY-MSL Management Consultants may lend itself to eliciting data on propensity and potential for employee participation. Such an approach requires the construction of specific climate questionnaires tailored to the company culture and validated before being administered to designated cross-sections or levels of people in the company.

The types of questions posed, relating, for example, to the planning style of the company may be as follows:

How successful do you think the company is in planning, forecasting, and monitoring the scope of its business?

Very successful   7 6 5 4 3 2 1 Very unsuccessful

Does planning for the achievement of objectives in your unit tend to be:

(a) Widely discussed?   7 6 5 4 3 2 1 Largely undiscussed?
(b) Oriented towards   1 2 3 4 5 6 7 Oriented towards the
    short term?   long term?

(HAY-MSL Ltd., 1977)[11]

Specific questions may also be posed in the areas of remuneration, management development, personnel policies, operations, clarity of objectives, or any other area which it is felt may feature as important in employee participation.

The resulting data so collected can be analysed to compare findings between specific variables such as length of service with the company, position or level in the hierarchy, size and location of units. This data may then be fed back to the company in a participative manner using discussion groups, an obvious advantage in beginning a process of greater involvement. Indeed, the total process of climate analysis will tend to increase the involvement of organisational members in organisational affairs. The approach adopted in such an analysis will vary according to the levels involved and the degree to which the company is unionised. We have already noted the attitude of the unions to employee participation. The extent of union involvement in climate analysis is clearly an area for preliminary negotiation.

This provides an approach to determining the nature and extent of participation required within a company. It is useful whether the requirement is limited to greater control over the work itself, the nature of supervision exercised on the part of a work group, or the creation of a high level committee or supervisory council with power to influence major strategic decisions.

It is as well to remember, however, that in times of accelerating social change, where shopfloor representative power is increasing, the involvement of junior and middle management may be decreasing. Little (1977)[12] has suggested that a number of companies are giving increasing priority in taking action to restore or strengthen managers' sense of involvement and influence upon the organisation's future. More attention is being paid in developing effort to employee participation projections to clarify their likely impacts on managerial accountabilities and on managers' perceptions.

As Little points out, most participation arguments assume that "managers" are already full "participants" in the running of the enterprise as their titles imply. In fact the contrary may apply as there is often no provision at all for managers to represent their views in a way that really influences their position. Furthermore, some managers are in the situation where, despite the fact that they have the in-depth knowledge of their business areas, trade union representatives have a closer involvement than they in respect of determination of the company's overall plans.

The impact of employee participation on managers has implications specifically in decision-making processes:

- an increased need to justify decisions;
- less unilateral decisions;
- the need to demonstrate consistency between one set of objectives/decisions and another;
- delayed decision making because of the increased number of reference points and interest groups.

Little concludes:

"That all developments in participation should be examined from the point of view of their impact on managers, not just on the shopfloor. There is also a need to create management participation: management's voice is critical in any participative structure since they constitute a large proportion of the Know-How and experience of an organisation, as the group which turns policy and planning into operational achievement."

A range of issues face the planner in coping with greater participation in company affairs. In reviewing the social need for participation, we have sought to focus attention on the range of possible alternatives for employee involvement, and to provide a framework of questions which may be asked to determine the degree and nature of participation in the company. Clearly the imposition of a structural form of participation required by any future legislation is likely to raise problems and issues of implementation within the firm. Such issues will be better resolved by the companies who have carried out some analyses of the propensity and potential for involvement and, who, in responding to the effects of increasing social change on the business, have already introduced meaningful forms of employee involvement.

References Chapter 17

1. HMSO (1977) *Report of the Committee of Enquiry on Industrial Democracy* (Bullock Report), HMSO, Cmnd 6706.
2. I. MacBeath (1973) *The European Approach to Worker Management Relationships*, British-North American Committee.
3. A. R. Berry (ed.) (1974) *Worker Participation: the European Experience*, Coventry and District Employers Association.
4. D. Harris (1974) The philosophy of trust: one company's path towards employee involvement, *The Times*, 20 May, London.
5. A. Coveny (1974) In talk presented to the IPM Croydon Branch, September 19. See also *Industrial and Commercial Training*, January 1974, p. 12.
6. G. Thomason (1971) *Experiments in Participation*, IPM publications, London.
7. H. A. Turner (1970) The trend of strikes, in K. Coates and A. Topham, *Workers Control*, a book of readings and witnesses for worker control, Panther, London.
8. K. F. Walker (1967) Workers' participation in management, *International Institute for Labour Studies Bulletin*, Vol. 2.
9. Tom Kilcourse (1976) Participation – an analytical approach, *Industrial Training International*, Vol. 11, no. 728, July–August.
10. A. Globerson (1970) Spheres and levels of employee participation in organisations (elements of a conceptual model) *British Journal of Industrial Relations*, Vol. 8.
11. HAY–MSL Ltd. (1977) Extracts from a company climate questionnaire, London.
12. Alan Little (1977) When is a manager not a manager?, *Journal of Chartered Institute of Secretaries*, September, pp. 17–19.

Further reading

G. Hespe and A. Little (1971) Some aspects of employee participation, in *Psychology at Work* (ed. P. B. Warr), Penguin, chap. 15.
D. Guest and D. Fatchett (1974) *Worker Participation: Individual Control and Performance*, Institute of Personnel Management.
A. Flanders, P. Pomeranz, and J. Woodward (1968) *Experiment in Industrial Democracy*, a study of the John Lewis Partnership, particularly chap. 3, Faber & Faber, London.

CHAPTER 18

Corporate Planning and Union
Involvement: The New Dimension

It is perhaps fitting that a book about corporate planning should have as its last chapter a study of a developing trend of concern to all planners — union involvement. This has political dimensions in that it is tied to ideologies about the role that organised labour should play (in the eyes of some) in directing corporate strategy. It has an international dimension in the growing movement for international co-operation between national trade unions. Above all, it has behavioural implications in that it postulates wider participation of employees who belong to unions and frequently involves full-time union officials who may otherwise have no connection with the company.

These trends are emerging, although the degree to which they will develop is a matter for conjecture. They are fed by the movement towards co-determination discussed in the previous chapter, but are unlikely to be satiated by this movement. For some the driving force is clearly one of the transfer firstly of power over and ultimately of ownership of business from the shareholders to the "workers". Others have a less-extreme objective, and believe in a true partnership of shareholder and worker.

As the future is a matter of conjecture we shall present facts to illustrate the trends, but shall not attempt dogmatic forecasts of what will happen. However, the planner will find his own scenarios emerging from the information provided.

Let us first look at what is happening in the development of international co-operation among unions and why this is important to national as well as multi-national companies. What is unlikely to happen is the birth of a true multi-national union with a rank-and-file membership of workers of different nationalities. This is because of the vast differences between union strengths, ideologies, and organisation between countries, the ambitions of union leaders, the lack of identification between workers of one country with that of another, and the fact that all national union ambitions can be achieved through a level of international co-operation which falls far short of amalgamation.

The mechanisms for international co-operation already exist in two sets of institutions: the international confederations of trade unions – of which there are four, and the international trade secretariats – of which there are 17 (plus 11 communist trade union internationals). The broad organisation of multi-national unions and how they work is shown in Fig. 18.1.

The international confederations have as their members the national confederations of trade unions, such as the United Kingdom's Trades Union Congress. They impact on national governments and international organisations such as the United Nations. The four international bodies are the International Federation of Free Trade Unions, the World Confederation of Labour, the World Federation of Trade Unions, and European Trade Union Federation. The first three divide on political and ideological grounds, and have as their members national confederations of a like persuasion.

International trade secretariats perform a different function and are worldwide co-ordinators of national trade unions, organised on broad industrial classifications (e.g. International Metal Workers' Federation, International Federation of Petroleum and Chemical Workers' Unions). Their members are those individual national unions which cover a like area of industrial activity. Their sphere of operations covers the relationship of their members with employers, and we shall demonstrate how they work later in this chapter. At an individual company level they are of more concern than the international confederations, and it is they who aim to become more involved in the strategy of the company.

Some indication of the new dimension of thinking is provided by a journalist's interview with Charles Levinson, Secretary General of the International Federation of Chemical and General Workers' Unions: "Bargaining today is retroactive, but that is no longer good enough. Our aim is to get a share of the pie. But what if you don't like the pie? The only answer is to get into the kitchen" (O'Shea, 1974[1]).

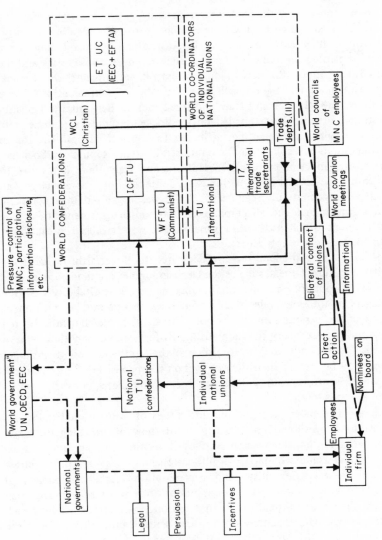

Fig. 18.1. How multi-national trade union action works.

Before considering the trade secretariats in more detail we should take a brief look at some of the differences between union ideologies and organisation which exist in Europe. In Austria and Germany, unions are largely organised on industrial lines, a direct contrast to Denmark and the United Kingdom who have a mainly craft-based organisation. France, Italy, Holland, and Belgium each have a number of confederations. There are five each in France and Italy and three each in Belgium and Holland. These confederations are divided on ideological grounds, sometimes religious in origin, and sometimes affiliated to political parties. The Italian confederations are split into Communist, Christian, Republican/Socialist, Neo-fascist, and non-political. In Holland and Italy there is a move to reduce the ideological gaps. Within these confederations there is largely an industrial organisation. Spain until 1977 was organised into company unions, which included all employees from top management down. The illegal unions which had sprung up alongside were legalised in that year, and a new pattern is now emerging.

Some union confederations are dedicated to the overthrowing of the capitalist system. Others, such as the German unions, are moderate, strong, and, in the opinion of some, more concerned with profitability than the managers of the companies with whom they negotiate. The position of unions in the various countries is not a constant. In Belgium, the United Kingdom, and Germany they are strong. In France and Italy they tend to be weak at an industrial level, although their influence on government policy may be greater than their impact on companies. (In Italy "worker" influence is strong and united on a company basis, although union membership is low.)

These differences highlight the difficulties of international union co-operation. They should not obscure the strategy of attacking the larger multi-national companies which is followed by the more aggressive of the international trade secretariats. Multi-national business is a prime target because its size, flexibility, and centralisation (some companies) of strategic decisions mean that national unions feel at a disadvantage when negotiating with multi-nationals. In addition, many trades unions feel, rightly or wrongly, that they do not have enough information about the multi-nationals with whom they deal. Transfer prices may conceal the true profitability of a local subsidiary, while some employees may not even be aware that they are in fact working for a multi-national. Others feel that the strategic decisions of a multi-national are often against the interests of workers in a particular country.

One of the earliest methods used by the international trades secretariats was the collection of information about multi-nationals for their members. Dossiers have been prepared on a number of multi-nationals. These may vary from relatively simple background statements about the company, its organisation and operation, to sophisticated analyses of products, markets, and decision-making processes.

Methods used to collect information may vary from the commercial intelligence methods as used by business throughout the world, to the collection of data from union members within a company. To this latter end some international trade secretariats have organised regular world industry and company conferences.

A notable example of these worldwide initiatives, which are as much concerned with union strategy as with the exchange of information, is provided by the automobile industry activities of the International Metalworkers' Federation. Councils exist for all the major car manufacturers, and as a result of their activities the Federation possesses a computerised data bank covering some 200 features of employment conditions in 47 worldwide plants operated by 15 different companies. In addition strategic analyses have been made of components flow within companies, so that those plants which are key to the entire multi-national operation are identified for strike action or disruption should this be desirable in the future.

An approach such as this, although not followed by all international trade secretariats, is certainly a factor which business should treat seriously. It is a skilled, planned approach, with nothing of a haphazard nature about it.

Information is not the only weapon used. Much union pressure is directed towards governments to act against multi-national companies.

"One policy the British Unions are adopting is to pressure the Government to pass legislation to bring about some accountability of multi-national corporations by seeking guarantees of behaviour by international companies investing in the United Kingdom or taking over British firms. There are limits as to what could be achieved by this policy because too many controls may result in multi-national corporations deciding to invest in less regulated countries." [Gennard, 1972[2].]

The exertion of pressure on national governments shows little evidence of success. The international unions movement has also attempted to have a legally enforceable international code of conduct for multi-national companies imposed. To achieve this the world confederations put pressure on the United Nations, the EEC and similar international bodies. The drive is therefore against a number of fronts. One of its first successes is the OECD guidelines for multi-national enterprises,[3] which lay down a broad code of conduct accepted by all governments (except Turkey) which belong to the OECD. Among other things, the guidelines provide standards of conduct on employment and industrial relations and the disclosure of information — all target areas for the multi-national trade union movement.

International union tactics have included direct action against individual companies, attempts to influence the actions of top management, and, in a few cases, a try for negotiating rights. At the lowest level, the action taken by the International Trade Secretariat may be little more than the dispatch of letters or telegrams to managements urging them to take certain decisions in the interests of the workers.

Some companies have found (see Hershfield, 1975[4]) that their labour dispute in one country has been publicised by the unions in other countries in an effort to reduce sales. This rather puny weapon is less damaging to most companies than direct action. For example, union officials of one country have joined those of another to assist in arbitration or court proceedings against the company. Employees have refused to work overtime to compensate for production lost in a "foreign" strike, or they have refused to ship goods, or receive goods, from the strike-bound country. Occasionally there have been sympathy strikes, although this is illegal in many countries.

One of the best-known examples of transnational co-operation is the St. Gobain action brought about by the International Federation of Chemical and General Workers Union (ICF). This has been described by many authorities. Our description is that of Turgendat (1971).[5]

"In 1969, St. Gobain workers in France, Italy, Germany, and the U.S. were due to re-negotiate their agreements with the company. On March 29 of that year delegates from the ICF unions concerned met at its headquarters in Geneva to co-ordinate their strategy. They were joined there by representatives from the company's plants in Belgium, Norway, Sweden, and Switzerland. The participants at the conference reached agreement on five points.

(1) To establish a standing committee to coordinate the negotiations in France, Germany, Italy, and the U.S.
(2) That no negotiations should be concluded in any country without the approval of the standing committee.
(3) That in the event of a strike in one country all unions would provide financial assistance if needed.
(4) That if the strike was prolonged, overtime would be stopped at other St. Gobain plants.
(5) That if the company tried to move production from one country to another in order to break or weaken a strike the move would be resisted.

"Several days later the German union, IG Chemie-Papier-Keramik, began negotiations with St. Gobain's German affiliate. It was offered a handsome package deal, including an effective eleven per cent pay rise plus various attractive redundancy and job security provisions. These not only represented a substantial advance by the German affiliate, but also provided ICF members with a useful precedent for negotiations with other St. Gobain subsidiaries. With the standing committee's approval, the union promptly accepted, but warned the company that its promises to the unions in other countries still held good.

"In Italy negotiations began on April 22 only to be broken off the following day until May 8. In the interim the Italian unions heard, through the ICF, that the U.S. St. Gobain workers intended to call a strike in three plants. They asked that it should be delayed until May 8 to coincide with the resumption of their talks with the company in order to subject it to a double pressure, and the Americans agreed. When the Italian negotiations re-started an impasse seemed imminent, and the unions called for a 72-hour strike. However, before the action took place a break-through was achieved, and a settlement reached, which, the unions claim, represented 'virtually a 100 per cent result in comparison to initial demands'. It included pay increases, a new basis for calculating production bonuses, and, most significantly, recognition by the company of the unions as the responsible bodies for negotiations on a company-wide basis.

"In the U.S. St. Gobain claimed that it could not concede the demands of the Glass and Ceramic Workers on the grounds that the U.S. subsidiary had failed to earn profits from 1966 to 1968. Accordingly the ICF sent the union details of St. Gobain's world-wide profits, which had risen sharply over the period, and the details of the agreements reached in Italy and Germany. Armed with this information the union argued that large concessions could also be made in the U.S. After a strike of twenty-six days negotiations were resumed, and the union secured a three-year contract with wage increases of nearly nine per cent a year, and various other benefits.

"Only in France, St. Gobain's home country, did the ICF have no practical effect. This was because the main French union, the Communist-controlled CGT, did not participate in the overall plan. It accepted an offer of a 3.5 per cent pay increase, and left the ICF member unions in France high and dry."

Levinson (1972),[6] architect of the action from the union side, writes: ". . . the action was not as spontaneous as it may have appeared to outsiders. The decisions taken stemmed from and were a direct application of the developing action programme of the ICF relative to multinational corporations." He believes "the Saint-Gobain strike stands at an important junction in trade union history".

Other successes are also claimed. Willatt (1974)[7] lists among his many examples the successful action in 1973 which prevented Honeywell-Bull of France from bringing in substitute engineers from West Germany, the prevention of redundancies at Zanussi in Italy, and in Ford UK in 1971 and General Motors USA in 1970 there were transnational union agreements about strike-breaking.

There have been reports that some multi-nationals have been quietly negotiating with the international trade secretariats. Philips of Eindhoven have held a number of meetings (not negotiations) with the European Metal Workers' Federation. The International Metal Workers also claim to have secured meetings with Ford in Detroit.

No doubt successes in negotiation will increase (although many companies would dispute the use of the word as a fair description of the meeting they have held with the international unions).

It is easy to dismiss this as a matter only for the multi-national companies, and of little concern to purely domestic organisations. In fact it is important to all, firstly because the pressure for unions to be involved in strategy also occurs at the local level, and would be reinforced by any concessions granted by multi-nationals. Secondly, any movements to international parity in terms and conditions of employment forced on the multi-nationals will soon spread to the purely national companies.

One of the difficulties is that the union understanding of corporate planning is currently very far from managements' understanding, which can be a source of difficulty in the future.

The Labour Research Department (1976)[8] carefully defines a corporate plan as "a contingency strategy as a positive alternative to recession and redundancies". This definition will not be found in any management textbook, and is very far away from the description of planning given in earlier pages of this book.

A further quotation from the same source shows more about the attitudes, and demonstrates why a definition was attempted.

"A challenging extension to the argument against worker directors in the private sector has come from the Lucas Aerospace Shop Stewards' Combine Committee. In a recently published corporate plan the combine committee has set out extensive proposals for alternative products that could be produced by the company in the event of further cutbacks in the aerospace industry. And, as a central part of this strategy the corporate plan includes among its alternative products . . . 'a number which would be socially useful to the community at large'. Explaining how such a strategy affects the debate on industrial democracy the combine committee state: 'Activities of this kind will, in our view, be far more significant in the long term than campaigns for worker participation or workers' directors.' This combined committee is opposed to such concepts and is not prepared to share in the management of means of production and the production of products which they find abhorrent. . . . There cannot be 'industrial democracy until there is a real shift in power to the workers themselves'."

Not all unions have the same objectives, and individual members of unions are highly varied in their opinions and beliefs.

In the United Kingdom the Industry Act 1975 adds some weight to the development of the trend for union involvement in strategy, although much of this Act is aimed at bringing about a closer relationship between government and the private sector (termed "partnership" by some and "intervention" by others).

"Britain's prosperity and welfare depend on the wealth generated by its industry and all those who work in it. It matters vitally to all of us that British industry should be strong and successful. We need both efficient publicly owned industries, and a vigorous, alert, responsible and profitable private sector, working together with the Government in a framework which brings together the interests of all concerned: those who work in industry, whether in management or on the shop floor, those who own its assets, and those who use its products and depend upon its success.' [Department of Industry, 1974[9]]

One of the features of the Industry Act is an increase in the amount and type of information that companies may be required to disclose to Government. The Act, considerably amended from the original Bill to be less stringent, provides for a formula of voluntary disclosure, which only becomes compulsory if the Minister follows a certain procedure, one step of which is to provide opportunity for the company and the unions to give their views.

In a summary to the Act, Robertson and Henderson (1975)[10] state:

"It is for the Minister to decide whether the information provided compulsorily to the Government should also be given to trade unions.

"After he has received the information he may:
(a) serve an additional notice on the company requiring the same information, or part of it, to be provided (after 28 days) to the authorised representatives of the unions; and
(b) serve a notice on each of these union representatives telling them whether or not the company is being asked to give them all the information. If the unions are to be denied some of the information they must be told of its general nature so that they can decide whether to appeal.

"But both the company and the union representatives must first be given the opportunity to put their views to the Minister."

There is an appeals procedure, and there are grounds (such as possible substantial injury to the company) on which a company may base an appeal. The intention is that the information would go to the unions recognised by the employer for negotiating purposes, and not to any other union. The representative authorised to receive the information may be a full-time union official and is therefore not necessarily a company employee.

The type of information subject to disclosure is carefully prescribed and includes forecasts as well as historical data. The list includes such items as sales, capital expenditure, the acquisition and sale of assets, capacity, output, and productivity.

The Industry Act provides for another form of discussion between company, employees, and government, in the planning agreement mechanism.

Planning Agreements are described by the Department of Industry (1974):[11]

"In their application to the private sector Planning Agreements will provide a new and improved framework for co-operation between the Government and leading industrial companies. A Planning Agreement will not be an agreement in the sense of a civil contract enforceable at law. It will, however, be given sufficient recognition by statute to enable the company concerned to rely on assistance promised under it. The Act which gives effect to the new system will also provide reserve powers to require the relevant companies to provide the Government and the workers in the firm with the information needed to formulate and monitor a Planning Agreement. There will, however, be no statutory requirement upon a company to conclude an agreement. . . .

". . . Employees and their representatives will have a major interest in the issues covered by Planning Agreements. The Government intend that the plans to be covered by an agreement will be drawn up by management in close consultation with trade union representatives from the firm. The framing and updating of agreements will thus involve a continuing discussion between management and the unions and will constitute an important advance in the part to be played by industrial democracy in the planning of company strategy. The Government envisage that union representatives from companies, while not formally parties to planning agreements, would also take part where there was interest in consultations on agreements with Government. "If consultation is to be effective, union representatives must be provided with all the necessary information relevant to the contents of Planning Agreements. . . ."

The results of the Planning Agreement initiative must be a disappointment to some and a relief to many. Under the voluntary system there has been no great rush of private companies to enter into discussions, and at the time of writing virtually no progress had been made. A more fundamental disappointment to many was the fact that planning agreements are voluntary. There is still a body of opinion that these should be compulsory, with Government and unions taking a directive line over management. The Industry Act represents a considerably more moderate view than some of the early statements of intent, and the statements of official policy on planning agreements make a very interesting contrast to the statements of the real intent made by certain politicians. The main reasons for the apparent failure are probably a feeling of mistrust over the degree of permanence in the Government's official policy mixed with a conviction that this form of agreement is irrelevant anyway.

On the other hand, the industrial strategy initiative, co-ordinated through the National Economic Development Office, has brought together management, government, and union representatives to work on strategy at an industry rather than a company level. Possibly this activity is seen as more relevant and with less distrust.

These various trends and pressures for more union involvement in company strategic planning will, of course, be greeted with widely varying degrees of enthusiasm, depending on personal political views. Managers as a whole are likely to resist the trends as much as possible: indeed, one portion of their corporate plans might be devoted to exploring how this aim might be achieved.

Our purpose is not to take a stand on whether or not the trends are desirable but to point out that they exist, and to examine some of the implications for planning if they continue.

The first implication is of nationwide importance and is the need for unions to obtain a good working knowledge of the true nature of corporate planning, the degree of uncertainty in all planning, and the need for plans to be changed, usually quickly, when circumstances prove that a decision was wrong or when an unforeseen opportunity arises. This improved understanding is needed among full-time union officials and company shop stewards. Certainly corporate planning is not what either the Labour Research Department or the Lucas Aerospace Combine Committee believe it to be.

There is another side to the coin. It is equally important for organisations to ensure that their managers generally are fully conversant with planning theory and practice. Under the new circumstances which may come about, this need would extend to supervisory levels of management. It may seem strange to argue for consistent training in a management tool which has been established for many years, but our experience is that many managers at all levels and in a wide spectrum of organisations have little or no idea of what corporate planning is about. Their definitions would be no better than the union view which was set down earlier in this chapter. This is a generalisation, to which there are numerous exceptions, but is correct for too many managers and too many organisations.

The reason for this organisational training need is that companies as a whole will need to look to the quality of their corporate planning. It is much easier to argue on the basis of a soundly researched, well-analysed, and well-prepared plan than on a loose collection of forecasts and off-the-cuff decisions. The trends imply that there will be an increasing tendency for management to have at the best to explain its strategy to Government and/or the unions, and at the worst to have to justify or defend them.

Implications would seem to be a greater emphasis on the importance of formal planning within organisations, and for plans to have a more secure analytical base. At the same time the behavioural aspects of planning cannot be ignored, because if this happens plans are likely to become academic, unsound, and ineffective. If management is to continue to manage it must seize a leadership position in the new situations as they emerge. This implies a greater degree of professionalism and the abandonment of any "I must be right because I am the boss" type of attitude. Management in the future is going to be much harder than it has been in the past (and it has never been easy) which means that those who are to succeed must obtain the maximum from a greater commitment to professionalism.

More than ever there is a need to involve management generally in the planning process. Middle management is already caught in a vice of pressure between top management and non-managerial employees. Unless care is taken they will end up by being the most ill-informed, demotivated, and uninvolved group of employees in any company. All the trends are in danger of exacerbating this situation. Corrective action from management could be an examination of the corporate planning process, and implementation of planning concepts which enable widespread management involvement.

One of the most worrying features of any extension, beyond management, to the groups which feel they have a right to be involved in corporate strategy, is delay. The more bureaucratic Government involvement becomes the more posturing there is over union and company attitudes, the more likelihood there is of paralysis from inaction. This is another reason why management should not only ensure that it has sound planning skills but also take a leadership position in the shaping of whatever consultative or co-determination measures are developed.

References Chapter 18

1. B. O'Shea (1974) New shape for unions in a multinational world, *Rydges*, Australia, October 1974.
2. J. Gennard (1972) *Multinational Corporations and British Labour: A Review of Attitudes and Responses*, British-North American Committee.
3. OECD (1976) *International Investment and Multi National*, Paris.
4. D. Hershfield (1975) *The Multi National Union Challenges the Multinational Company*, The Conference Board Inc.
5. C. Tugendhat (1971) *The Multinationals*, Penguin, 1971 edition, p. 225.
6. C. Levinson (1972) *International Trade Unionism*, Allen and Unwin, pp. 9 and 21.
7. N. Willatt (1974) Multinational Unions, *Financial Times*.
8. Labour Research Department (1976) *Industrial Democracy: A Trade Unionist's Guide*, pp. 27–28.
9. Department of Industry (1974) *The Regeneration of British Industry*, White paper presented to Parliament by the Secretary of State, HMSO, p. 1.
10. D. Robertson and J. Henderson (1975) *A Guide to the Industry Society*, p. 14.
11. Department of Industry (1974) op. cit., paragraph 11, p. 3, and paragraphs 19 and 20, p. 5.

Index